Real World Java EE Patterns

Rethinking Best Practices

Adam Bien (blog.adam-bien.com)

press.adam-bien.com

Real World Java EE Patterns – Rethinking Best Practices

by Adam Bien

Published by press.adam-bien.com

For more information or feedback, contact: abien@adam-bien.com

Cover Designer: Kinga Bien (www.graphikerin.com)

Editor: Michael Koch (www.mkp.com)

Printing History:

June 2009 Iteration One (First Edition)

ISBN 978-0-557-07832-5

Table of Contents

0

Preface

Most of the Java EE 5 projects keep using the old, superfluous J2EE patterns and best practices. J2EE was intrusive—the separation of the technical infrastructure and business logic required the introduction of *patterns*, which were mostly workarounds for the J2EE shortcomings.

I'm freelance *coding architect*, working on the architecture, design, and implementation of enterprise applications. With the advent of Java EE 5, I was able to remove a remarkable amount of patterns, indirections, and layers—without sacrificing the functionality. Even though I mostly deleted only superfluous code, my clients were delighted by the results. I sometimes give trainings and workshops about various Java, Java FX, and Java EE topics. We were able to cut production time in half with Java EE 5 for comparable tasks, without strange workarounds and patterns—it is a really good productivity indicator.

The Java User Group Hamburg invited me in May 2008 to talk about a Java EE 5 topic at Lehmann's bookstore in Hamburg [http://www.lob.de]. I submitted a talk with the title: *"Pragmatic Java EE 5 Hacking: Rethinking Best Practices with code/deployment / demos and few slides"* [http://www.adam-bien.com/roller/abien/entry/free_jug_session_pragmatic_java]. More attendees came, than I ever expected. The talk was supposed to last about one hour—I was done after about five hours, including an open-ended, discussion.

Its sounds like a good title for a Book:

"Pragmatic Java EE 5 Hacking - Rethinking Best Practices"

Nice Topic.

Roberto Carlos Gonzalez Flores on May 13, 2008 at 08:51 PM CEST #

Roberto,

indeed - I'm in the process of thinking about it.

regards,

adam

Adam Bien on May 13, 2008 at 09:40 PM CEST #

Someone mentioned during the talk, "you should write a book about that." I was able to get O'Reilly interested in the topic during a podcast at the JavaOne 2008 conference, but publication would have been deferred to 2010, so I decided to self-publish the book: http://press.adam-bien.com.

The goal of this book is to question already established J2EE best practices and discuss the alternatives with working code.

- **Chapter 1**, **A Brief History of J2EE and Chapter 2,Understanding Java EE Core Concepts,** introduce you to the Java EE 5 world and help dispel some of the misconceptions around Java EE 5. You will learn about common principles such configuration by exception, Dependency Injection, interceptors, JPA and EJB features. I even started with a brief Java EE history to explain the multi-vendor Java EE origins and the reason for the variety of available APIs—topics that have been part of my past talks. If you are a Java EE savvy developer, you can skip Chapters 1 and 2 and start with Chapter 3.

- **Chapter 3, Rethinking the Business Tier,** focuses on patterns for the business tier. Serviceoriented as well as domain driven patterns and best practices are discussed with many aspects, variants and strategies. Because of "rethinking" I will not only introduce fresh ideas like integration of scripting functionality with JSR-223 into EJBs or stateful gateways with "open" EntityManager, but also retire the majority of the J2EE patterns.

- **Chapter 4, Rethinking the Integration Tier,** discusses some controversial patterns like Data Access Object or Data Transfer Object , EJB 2 to EJB 3 migration strategies and even a generic Java Connector Architecture (JCA) implementation.

- **Chapter 5, Infrastructural Patterns and Utilities,** describes universal patterns, that cannot be uniquely associated with a particular layer. You will find crosscutting functionality like extensions of Dependency Injection (e.g. Guice integration), JNDI lookups , singleton implementation, startup services, additional monitoring utilities (thread tracking, precondition checks) which can be applied to any layer.

- **Chapter 6, Pragmatic Java EE Architectures,** summarizes the pattern language and combines the patterns into two opposite configurations, service-oriented and domain-driven architecture. In an enterprise context, however, nothing is simple black and white. You will have to find a pragmatic way in between the two extremes to produce efficient, lean, and clean code.

I've used these patterns in recent projects without consistent naming. In the majority of projects, discussion started with architects, designers, and sometimes developers and we ended with another name pointing to the same old definition. As long as the name of a pattern in a project, or even company is consistent—it's fine. The patterns facilitate the communication and make the documentation leaner.

I open sourced all the examples at kenai.com—a really interesting collaboration platform: http://kenai.com/projects/javaee-patterns.

The main motivation behind this book was forcing myself to re-implement concepts from my projects in a business logic–neutral way (and without the NDA restrictions) and learning new approaches. I can use them now in my workshops and training as well.

During the process of writing, I got some better ideas and refactored some patterns and re-introduced them back into my projects. I'm always open for feedback and discussion—to learn from you, the reader. Just drop me an email (abien@adam-bien.com) and I'll be sure to incorporate them in a future update of the book. Also, keep an eye on my blog (http://blog.adam-bien.com) where I will continue to cover the topics discussed in this book.

Special thanks to my wife Kinga for the great cover (although the colors were my idea—she didn't like them), my technical reviewer Patrick for technical review, and Eileen Cohen for pointing me to my editor, Michael Koch (www.mkpub.com), who helped me clean up my manuscript, cut redundancies, and eliminate my "German-isms."

Adam Bien

En route from Munich to Hamburg, June 2009

1

A Brief History of J2EE

If you're new to Java Platform, Enterprise Edition or Java EE, you might be wondering about the platform's complexity and APIs. The Java EE platform is not the product of a single company; it is an abstraction of many established products, libraries, and frameworks. In fact, distributed computing, not Java EE, makes our daily work so challenging. For a better understanding of what's behind the history of Java EE, I will start with its history and explain the basics of synchronization and transactions—the basics of our distributed world.

If you are a Java EE expert and already know the advantages of transaction management, isolation levels, and concurrency control, you can safely skip this chapter.

The Rise and Fall of Applets

The beginnings of Java EE can be traced back to the introduction of Java applets in the first Java release in 1995. When Netscape introduced support for applets in its Netscape Navigator browser in the mid-1990s, Java quickly gained in popularity. Everything was turned into applets, even simple static pages became animated. Although applets quickly gained in size and became more sophisticated,most of their functionality was handled on the back end, making client server communication essential for even simple operations. The introduction of Remote Method Invocation (RMI) in the Java Development Kit (JDK) 1.1 at least addressed the need for a transparent client-server communication, but it didn't solve it entirely.

Java Database Connectivity (JDBC), also introduced in JDK 1.1, facilitated the implementation of low-level access to relational databases and even helped control local transactions. Several applets shared a single, remote server instance, which accessed the database using JDBC. And that's when things became problematic. RMI code isn't thread-safe. Only one instance of the `UnicastRemoteObject` was bound to a particular port, which was shared among different users or threads. This instance was actually a distributed singleton and maintained the connections to the database as well. Database transactions could only be managed using the particular `java.sql.Connection` instance; the Java Transaction API (JTA) had yet to be written. Access to the shared connection had to be serialized to ensure consistency, but demand for scalability increased significantly at the same time.

By the time the browser wars were in full swing, it became significantly harder to built cross-browser applets. Proxy servers and firewalls were not Java Remote Method Protocol (JRMP) friendly—communication problems between applets and the back end were common. The advent of a new architectural paradigm, the *ultra-thin client* (UTC), coupled with an increasing number of incompatible JDK versions, often from different vendors, contributed to the demise of applets.

The UTC Paradigm: Moving Beyond Applets

The basic idea behind the UTC was as simple as it was radical: move—the entire business logic to the server and limit the client's responsibilities to presentation logic and user interaction. The introduction of the Servlet API and—the Java Web Server (JWS), the precursor of an application server, in 1997 were intended as the UTC backbone. Servlets, although not thread-safe, were multithreaded and able to dynamically generate HTML output. Curiously, the user interface of the JWS admin console was implemented using applets.

Database access was still implemented using plain JDBC. The association of user request and its transaction became important again for database consistency. Most applications used the `java.sql.Conneciton#setAutoCommit(true)` strategy to start a new transaciton for every single statement. A user request initiated a series of fine-grained, independent transactions.

This approach is comparable to not having transactions at all, because other users (transactions) were able to see immediately all the changes performed inside a parallel web request. As long as the application was only sequentially unit tested (which was not common then neither) in a single thread, everything worked just fine. Trouble started during integration tests if not in production. Server crashes often led to inconsistent or corrupted databases. It was hard to provide a reasonable level of isolation between different transactions. Even user actions interfered under load. The introduction of Enterprise JavaBeans (EJB) technology and the Java Transaction API (JTA) around 1997/98 helped make transactions more logical or business-oriented.

EJB: Introducing Consistency

The EJB API is a server-side component model. An EJB 1.0–2.x consists of a Java class (the Bean class), one factory interface (the home) and the remote interface (the remote view). Clients are able to access the EJB remotely via Common Object Request Broker Architecture (CORBA). An applet could access an EJB instead of the RMI server. This often underestimated feature, however, was the solution for the concurrency and consistency problems.

Because EJBs are always executed in a dedicated thread, they appear as single-threaded to the developer. For every thread (that is, user request or transaction) a new EJB instance is created (or reused from the pool)—there is no shared state between calls. The EJB specification even prohibits the use of the synchronization primitives and threading functionality inside session beans.

The programming model is rather *procedural* (sometimes also referred to as service oriented). The methods of a stateless session bean (SSB) process some input data and give it back to the caller. Even stateful session beans (SFSB) do not brake the rule—the container still prohibits concurrent access to a stateful instance. Because an SSB can only be executed in a single thread, you do not have to care about thread synchronization either.

The single-threaded programming model combined with declarative transactions solved the inconsistency problem as well—now the database connection can be accessed only by a single thread at a time. The EJB container starts a transaction before a bean method is invoked. The implementation of the method is executed in an atomic manner. Either every single step is successful and the coarse-grained transaction committed, or it is going to be just rolled back. The container manages the transactional resources for you. For example,— only one database connection is returned to the caller inside a transaction, even when it is requested several times from the connection pool.

Relational databases were not the only Enterprise Information Systems (EIS). Message-oriented middleware (MOM), ERP systems with proprietary interfaces, and even monolithic systems without any public interfaces had to be seamlessly integrated. On the legacy hosts, servers such as MQ Series or BEA Tuxedo continue to be used for asynchronous communication (messaging). Messaging is often also introduced just for the decoupling purposes between producer and consumer. Applets, EJBs, and Servlets operate according to the request-response communication style. The client invokes an EJB method and waits until the response is received. The procedural programming model is convenient, but messaging appears to be even more intriguing. The messaging APIs are indeed simple. The hot spots are error handling and proper transaction control. It's impossible to send a request and receive the response in a single transaction and it is also hard to deal with syntactical incorrect messages. Both problems don't exists in the procedural, type-safe communication, but have to be addressed in message-oriented architectures.

JMS: A Messaging System of Its Own

Although messaging was heavily used on the back end—a standard Java API did not exist at that time. In 1998 the Java Messaging System (JMS) API was introduced. It was to a high degree influenced by the IBM MQ Series product, but the API itself is vendor-neutral. The JMS API remained largely unchanged until today.

In parallel the product Novell Directly Services (NDS), integrated with the operating system Netware (with applet-based admin console), pushed the standardization of directory access; the Java Naming and Directory Interface (JNDI) was born. It was mainly used as an LDAP abstraction, for authorization and authentication purposes.

Servlets, JMS, JNDI, JTA, and EJB were fully independent specifications—available in different releases and versions. The available application servers combined those specs with different versions, which made porting an application a nightmare. Even worse, portable XML deployment descriptors weren't even invented yet. The EJB 1.0 deployment descriptor was a serialized Java class. It was hardly possible to port an application from one application server to another. The problem was not the code, but the portability of the server-specific configuration.

J2EE: A New Standard Is Born

The introduction of Java 2 Enterprise Edition (J2EE) in late 1999 solved the incompatibility issues. All APIs were bundled under a common name—and the application server vendors had to certify their products. The J2EE 1.2 release included the following APIs:

- Servlets 2.2

- Java ServerPages (JSP) 1.1

- Enterprise JavaBeans 1.1

- JDBC 2.0

- RMI-IIOP 1.0

- Java Message Service 1.0

- Java Naming and Directory Interface 1.2

- Java Transaction API 1.0

- JavaMail 1.1

Bundling the API into one consistent release improved the compatibility story slightly. At least you could rely on the existence of a standardized set of APIs. The development experience, however, was far from being perfect. The developer had not only to rely on the lowest common denominator, the APIs left too much room for interpretation. The EJB 1.1–2.0, and especially the entity beans with container-managed persistence 2.0 (CMP 2.0) were underspecified.

Important features such as pool settings, isolation levels, lock behavior, generation of primary keys and so on were not specified. The application server vendors had to extend the functionality of the common core. For this purpose, in addition to the standard deployment descriptors, further configuration was added. The write once, run anywhere (WORA) idea of the J2EE platform was less and less practicable. Although the compiled application ran on different application servers without change or recompilation—the realization of the business logic was highly dependent on the proprietary extensions of a particular application server. These extensions weren't standardized, the configuration was very different and the applications hard to migrate. It took a considerable amount of resources to migrate and test the business logic in a migration project. There were huge differences between the nonfunctional aspects such as clustering or fail over.

Furthermore the EJB spec was not very concise and didn't follow the "dry" (don't repeat yourself) principle. The information about an EJB component was spread across a remote interface, home interface, the Bean class and the deployment descriptor. Refactoring was very unproductive and tedious without tools, and the IDEs weren't very good in refactoring at that time. The deployment descriptors had to be kept in sync with the code as well.

Even when implementing simple tasks, developers had to deal with a considerable amount of overhead. The Bean class had to implement the `javax.ejb.SessionBean` interface and forced the implementation of all life cycle methods. The `ejbActivate` and `ejbPassivate` methods were only invoked in stateful session beans, although most of the deployed session beans were stateless:

```
public class HelloWorldBean implements SessionBean {

    public void setSessionContext(SessionContext aContext) {      }
    public void ejbCreate() {}
    public void ejbActivate() {} //SFSB only
    public void ejbPassivate() {}//SFSB only
    public void ejbRemove() {}

    public void sayHello() {
        System.out.println("Hello!");
    }
}
```

The business method, sayHello, is just a fraction of the overall code. This method was declared in an interface as well:

```
public interface HelloWorldRemote extends EJBObject {
    void sayHello() throws RemoteException;
}
```

Every method had to throw a (checked) RemoteException. This interface was not directly implemented by the Bean—the compiler was not able to check the signatures which led to frequent deployment errors. Such deployment errors were hard to find and it increased significantly the round trip times. In addition to the code, a deployment descriptor had to be provided. The XML deployment descriptor was the glue for all the disparate parts—already existing information had to be repeated again in this place. In a worst-case scenario, even the signature of the method was listed in the descriptor, as shown in the following example:

```
<ejb-jar>
    <display-name>HelloWorldEJB</display-name>
    <enterprise-beans>
        <session>
            <display-name>HelloWorldSB</display-name>
            <ejb-name>HelloWorldBean</ejb-name>
            <home>...helloworld.HelloWorldRemoteHome</home>
            <remote>...helloworld.HelloWorldRemote</remote>
            <ejb-class>...helloworld.HelloWorldBean</ejb-class>
            <session-type>Stateless</session-type>
            <transaction-type>Container</transaction-type>
        </session>
    </enterprise-beans>
    <assembly-descriptor>
        <container-transaction>
            <method>
                <ejb-name>HelloWorldBean</ejb-name>
                <method-name>sayHello</method-name>
            </method>
            <trans-attribute>RequiresNew</trans-attribute>
        </container-transaction>
    </assembly-descriptor>
</ejb-jar>
```

The descriptor was intended to be created by the developer, extended by the assembler and fine tuned by the deployer. In practice it was rarely the case. In general the developer was responsible for the whole process. Even settings like transactions, state management, or remoting were stable and didn't change frequently.

Within an enterprise context, the XML descriptors were created once and never touched again (at least for configuration purposes). In most cases, a proprietary descriptor was required as well—it was highly vendor dependent. The last required interface was the factory, EJBHome. It was the entry point to the remote interface:

```
public interface HelloWorldRemoteHome extends EJBHome {

    HelloWorldRemote create()  throws CreateException, RemoteException;

}
```

Even for simple logic, the developer had to create and maintain all the required infrastructural artifacts. The business code was highly dependent on the EJB API. The separation between the functional realization and the platform was not given. Many patterns, idioms, and indirections were introduced—just to encapsulate an unstable infrastructure. Although session beans were verbose and the programming harder than necessary, the additional benefit was huge. Remoting, single-threaded programming model, state management, transaction, and concurrency control could be applied declaratively, without any coding. Nonetheless, session beans are transient components without direct support for persistency.

JavaBlend

Even before the advent of J2EE, or even EJB, around 1998, the JavaBlend product was introduced to simplify object-relational mapping. It was very ambitious: ODMG 2.0 compliance with Object Query Language (OQL) support. JavaBlend aimed for the elimination of the object-relational impedance mismatch. Even visual tool support was provided to map the objects to relational tables and design dependencies. The persistent classes were actually plain old Java objects (POJOs), with only few dependencies on the JavaBlend API. The programming model was very similar to Java Data Objects (JDO) and required post-processing of the byte code. It was mainly motivated by performance optimization. Interestingly enough, the JavaBlend programming model was very similar to today's Java Persistence API (JPA).

Unfortunately, neither JavaBlend nor JDO made it into the J2EE spec. Entity beans with bean-managed persistence (BMP) as well as CMP were introduced instead. IIn contrast to the cleaner JDO and JavaBlend APIs, CMP entities were highly dependent on the platform. The programming model was resembled that of session beans, rather than the object-oriented POJOs. The developer had to provide the same artifacts as for the development of session beans, namely: the remote, home, interfaces, and bean classes and the deployment descriptor. In the first container-managed persistence (CMP) version (in EJB 1.1) persistent entity beans were intended to be accessed remotely. Because entity beans were active enterprise beans, they were also able to handle the transactions. This was the biggest misconception, which lead to chattiness and inconsistency. In a worst-case scenario, every fine-grained getter or setter caused a new transaction. This fact was also the reason for the introduction of many best practices, such as Session Façade.

In particular the problem of information duplication and the lack of encapsulation of the technical details, inspired the community to think about the alternatives. Hibernate was created as a powerful and lean alternative for the cumbersome J2EE persistence. In contrast to the CMP entity beans, Hibernate was POJO-based and object-oriented, and it supported polymorphic queries.

The JavaBean-based Spring framework encapsulated effectively the infrastructure and introduced a concept called *Dependency Injection*. The mix of these frameworks became very popular. It was often used as a viable alternative to the official J2EE stack.

Looking Beyond Java EE

Java EE was introduced in 2006, after a long period of debates and drafts. It makes intensive use of Java SE 5 features, including annotations, generics, and enums. Java EE 5 persistence was highly influenced by Hibernate. Gavin King, the founder of Hibernate, participated in the JPA Expert Group. The Dependency Injection (DI) pattern and the convention over configuration principle inspired by the Ruby on Rails framework also influenced the specification. Java EE 5 revolutionized session beans and introduced a viable replacement for the entity beans, the Java Persistence API (JPA). Nonetheless the remaining APIs, especially JTA, JMS, JNDI, and Servlets, were left unchanged.

The EJB 3 programming model was totally refurbished. All the redundant, infrastructural plumbing became optional. In fact, the entire coupling to the infrastructure was removed. To provide the same functionality as in EJB 2.1, only one business interface and a bean class are needed. The only dependency on the API is the use of the annotations @Stateless on the class, and @Local on the interface. No deployment descriptors are necessary. However, they can still be used to override the settings provided by the annotation.

The business interface is just a usual Java interface. No checked exceptions on methods, or inheritance from technically motivated interfaces (such as EJBObject) are necessary:

```
@Remote
public interface HelloWorld {
    public void sayHello();
}
```

The bean class directly implements this interface, which allows the compiler to verify the method signature again. Most of the errors can thus be recognized during the compilation and not at deployment time. Furthermore, it becomes fairly easy to deploy common POJOs as EJB 3 components.

```
@Stateless
public class HelloWorldBean implements HelloWorld {
    public void sayHello() {
        System.out.println("Hello!");
    }
}
```

The transaction management does not have to be specified, Container-managed transactions (CMT) with the `Required` attribute is the default. The principle convention over configuration goes even further and makes premature configuration superfluous. I will cover the core Java EE 5 concepts in Chapter 2 in greater detail.

Server-side Java: The Core Principles

The essential complexity in Java EE is caused by its distributed nature. A common Java EE application consists of at least four, often distributed, layers:

- **The browser:** It renders the data and caches the user input in hidden fields or even JavaScript objects. It is responsible for synchronous and asynchronous communication with the back end.

- **The presentation:** It is usually the web container. The user interface can be generated by JSF or other alternative frameworks such as Web Beans, Google Web Toolkit, Wicket, Tapestry, or many others. Client-specific objects, such as backing beans in JSF, are used in the web container for caching and transformation purposes.

- **The business container:** This can be an EJB, Guice, Spring, or another container. EJB 3 comes with a Java EE 5 compliant server. A business container is mainly responsible for keeping the consistency, hosting the business logic, and providing persistence services. It caches the JPA entities, at least for the period of a transaction. The business container is transactional and synchronizes the cached state with the database. In case messaging or access to legacy services is used, the container has to synchronize and coordinate such transactional resources as well.

- **The undefined back end:** If you are lucky, you have to access only a standard, relational database via JDBC. In this particular case, you can rely on standard Java EE persistence, JPA. In other cases, the back end consists of heterogeneous systems, services, and interfaces. Most of the systems are not accessed by the Java EE server exclusively, which makes caching and data synchronization especially challenging.

Every layer uses, transforms, and caches the data. The browser even relies on another language—JavaScript for that purpose. The main challenge of every distributed system is to keep all the data synchronized and consistent.

Even if your Java EE architecture is simplistic and only consists of one single EJB with a persistent JPA entity, you will have to deal with the data distribution and synchronization in these layers. An additional problem is the massive parallel nature of a Java EE application. Many users can access the same, also cached, resource or entity at the same time in parallel.

Java EE applications are multithreaded by nature and run on multiprocessor, multicore hardware. In addition, a Java EE application is often clustered; it runs on different application servers in a cluster, and thus JVM instances at the same time. It can be especially challenging for components with a conversational state or persistence. The state has to be distributed or replicated between nodes in a consistent manner.

Different mechanisms are available to overcome the problem of data distribution. Most of the currently available application servers rely on synchronous or asynchronous replication, cache invalidation, and so called *sticky sessions*; the caller returns over and over again to the same cluster node with an existing stateful component.

Most of the resources you access (for example, `EntityManager`) are not even thread-safe. The solution to the problem is older than Java itself—transactions.

The Case of Transactions

A transaction is but a unit of work. Regardless of whether a transaction is successful it has to remain atomic. In a Java EE environment, a transaction is associated with a thread—which means everything that is synchronously invoked from the entry point is invoked in the transaction scope. You only have to configure the transactions properly. The rollback of the transaction causes the rollback of all resources accessed in the particular thread.

The problem starts with the introduction of the transient state. Even Servlets are not thread-safe, so that access to the `HttpSession` has to be synchronized. The synchronization is already solved by many available web frameworks. For example, JSF already manages a stateful backing bean for you. The real problem comes with persistent state. Now you not only have to synchronize access to a persistent resource, but also have to decide when the state of your persistent entity has to be written back to the database. Only then your changes will be visible to other transactions and users.

Even in a very simple create, read, update, and delete (CRUD) application, multiple transactional resources are involved. First a JPA entity is created, passed to a session bean, and persisted using an injected (I will cover injection later) `EntityManager` instance. However, the `EntityManager` is not the database, it is only responsible for the object-relational mapping. In step 1, it only stores the entity bean internally and then waits until the end of the transaction. Only after the transaction commits successfully, does the `EntityManager` flush its state to a relational database using a `DataSource` and the `java.sql.Connection`. The database transaction is committed by the container. It commits not only the single database transaction, but all other resources as well (including JMS, other databases, legacy and connections). As long as you have a reference to an attached entity and you are inside a transaction, you can change the state of the entity—and you will see the changes after the commit:

```
@Stateless
public class BookMgrBean implements BookMgr {
    //injected by the container
    @PersistenceContext
    private EntityManager em;

    //transaction begin
    public void create(Book book) {
        em.persist(book);
        book.setDescription("new state"); //visible in the DB
    }
    //transaction commit
```

In a Java EE environment, a transaction is wider scoped than just a single resource access such as `java.sql.Connection`. This lets you invoke several methods in the EJB container within a transaction and modify several JPA entities in an atomic way. At the end of this activity, all your modifications in all session beans performed in the scope of the transaction (or request/thread) are flushed to the back-end resources. Everything that is going to be executed synchronously (in the same thread), inherits the transaction and involves (enlists) its resources to the transaction.

The application server acts as a transaction coordinator which starts a transaction, before even accessing a back-end resource. The application server accesses each resource and manages the transactions for you. In case something in the process goes wrong, it is going to roll back all involved resources. Transactions are even useful in a single-threaded application—fine-grained operations can be grouped into logical units and executed all at once atomically. Admittedly transactions were not created for grouping related activities into logical chunks in a single-threaded environment. They are especially essential in multithreaded environments.

The Concurrency Problem

A Java EE application server is designed to be executed in a multithreaded way. For this reason your application will have to deal with parallel access to a transactional resource. In general, it is a good idea to keep the local changes hidden until all changes are performed consistently and successful.

Otherwise another thread (that is, the user) would see the half-performed logical transaction and rely on its outcome. It becomes problematic in case the first transaction encounters a problem and is going to be rolled back. This would be fatal—a dependent transaction may already rely on the result and perform its own independent unit of work.

Just imagine an order-processing system. The order should only be shipped, in case the customer confirmed the order, his credit card was charged, and the product is in stock. Even if the shipment is triggered by the confirmation, the confirmation should only be visible for other threads after the credit was charged and the product checked out from stock.

It is a business, and not a technical, decision how isolated such transactions have to be. The degree of independence and isolation of a transaction can be configured—all transactional resources do support isolation levels.

An *isolation level* determines how independent one transaction has to be from another. A higher isolation level implies serial execution, a lower isolation level implies higher throughput, but less isolation and consistency. In fact, a very high isolation level (SERIALIZABLE) denotes serial access to a transactional resource, the lowest (NONE) no restrictions at all. With the NONE isolation setting, all transactions would immediately see all changes performed by another transaction, which is the same behavior as without transactions. Table 1 summarizes the various isolation levels.

Table 1: Isolation Levels

Isolation Level	Description
READ UNCOMMITTED	Already written, but still uncommitted data is visible for other transactions. If any of the changes are rolled back, another transaction might have retrieved an invalid row. This setting can even be problematic for read-only applications such as reporting. Reports created with READ_UNCOMMITTED can be partially based on stale or even non-existing data.
READ COMMITTED	Only committed data is visible to other transactions. The isolation is higher, because the stale data is isolated until the commit—and only then visible to others. You can rely on the consistency of the read data; however, the data remains consistent only for the length of the read operation. When you re-execute the same query in the current active transaction, you might see different results.
REPEATABLE READS	On this level, a query operation with the same parameters ensures the same results. Even if other transactions committed the changes, which affected some rows in the result set, it will not change the result set. Although delete and change operations are not visible in the result set, new rows can still be added by another transaction and appear in the result.
SERIALIZABLE	This is the highest possible level. The name is derived from serial access, no interferences between transactions are allowed. Rereading a query always returns the same result, regardless of whether the data was changed, added or deleted. This level is very consistent and very costly. Read and write locks are needed to ensure this consistency level. The price for the consistency is high as well: the lowest scalability (because lack of concurrency) and increased chances for deadlocks.

In a Java EE environment, the isolation levels are only indirectly exposed to the developer. In general, all transactional resources can be configured using isolation levels. Isolation levels can be configured for all transactional resources such as DataSources, JMS factories or destinations, JCA connectors, or distributed caches directly in the application server or in the resource itself (for example, directly in the database).

Without isolation levels, the only remaining benefit would be the logical grouping of cohesive actions to one atomic unit. In general, the application server waits until the end of the transactions and then writes the cached state to the back-end resources. However, you shouldn't rely on this rule—it is configurable. For example, the `FlushModeType.AUTO` setting of `EntityManager` and `Query` cause the changes to JPA entities to be flushed to the database immediately, whereby `FlushModeType.COMMIT` only prescribes the synchronization at the end of the transaction.

Regardless at which time the transactional cache (for example, the state of the `EntityManager`) is flushed to the database, nothing prevents other users to access the same entity. This leads to further challenges. Several existing copies may exist in parallel and result in lost updates, where one transaction could override data from another. One of the solutions to this problem is very similar to the `synchronized` keyword—only one transaction can access the resource exclusively, all the others have to wait.

Locking for Consistency

Exclusively locking resources is rather pessimistic. It is assumed that an interference between transactions will happen. The consequences of this assumption are rather high too; only one transaction at a time can access a resource (for example, a row in a table or even the entire table). Pessimistic locks are one available option in the world of transactions and also the Java EE platform. Locking resources exclusively fits not very well into the multithreaded nature of a Java EE server. Only one thread (transaction) at time would be able to access the resource, all others would have to wait.

This approach hardly scales. It is getting even worse in a clustered environment. Different application server instances access now a common resource, which means not only the transactions from one server, but all servers in the clusters have to be blocked. This increases not only the probability of deadlocks, but makes the implementation of failover harder than necessary. What happens in case one application acquires a lock to a database table and then dies? Just restarting the application server wouldn't solve the problem, because the resource is still locked. You will have to wait, until the lock will be freed by a timeout. Fortunately, a more optimistic approach is available. The term *optimistic* - implies low probability of parallel write-access to the same resource at the same time. Most applications read significantly more than they write. The write modifications often access different rows or even resources. This is also the reason why most of the version control systems operate without locking in optimistic mode. Optimistic locking is sometimes referred to as optimistic concurrency. Regardless of how low the probability of inconsistency really is, there should be a consistent recovery strategy.

As already mentioned, optimistic concurrency operates with almost no locking. A data set is fetched in a short read transaction from database and then it becomes disconnected. In a Java EE environment such a data set is converted to a JPA entity. In case the read entity was modified, it has to be flushed back to the database. At this point the state of the application could become inconsistent, because another transaction could have modified, or even deleted, the entity already. It is essentially important to check whether the database was changed in the meantime. This can be accomplished in a number of ways:

- **Preventing other transactions to access the resource:** This approach works, but is not really optimistic.

- **Checking the current state of the database using the "before image":** In this case the state of the database is captured at read time and associated with the entity. During the modification (update or delete), the state of the current database row will be compared with the captured one. In case it matches, the database is going to be updated; otherwise an exception will be thrown.

- **Checking the current state of the database using a proxy or synthetic column:** This strategy is very similar to the previous one but more lightweight. Instead of capturing the entire row, only a proxy row (version row) is associated with the data set or entity. This row is added to the where clause and compared with the current state of the database. In case the version row of the modified data set is equal to the row in the database, the update operation is performed and the version changed. Numeric types are usually going to be increased, timestamps just refreshed. This strategy can be understood as an optimization of the second one.

The first strategy isn't optimistic. The second one is mostly used in legacy systems and custom persistence frameworks. Only the last one is used in Java EE:

```
@Entity
public class Book{
    @Id
    @GeneratedValue
    private Long id;
    private String title;
    @Version
    private long version;
                        //...other fields
```

The @Version annotated attribute represents such a synthetic field. It is mapped to a database column. Furthermore, it is compared with the database on every write (as well as delete) operation and finally changed by the JPA provider. You only have to keep the value of the field associated with the entity for the length of the entire business transaction.

The business transaction can be understood as a logical step that can be realized by one or more technical transactions. Carrying the value of the version field with the entity is necessary in case it becomes detached from the store and transferred to the presentation tier. In this case, the value of the version field has to be bound to the view and converted back to the entity. Otherwise the relationship between the logical activity and the technical transactions is lost.

In some architectures, the entity is never exposed to the presentation tier. A dedicated Data Transfer Object (DTO) transports the information between the layers instead. In this particular case, the version field has to be copied back and forth between the entity and the DTO.

Optimistic concurrency solves the following challenges:

- **Mapping of long-running, business activities to a sequence of fine-grained, technical transactions:** Often it is not possible to execute a business transaction in a technical one, because of its duration. Everything that takes longer than a few seconds has significant impact on scalability and robustness.

- **Preventing lost updates:** Different user transactions modify distinct attributes of the same entity or table. Without optimistic locking the entity from the latter transaction would overwrite the already changed attributes of the first one. Because they are two independent technical transactions, such a behavior would be perfectly valid from a technical perspective. Such behavior is, however, not acceptable from a business perspective.

- **Preventing inconsistencies in a clustered environment:** Every cluster node acts mostly independently, caches the data, and synchronizes itself with the database. In this case, the cluster nodes concur for the same resource.

- **Preventing deadlocks:** This goal is achieved only indirectly. Because the resource (for example, a database) is locked only for the duration of the update operation (that is, for a very short period of time), the chances of a deadlock are lowered.

Collisions happen but I haven't covered the recovery yet. A collision does result in stale data. Actually, it is very similar to collision in your version control system, in case your colleague modified accidently the same file as you. The same strategies can be applied in both cases:

- Merging the cached data with the database

- Overriding the database

- Rejecting the cached data

A collision is manifested as an unchecked exception (`javax.persistence.OptimisticLockException`), which leads to the detachment of all entities. The exception has to be caught and one of the recovery strategies initiated after this step. The only Java EE specific occurrence is the `OptimisticLockException`; the challenge, as well as the solution, is fully Java EE independent.

The distribution of an application into several JVM processes or address spaces makes maintenance of the consistency even more challenging. Method parameters and return values will be copied, sometimes even transferred, from one JVM to another.

Distribution, Latency, and the Fallacies

James Gosling's and Peter Deutsch's *Fallacies of Distributed Computing* are independent of the computing platform, language, or system. Of importance for the system architecture are the first, second, and seventh item:

- The network is reliable

- Latency is zero

- Bandwidth is infinite

- The network is secure

- Topology doesn't change

- There is one administrator

- Transport cost is zero

- The network is homogeneous

The latency, often referred as *ping time*, has significant impact on the performance of a system. High latency paired with too fine-grained methods can even make it unusable. A remote method call is magnitudes slower than a local one. Reduction of remote calls helps to deal with this fact. A remote method has to be coarser than a local one. The introduction of remote façades is just a natural reaction to the higher cost of network invocation. The purpose of the façade is the aggregation of fine-grained local calls, and exposing them as a single coarse-grained operation. This approach is necessary; otherwise the latency of every single method will be cumulated. The application could even become unusable in this case, which is a key reason why the remote view of CMP entity beans was ridiculous. Every single setter and getter invocation would cause remote communication. For the update of a single database row, several remote invocations would be necessary.

A much harder problem is object serialization for transport purposes. The data of an object is going to be serialized, transferred over the wire, and finally deserialized on the other end. At this point, an additional copy of an entity was introduced. Now we have one object instance in the database, one cached in the `EntityManager`, and another one was copied during the distribution. Data consistency can still be ensured with optimistic concurrency; however, every additional copy increases the chance of a collision. Furthermore, the copies have to be merged back after every modification. This hits not only the performance and memory consumption, but also introduces an additional layer of complexity. The first fallacy is inconvenient as well. A distributed communication is unreliable by nature. A network failure can simply happen—it causes nasty exceptions and sometimes a rollback of the entire transaction. This is the reason why in EJB 2.x every remote method throws a `java.rmi.RemoteException`. It is checked, so the developer has to deal with the exception—even if it is not always possible to recover in defined way. In the EJB 3 specification the exception disappeared from the business interface, which means it is invisible for the user of the remote interface. Nonetheless, the problem isn't really solved, only hidden. The exception still can happen, but it is wrapped in an unchecked one.

One of the biggest problems of every distributed system is its partial failure. A distributed system is comprised of processes, which to some degree are independent of each other. The failure of one subsystem does not necessarily entail the consistent shutdown of all dependent parts. The dependent subsystems are still able to accept requests, but are no longer able to handle them. This is one of the essential problems of a distributed system. A single-process system becomes just completely and consistently unavailable. Sometimes it is the best error recovering strategy.

In the context of Java EE most annoying errors are caused by the failure of back-end resources. Resources involved in a distributed transaction coordinated by the application server are especially sensitive. A not-responding participant can lead to hanging transactions, deadlocks, heuristic exceptions and even the failure of the transaction coordinator. Such scenarios are hard to test. Such errors are even harder to be reproduced in the integration environment. Timeouts, blocking requests, and inconsistencies often only occur under certain, often unknown, circumstances and heavy load.

Summary

You can start without Java EE or other similar framework like .NET, Spring, Guice, or even systems such as CICS, but you will have to implement the concurrency, transactions, locking, sessions on your own. It's likely that the end result will be more complex, than a full-blown Java EE solution. If you understand the concepts of distributed computing and know the challenges, Java EE becomes suddenly a breeze. Instead of coding, you can mostly rely on the provided defaults or configure the desired behavior declaratively. In addition you will gain with Java EE vendor independence. Your business logic will be clearly separated from infrastructure, which can be provided by (as of summer 2009) thirteen certified application servers and even the Spring framework itself.

Building distributed, robust systems is hard. You have to be aware of the nature of distribution, per-value and per-reference semantics, and exception handling. You have another option—don't distribute your system. Deployment of the entire application to a single JVM solves the challenges in an elegant way—the fallacies of distributed computing doesn't apply any more. The system isn't distributed; you can work with the objects in transparent way. You can partially achieve that even with Java EE 5—you can run as many layers as possible in as single process.

2

Understanding Java EE Core Concepts

Java EE is a vast improvement over J2EE. Although the underlying principles of the J2EE 1.x and Java EE specs are similar, experienced J2EE developers have to rethink best practices when using the EJB 3 programming model. Concepts such as lifecycle management of session beans, remoting, transaction handling, or state management have not changed. The improvements in the programming model and persistence, however, are dramatic. And although the web tier API didn't change in Java EE 5, it has been significantly refactored in Java EE 6.

Although the EJB 3.0 spec is lean and sound, the same amount of metadata is required as with the EJB 2.1 predecessors. Nonetheless, the way how the information is derived and leveraged has changed. Instead of configuring the obvious, only the deviation from the default has to be specified. The default case is covered already by the self-contained metadata such as class name, method name, attribute names, and suitable defaults. The defaults suffice in about 80 percent of all cases; specific requirements can still be met with annotations or, if necessary, be overridden using XML descriptor files.

This chapter explains some of the less obvious principles and practices of the EJB 3.x programming model, including convention over configuration, Dependency Injection, and interceptors. It also provides answers to common questions that tend to preoccupy both experienced J2EE developers as well as developers new to the Java EE Platform.

Convention over Configuration

Convention over configuration (CoC) is a software paradigm borrowed from the Ruby on Rails community. The principle is simple: decrease the number of decisions that developers need to make through default configurations and only define behaviors that deviate from the established convention. In Java EE terms this means that plain classes with a limited set of annotations (or modifiers) took the place of large deployment descriptors and XML configuration files.

Annotations were introduced in Java 5 SE, but the trend towards simplifying coding practices through conventions that combine code and metadata was already apparent in J2EE. XDoclet (an open source JavaDoc-driven code and configuration generator) leveraged the necessary information from the session bean class using custom JavaDoc tags. The redundant infrastructure such as home, remote interface, deployment descriptors, even value objects were generated from the metadata provided in the JavaDoc comments.

The custom JavaDoc tags are similar to annotations, but have many drawbacks, including:

- **Lack of compiler checks:** It is possible to misspell the tags – names and types aren't checked by the compiler, but during the deployment cycle.

- **Lack of structure:** Tags alone are not enough. In most cases additional information such as the name of the bean or the transaction level had to be provided as an attribute of the tag. This can be simulated by JavaDoc, but cannot be enforced by the compiler. It is impossible to prescribe mandatory attributes and default values.

- **Lack of type safety:** The attributes are not just strings. The metadata is mainly comprised of constants or enumerated values in Java EE (for example, `@TransactionAttribute(TransactionAttributeType.MANDATORY)`). The compiler is not able to check the syntactic correctness of the attribute in plain JavaDoc as is the case in annotations.

The introduction of annotations improved dramatically the usability of metadata in Java classes, interfaces, fields, and methods. Instead of relying on the JavaDoc and deployment process, the compiler checks for syntactic correctness, the availability of the default values, and correct typing. No additional tools or specific IDE extensions are required.

EJB 3.x and JPA specifications rely heavily on annotations. In fact, all the information stored previously in deployment descriptors is now available in the form of annotations. They are supplemented by metadata derived via reflection from the byte code and suitable defaults. The mix of convention and metadata derived from the components minimizes the need of providing additional information in the form of annotations or XML configuration files.

In fact annotations are used as markers to introduce an EJB or persistent entity. The intention of such annotations is identical to the Marker Interface or Tag Interface patterns. The interfaces `java.io.Serializable` and `java.rmi.Remote` are classic examples of this pattern. An annotation does not extend the type, as is the case with the tag interface pattern, but instead provides additional metadata at runtime.

During the deployment phase, the container searches for the additional metadata and treats the classes accordingly. For deployment of a session bean, for example, only the annotation `@Stateless` or `@Stateful` has to be defined. The XDoclet metadata included in JavaDoc has been replaced by annotations.

```
/**
 * @ejb.bean name="HelloBean" type="Stateless" view-type="local"
 */
public class HelloBean implements SessionBean {
```

The annotations introduced with Java EE 5 are lean and explicit—it now suffices to mark an ordinary Java class with the annotation `@Stateless` to make it an EJB:

```
@Stateless
public class HelloBean {}
```

The container recognizes it as a stateless session bean and applies the predefined (or conventional) behavior such as transactions, state, security aspects, and remoting. The stateless nature of the `HelloBean` class is explicitly configured using the annotation `@Stateless`. The transactions, however, do not have to be explicitly specified. The setting

`@TransactionAttribute(TransactionAttributeType.REQUIRED)` is silently applied, although it isn't explicitly specified. It causes every method to be executed in a transaction. If a transaction already exists it will be reused; if no transaction exists it will be started for you. You can specify this annotation explicitly, override it with an XML deployment descriptor, or rely on the default settings.

Even the implementation of the interface is no longer necessary. All public methods are automatically exposed to the client (the user of the bean). The client acquires an instance of the bean either via a JNDI lookup or using Dependency Injection.

Dependency Injection

Dependency Injection (DI) refers to the process of supplying an external dependency to a software component; in Java EE terms, this means that the EJB 3 container manages the dependencies for you. Instead of performing lookups, using factories, or even writing custom code, all you have to do is declare the need for a particular resource.

For example, instead of writing custom code like this:

```
Service service = ServiceFactory.getInstance().createService();
```

Or this:

```
try{
    Context ctx = new InitialContext();
    Object proxy = ctx.lookup("service");
    ServiceHome home =
(ServiceHome)PortableRemoteObject.narrow(proxy,ServiceHome.class);
    Service service = home.create();
}catch(Exception ex){ /* omitted */}
```

You just have to declare the dependency and the need for automatic association with a given instance as `@EJB` annotation:

```
@EJB
private Service service;
```

The container does the work for you. It scans for the annotation and injects the implementation before a single business method is invoked. The process of acquiring an implementation of an interface and associating it with a field is completely factored out from the application code, making the application code leaner and less error-prone. Possible misspellings of JNDI names, necessary exception handling, or castings are gone.

Take a look at the previous three factory samples. In the first sample, (`ServiceFactory. getInstance().createService()`), the decision which implementation of the `Service` interface will be injected is encapsulated in the factory (instead of you externalizing and storing the fully qualified name in a configuration file). The second sample (`InitialContext#lookup`) looks up an EJB 2.*x* bean. (Although the bean doesn't implement the interface directly, I specified a particular bean class in an XML deployment descriptor file.) The third (true DI) sample needs the fully qualified name of the implementation as well. The container has to decide which implementation to inject. In case there is only one implementation of the interface, you do not have to specify it—CoC does it for you.

Note: In some cases you will have more than one implementation for a given bean interface. In those cases, the container will have to differentiate between both possibilities. Pure conventions are not enough; the developer will have to provide at least a hint, which class to use.

In the following example, an implementation of the Service interface is injected by the ClientBean:

```
@Stateless
public class ClientBean implements Client {

    @EJB
    private Service service;

    public String getHello() {
        return this.service.getMessage();
    }
}
```

For demonstration purposes, I introduced more than one implementation of the interface, so that the convention is explicitly violated. The two implementations return different messages.

```
@Stateless
public class DefaultService implements Service {

    public String getMessage() {
        return "Hello from: " + this.getClass().getName();
    }
}
```

The name of the EJB is derived from the simple (not fully qualified) class name. Therefore two different beans, DefaultService and SpecificService, are going to be deployed:

```
@Stateless
public class SpecificService implements Service {
    public String getMessage() {
        return "Hello from: " + this.getClass().getName();
    }
}
```

The deployment will fail in the early stage with the following error:

```
Cannot resolve reference Unresolved Ejb-Ref
com.abien.samples.di.client.ClientBean/service@jndi:
@null@com.abien.samples.di.service.Service@Session@null because there are 2
ejbs  in the application with interface com.abien.samples.di.service.Service
```

The problem can be solved either by hardcoding the dependency with annotation attributes or by using the optional descriptor file ejb-jar.xml. The first case is simple, you only have to set the attribute in the @EJB annotation and specify the EJB name:

```
public class ClientBean implements Client {
```

```
@EJB(beanName="DefaultService")
private Service service;
```

Using the optional descriptor file is more labor-intensive; instead of changing the code, you have to resolve the dependency in the deployment descriptor:

```
<ejb-jar ...>
    <enterprise-beans>
        <session>
        <ejb-name>ClientBean</ejb-name>
        <ejb-local-ref>
            <ejb-ref-name>...di.client.ClientBean/service</ejb-ref-name>
            <local>com.abien.samples.di.service.Service</local>
            <ejb-link>DefaultService</ejb-link>
        </ejb-local-ref>
    </session>
  </enterprise-beans>
</ejb-jar>
```

This approach is more flexible and allows for the dependency to be resolved externally, without code modification. The declaration of the dependency remains unchanged – no additional attributes have to be provided.

Using the descriptor file is more suitable for testing purposes or product customization. You can even use an XML deployment descriptor to override existing annotations. This is especially convenient if you want to try a specific configuration during integration tests. Just be sure to remove the deployment descriptor in production.

Similar principles can be applied for the injection of resources such as EntityManager, JMS destinations and ConnectionFactory objects as well. The Dependency Injection can be either configured with annotations or in deployment descriptors. For the persistence, however, an additional file called persistence.xml is needed. The injection of the EntityManager without specification of the persistence unit works only in case there is only one persistence unit specified in the persistence.xml file:

```
@Stateless
public class BookServiceBean implements BookService {

/*no additional information; works only for one persistence unit in the
persistence.xml file*/
    @PersistenceContext
    private EntityManager em;

    public void create(Book book) {
        this.em.persist(book);
    }
}
```

In all other cases it has to be resolved, either with an attribute of the annotation or again in the deployment descriptor. It is not uncommon to have more than one persistence unit with different configurations available. Every injected EntityManager instance is related to a persistence unit and is independent of others. Different `EntityManager` instances have distinct caches and can be configured differently in the `persistence.xml` file. An `EntityManager` instance responsible for access to the master data could use aggressive caching, whereby the `EntityManager` instance for the operational data could be configured with, for example, a "weak" reference cache, or the instance responsible for export/import could be deployed with no cache activated at all.

That Java Persistence API (JPA) can be used outside the container as well. This feature is especially useful for testing purposes. However it requires another persistence unit with dedicated JDBC driver configuration and `RESOURCE_LOCAL` transaction handling. It is just another example for several persistence units inside a `persistence.xml` deployment descriptor. In the following example, both persistence units are identical, with the exception of the database schema generation. The persistence unit `DaC` drops and creates all tables on deploy and undeploy, respectively. The persistence unit `None` relies only on the existence of the schema.

```
<persistence ...>
  <persistence-unit name="DaC" transaction-type="JTA">
    <provider>oracle.toplink.essentials.PersistenceProvider</provider>
    <jta-data-source>jdbc/sample</jta-data-source>
    <properties>
      <property name="toplink.ddl-generation" value="drop-and-create-tables"/>
    </properties>
  </persistence-unit>
  <persistence-unit name="None" transaction-type="JTA">
    <provider>oracle.toplink.essentials.PersistenceProvider</provider>
    <jta-data-source>jdbc/sample</jta-data-source>
    <properties>
    </properties>
  </persistence-unit>
</persistence>
```

The injection of the `EntityManager` instance has to be explicitly configured in case it is arbitrary and cannot be inferred from the convention. The most flexible, but also most tedious way is the resolution of the dependency in the deployment descriptor.

```
<ejb-jar ...>
    <enterprise-beans>
        <session>
            <ejb-name>BookServiceXMLBean</ejb-name>
            <persistence-context-ref>
<persistence-context-ref-
name>...persistence.BookServiceXMLBean/em</persistence-context-ref-
name>
                <persistence-unit-name>DaC</persistence-unit-name>
            </persistence-context-ref>
        </session>
    </enterprise-beans>
</ejb-jar>
```

The relation between the injected `EntityManager` instance and its persistence unit can be maintained in the ejb-jar deployment descriptor without recompilation of the session bean and is therefore especially interesting for integration tests or customer-specific settings in product development. On the other hand the deployment descriptor is an additional artifact which has to be created and maintained, so this approach comes not for free. Especially refactoring can be challenging, because the IDE has to keep the source and XML configuration consistent.

For static resolution, annotations are more appropriate and efficient. The name of the persistence unit can be easily set in the `@PersistenceContext` annotation. No additional deployment descriptors are required for this purpose.

```
@Stateless
public class BookServiceAnnotationBean implements BookService {

    @PersistenceContext(unitName="DaC")
    private EntityManager em;

    public void create(Book book) {
        this.em.persist(book);
    }
}
```

The injection of resources works slightly different. Although the principle is the same the data sources, JMS resources, or mail sessions are injected using the `@Resource` annotation.

```
@Stateless
public class DataSourceInjectionBean implements DataSourceInjection {
    @Resource(name = "mail/Context")
    private Session mailContext;

    @Resource(name = "jms/Queue")
    private Queue queue;
    @Resource(name = "jms/ConnectionFactory")
    private ConnectionFactory eocFactory;

    @Resource(name="jdbc/sample")
    private DataSource ds;

    public void accessResources(){
        //use the datasource
    }
}
```

The deployed resources are uniquely identified by the JNDI name, which is used in the previous example for injection, instead of a traditional lookup. The `mappedName` attribute could be used in this example as well, even though it is product specific.

Aspect-Oriented Programming and Interceptors

The idea behind aspect-oriented programming (AOP) is the strict separation between pure business logic and reusable, crosscutting code. The reusable, crosscutting code, or aspects, is provided once and reused in different places. The reuse, however, happens externally, the business logic classes do not even know that they are decorated with additional functionality. In fact, AOP could be explained as flexible and configurable decorator (or interceptor), which can be applied to methods, attributes, or constructors in a declarative manner.

The EJB container comes already with some built-in, highly reusable aspects. The availability of remote EJB via SOAP-based web services, RESTful services, or even IIOP remoting is nothing else than decoration of an existing functionality with the crosscutting aspect of remoting. Transaction and exception handling, security, concurrency, state management, and even persistence are classic aspects. Aspects actually existed from the beginning of the J2EE platform —long before the acronym AOP became popular. Application-defined aspects were introduced with the EJB 3.0 specification. In J2EE 1.4 only the web container was able to intercept incoming requests with a Servlet filter.

In a Java EE application, session beans tend to implement the major portion of business logic. This logic is rather functional, or even procedural. Session beans are the natural place for the utilization of AOP ideas. Session beans mainly consists of methods and a default constructor. Attributes are very rare and mostly used together with stateful session beans. All other attributes are not client specific and shared by all instances. References to `EntityManager` instances, JMS resources, or other EJBs are typical examples for such a technical state.

The Java EE aspects are called *interceptors*. Comparing them to fully-fledged AOP frameworks is not suitable because they are optimized for the use with EJB and are thus rather limited. An EJB interceptor can only be applied to methods of a particular EJB. It is not possible to apply interceptors to constructor invocations or attribute access.

Interceptors are nevertheless sufficient for most common use cases. An interceptor can be enabled either with an annotation or through a deployment descriptor. From the conceptual point of view its activation is identical to the DI approach: either annotations or deployment descriptors can be used.

An EJB 3 interceptor is just a Java class with an annotated method:

```
public class TracingInterceptor {
 @AroundInvoke
 public Object trace(InvocationContext ic) throws Exception{
  System.out.println("Method: " + ic.getMethod());
  return invocationContext.proceed();
  }
}
```

The interceptor has full control over the execution, it is able to invoke the method, change its parameters and return values, invoke the method several times, transform exceptions and so on. The realization of the interceptor is independent of the actual business logic. An interceptor is activated for a particular EJB using the `@Interceptors` annotation.

```
@Stateless
@Interceptors({TracingInterceptor.class, PerformanceMeasurement.class})
```

```
public class HelloBean implements Hello {

    public String sayHello() {
        return "Hello from Bean";
    }
}
```

The value of the annotation is an array of classes. The order of the array is equivalent to the order of the interception. Because the @Interceptors annotation refers to the interceptors as classes and not as strings, the IDE and the compiler ensure the consistency and provide autocompletion and refactoring support.

On the other hand, because the interceptors are declared in the business code, every change requires recompilation and redeployment of the whole application. This could become a problem for utility interceptors, which are only needed in the development phase or only activated for troubleshooting.

Fortunately, interceptors can be declared and applied in the standard deployment descriptors as well. In the following example, the first part of the configuration is the actual declaration of the interceptor. It is needed only once. In the second part, the already declared interceptor can be applied to all beans from the ejb-jar, a particular bean, or a specific, overloaded method.

```
<ejb-jar …>
<!-- declaration (needed once) -->
    <interceptors>
        <interceptor>
 <interceptor-class>...PerformanceMeasurement</interceptor-class>
        </interceptor>
    </interceptors>

<!-- interceptor activation -->
    <assembly-descriptor>
        <interceptor-binding>
            <ejb-name>HelloBean</ejb-name>
            <interceptor-order>
     <interceptor-class>...PerformanceMeasurement</interceptor-class>
            </interceptor-order>
        </interceptor-binding>
    </assembly-descriptor>
</ejb-jar>
```

The XML configuration is not only more flexible, but also more powerful. The deployment descriptor allows the configuration of default interceptors, which intercept all beans in the module (ejb-jar).

You should have really good reasons for the introduction of XML deployment descriptors. Deployment descriptors are harder to create and maintain and have to be treated as plain source code. Although the application is more flexible and configurable with externalized XML configuration, once deployed this advantage will lose its importance. No one will change XML configurations without a test phase in production—the additional flexibility is therefore only interesting in the development phase. The XML configuration has to be maintained and versioned together with source code. Therefore XML becomes as important as source code itself and has to be maintained with the same care.

Another argument for the annotation-driven approach is the lower amount of implicit behavior behind the scenes. The relation between the main concern (the session bean), and the crosscutting concern (the interceptor) is self documented. The refactoring of the interceptor such as renaming, moving to other packages and so on can be performed in every standard IDE without Java EE or EJB support.

Interceptors are not just POJOs, they come with some interesting features. They participate in transactions and support Dependency Injection. An interceptor is even able to use the functionality of another EJB directly via DI. In the following example, a session bean is injected into an Interceptor.

```
public class AuditInterceptor {

    @EJB
    private Audit audit;

    @AroundInvoke
    public Object trace(InvocationContext ic) throws Exception{
        String info = ("Method: " + ic.getMethod() + "\n");
        info += ("Object: " + ic.getTarget().getClass().getName());
        this.audit.audit(info);
        return invocationContext.proceed();
    }
}
```

It is really convenient to access already existing logic of an EJB—with all its provided services such as transactions, concurrency, or security. This Dependency Injection can be configured in the same manner with annotations or XML, or by relying on convention and using the default implementation. The `AuditInterceptor` class is a ubiquitous and rather trivial example for AOP.

Interceptors can be used for a variety of purposes, including:

- **Ensuring the preconditions:** Interceptors have access to the intercepted EJB. Therefore it is easy to access not only the methods, but their parameters with annotations as well. It is relatively easy to evaluate the annotations and ensure the validity of the parameters; for example, the annotation `@NotNull` already implies that the method should be invoked with a non-null parameter. With this approach the validation of the preconditions could be easily moved from the EJB into a reusable interceptor.

- **Ensuring the service level agreements (SLAs):** This case is very similar to the previous one. You could measure the performance of a method and escalate all too slow invocations using, for example, JMS Topic wrapped in a session bean. This lightweight monitoring capability is especially important in SOA environments, where multiple clients have to rely on the availability of a single, reusable service.

- **Enhancing the DI capabilities:** An interceptor is able to access the intercepted EJB instance directly. So it is able to access its fields and search for annotations. Additional values can be injected directly into the fields or methods of a session bean. The framework Seam uses this approach to introduce own Dependency Injection semantics. The integration with Google Guice can be approached in this way as well.

- **Transforming or filtering exceptions:** An interceptor invokes a method of the next participant in the chain. It wraps the invocation, so it is capable to catch any encountered exceptions, swallow them, or re-throw a clean version of an exception. This is particular useful for dealing with legacy connectors with exceptions in the "cause". Not all exceptions, however, can be easily caught in an interceptor. Some exceptions, such as `javax.persistence.OptimistickLockException`, might occur at the end of a transaction. Because the interceptors are involved in the same transactions as well – it is not possible to catch such exceptions.

Interceptors help you to realize non-functional requirements without touching the business code. They aren't as powerful as fully fledged AOP languages, but sufficient for most of the use cases. I will cover the examples above in greater detail in Chapter 5 when discussing the ThreadTracker, Dependency Injection Extender, or Payload Extractor patterns. In an enterprise environment, AOP and interceptors are less common than you may think. The Java EE container comes already with a bunch of useful aspects, which can be enabled declaratively without any coding. In fact, a Java EE developer should not even know that persistency, transactions, concurrency, or conversational state are aspects.

EJB 3 and JPA Support

The support for JPA in EJB 3 goes far beyond pure Dependency Injection. The injected `EntityManager` instance is managed by the container. This task is trivial in a single-threaded environment, but Java EE is a multithreaded, concurrent environment. The EJB container does the bookkeeping and manages the `EntityManager` instance in a transactional manner behind the scenes.

The previously introduced session bean example is more complex to realize in a web container environment:

```
@PersistenceContext
private EntityManager em;

public void create(Book book) {
    this.em.persist(book);
}
}
```

Since the `EntityManager` instance isn't thread-safe, it cannot be cached or stored between requests. Before every method invocation, it has to be obtained from the `EntityManagerFactory` (which is thread-safe) and closed after every method invocation. The same is true for exceptions; the `EntityManager` has to be closed in the `finally` block. The following example demonstrates the manual management of `EntityManager` in web container:

```
@PersistenceUnit EntityManagerFactory emf;
```

```
@Resource UserTransaction utx;

...
public void create(Book book){
  EntityManager em = emf.createEntityManager();
  try{
    utx.begin();
    em.joinTransaction();
    em.persist(book);
    utx.commit();
  } catch(Exception exe){
                                    //handle exception
    try {
      utx.rollback();
    } catch (Exception e) {}
} finally {
    em.close();
  }
}
```

Some of the methods in the EntityManager interface (injected with TRANSACTION scope) require an active transaction. They include persist, merge, remove, flush, and refresh. These methods throw an exception, TransactionRequiredException, if there is no transaction and the persistence context is transaction-scoped.

Regardless of whether the application runs in a web container or not, you have to start transactions anyway. In a managed environment, the transactions are started for you; it just happens behind the scenes before every method invocation (the convention is REQUIRED transaction scope for the business methods). In a web container you will have to inject the UserTransaction instance and associate the current transaction with the EntityManager instance using the joinTransaction method.

Transactions are required infrastructure for the EntityManager interface. Transactions are not only required for consistent database access, but do control the time of detachment of the JPA entities.

The Transaction mode

The PersistenceContextType.TRANSACTION is the default configuration. If you are injecting the EntityManager into a stateless session bean, this setting is used by convention. In fact, it is the only possible option for stateless session beans. After every transactional method call, the EntityManager gets closed and cleared. All attached or managed entities become detached. Changes to those entities will be not synchronized with the database. This behavior is caused by transactions and not method invocations. If the first stateless session bean opens a transaction and invokes another session bean with TransactionAttribute.REQUIRED or TransactionAttribute.MANDATORY, all entities remain attached for the duration of the whole transaction.

You can cascade the session beans in arbitrary depth in the context of a single transaction, without loosing the consistency. This gives you great flexibility in designing the business logic. It is just enough to start a transaction in the boundary / first session bean (BookFacadeBean). The transaction will be propagated automatically to the invoked session beans (BookServiceBean) or finer services. Remember, inside the transaction all JPA entities will remain attached, regardless of how many nested session bean methods are invoked. In the following example, a service is invoked in the context of a transaction:

```
@Stateless
@TransactionAttribute(TransactionAttributeType.MANDATORY)
public class BookServiceBean implements BookService {
    @PersistenceContext
    private EntityManager em;

    public Book find(long id){
        return this.em.find(Book.class,id);
    }
}
```

All the changes performed to an attached entity will be automatically and transparently synchronized with the database for you. No additional merging is required. This saves a lot of boilerplate code. The change performed by any of the subsequent invocations is visible immediately to all other transaction participants. You are always working with the entity per reference, so the EntityManager#find method of any session beans involved in the active transaction will return the same instance of the entity.

```
@Stateless
@TransactionAttribute(TransactionAttributeType.REQUIRES_NEW)
public class BookFacadeBean implements BookFacade {

    @EJB
    private BookService bookService;

    public void update(long id,String name){
        Book found = this.bookService.find(id);
        found.setName(name);
    }
}
```

This is actually the natural, expected behavior of a stateless session bean and it is consistent with J2EE best practices. Most of the J2EE architectures relied on the value object, renamed later to Data Transfer Object (DTO) pattern. All parameter and return values were copies of the actual CMP 2.0 entities. This was necessary because CMP 2.0 entities could not be serialized, it was simply not possible to transfer them to a remote JVM.

The behavior of a transaction-scoped EntityManager is similar, except all the JPA entities do not have to be copied. As soon as they become detached or unmanaged, they can be used as DTOs. Dedicated DTOs became optional, but can still be used for additional decoupling of the persistence layer from its clients.

To summarize:

- The transaction scope is the default setting and suitable for most applications.

- The `EntityManager` maintains an internal cache for the durability of the transaction. All entities referenced from the cache are managed; changes to those entities will be synchronized with the database at the end of the current transaction.

- Between method invocations another instance of stateless session beans can be associated with the caller. Therefore the `EntityManager` has to be cleared or closed after every call. The closing and clearing of the `EntityManager` causes the detachment of all managed entities in the transaction.

- After completing a transactional method, all entities become detached. Therefore all entities returned to the caller can be treated as DTOs. Changes to their state will not be synchronized with the database.

The Extended mode

The extended mode is similar to the transaction mode except that the `EntityManager` is not going to be cleared after every transactional call; instead all entities remain attached as long as the stateful session bean lives. Because the cache is not cleared after every transaction, the state of the session bean becomes client-specific. This is the reason, why this mode only works with stateful session beans. Only a 1:1 relation between the client and an `EntityManager` instance guarantees that all client requests will be routed to the same stateful session bean instance. Any modification to the entities will be synchronized at the end of the next transaction. So a commit of a transaction implies a save operation and the rollback an undo operation.

The extended mode is therefore very similar to the application scope `EntityManager`, which is entirely managed by the application. In both cases the cache is not cleared automatically; instead, clearing the cache is the responsibility of the developer.

A stateful session bean is able to keep client-specific state, and thus hold an attached JPA entity for caching purposes. This makes it even accessible without the invocation of `EntityManager`. Once located, the JPA entity can be easily modified, even outside of an active transaction.

In the following example, a JPA entity is cached in a stateful session bean and accessible via a simple getter. It is important to return the entity per reference through a local interface. Through a remote interface, all return values would be copied which would destroy the idea of transparent persistency. A copy would have to be merged with the `EntityManager`..

The `Book` entity has to be located only once. All relations, regardless whether eager or lazy, can be traversed from the `Book` entity, even outside of the session bean.

```
@Stateful
@Local(BookFacade.class)
@TransactionAttribute(TransactionAttributeType.NEVER)
public class BookFacadeBean implements BookFacade {

    @PersistenceContext(type=PersistenceContextType.EXTENDED)
    private EntityManager em;

    private Book currentBook;

    public Book find(long id){
```

```
            this.currentBook = this.em.find(Book.class, id);
            return this.currentBook;
        }

    public void create(Book book){
        this.em.persist(book);
                            this.currentBook = book;
        }

    public Book getCurrentBook() {
        return currentBook;
        }

    @TransactionAttribute(TransactionAttributeType.REQUIRES_NEW)
    public void save(){
        //nothing to do here
        }
}
```

The transaction setting of the BookFacade may appear a little esoteric at the first glance. On the class level the TransactionAttributeType.NEVER is used. Therefore it is guaranteed, that no method of the bean will be invoked in an active transaction. The method save, however, overwrites this rule with the setting TransactionAttributeType.REQUIRES_NEW at method level, which in turn starts a new transaction every time. The method create in turn was not annotated with TransactionAttributeType.REQUIRES_NEW even though the EntityManager#persist method is invoked inside. This invocation will not fail with the TransactionRequiredException. It will not fail because on an EntityManager with an EXTENDED persistence context, the persist, remove, merge, and refresh methods may be called regardless of whether a transaction is active or not. The effects of these operations will be committed to the database when the extended persistence context is enlisted in a transaction and the transaction commits. It actually happens in the empty method save.

The method save is annotated with TransactionAttributeType.REQUIRES_NEW, but comes without any implementation. The most interesting part happens after the method is invoked; the active transaction is going to be committed. The EntityManager is joined by the container to the transaction. It takes part on it. The reaction of the EntityManager to a commit operation is the synchronization of all the attached or managed entities with the database. This explains the empty body of the save method. The interesting stuff happens before and after the method—a perfect sample for an interceptor, or a crosscutting concern.

The invocation of the method save causes a flush of all modified entities to the database. Every change performed before this invocation is persisted after it. The implementation of a simple, one-level, undo mechanism is very simple as well:

```
public void undo(){
    this.em.refresh(this.currentBook);
}
```

The state of the current entity, and thus all performed changes, will be undone and replaced with the current state of the database. However, this is not a real undo operation. The state of the database could be newer than the actual state before all the local modifications.

The approach with the EXTENDED EntityManager significantly minimizes method calls for the purpose of synchronization. It integrates well with web frameworks such as JavaServer Faces (JSF), where data binding allows declarative synchronization between the view and the domain model.

The Extended Mode and Concurrency

The obvious problem in a concurrent environment of a stateful session bean is its caching behavior. The cache of the EntityManager is completely disconnected from the database. Database changes will be not automatically propagated to the local cache or the stateful session bean. Ensuring the consistency is the responsibility of the application developer.

Every session, or stateful session bean, instance is completely independent of another one. Multiple sessions and independent caches may exist in parallel. Concurrent access to the same stateful session bean instance, however, is not allowed.

Both sessions can contain entities with the same identifier. So entities from different sessions may actually refer to the same record in the database. Because the sessions are independent of each other, the cache can become inconsistent.

The problem can be solved in one of two ways: with pessimistic locks or optimistic concurrency. The pessimistic locking would massively hurt the scalability and performance of your application, so the only viable solution remains optimistic locking.

The data in the cache could become stale, but during the write operations (or, more precisely, at the end of the next transaction) the version field in the database will be compared with the @Version field in the entity. If it matches, the write operations will be performed; if not the exception OptimisticLockException will be thrown.

Hence "lost updates" between caches and users are detected at the end of a transaction; the recovery from such an optimistic collision is not convenient for the end users. Such a collision can occur after several minutes, but can also take hours. An OptimisticLockException causes the detachment of all managed entities, so all changes get lost and have to be merged or reloaded from the database.

This challenge can be approached by providing functionality for refreshing the state of the session from the database. The method refresh with cascading relations does the heavy lifting. All associated entities will be refreshed with the database state. Although all entities remain attached and possible local changes will be lost.

For non-trivial applications a more practicable merge strategy is needed. The conflict resolution strategies are identical to version control systems such as CVS or Subversion configured to operate in optimistic manner:

- Local cache overwrites the database

- Database overwrites the local cache
- The end user has to merge local changes with the database manually

These different solutions should be communicated in the early development stage to the domain experts and customer. Each choice requires changes to the user interface and page flow. This can become quite expensive in later iterations. The choice of the right strategy is a business decision, so it cannot be decided by the developer; it has to be made by the domain experts.

The problem of disjoined, independent caches is not specific to stateful session beans or extended `EntityManager`. Every clustered application server has to deal with the same problem, having independent caches of each cluster node.

Application servers usually broadcast messages to neighbor nodes that invalidate the changed (dirty) entity. This lowers the probability of `OptimisticLockExceptions`, but does not completely avoid them. The notifications are performed asynchronously in most cases.

The Problem with Lazy Loading and Transparent Persistence

The transaction-scoped `EntityManager` detaches all managed entities after each transaction. Because a transaction-scoped `EntityManager` can be only be used from a stateless session bean a transaction in this context is synonymous with method invocation. All return values of stateless session beans are detached and not managed entities—they are comparable to DTOs.

A detached entity is no more able to transparently load its dependent entities. Any attempt to invoke a method of lazy-loaded relations will result in a runtime, provider-dependent exception. To overcome this problem all lazy relations have to be loaded inside the stateless session bean method before the transaction ends. Another solution would be to use eager relations exclusively, but then more objects than needed would be loaded in every method. In the worst case, the whole database would be fetched eagerly inside a transaction.

The JPA specification foresees *fetch joins*, specific queries that eagerly load the relations, to solve this problem. Regardless which approach you are choosing to load the relations eagerly before detaching, the challenge here is to know in advance which relation path is actually needed for a particular use case.

An extended `EntityManager` is more flexible at this point. Because the entities are not going to be detached after every transaction and thus invocation, the decision which relation has to be loaded, can be significantly deferred. Accessing the entities through a `@Local` interface per reference makes even such a decision completely obsolete. Because the entities remain managed, the relations can be conveniently loaded at any point. Even in the presentation layer (for example, in a JSF component) a lazy relation can be loaded just by accessing the method or field. Setting all relations as *lazy* is not necessary—the convention is already suitable. The X:1 relations are loaded eagerly and all 1:N relations lazily by default. This convention is appropriate for most use cases. Especially the default `EAGER` setting of the 1:1 relation should be changed to `LAZY` only rarely.

A `@OneToOne` relation points directly to another entity. The on-demand fetching can only be achieved with byte code manipulation. The performance gain is minimal; only one entity is loaded on demand. For the dedicated loading of the `LAZY` relation at least one additional SQL statement is needed. Lazy loading of single valued relations is only suitable for huge and rarely used child entities. A good example of that would be an entity with @Lob fields in it. Only then this approach may pay off. The default fetch strategy in @OneToOne relations is already set to EAGER, so there is no need to specify it explicitly.

```
@OneToOne(fetch=FetchType.EAGER)
private ChildEntity entity;

@OneToMany(fetch=FetchType.LAZY)
private Collection<ChildEntity> entities;
```

On the other hand, @OneToMany relations come already with LAZY fetching as default, which is reasonable as well. The *many* side of the relation can have hundreds, thousands, or even millions of dependent entities. Loading them on demand can increase the performance and lowers the memory consumption. This optimization, however, is only suitable for rarely needed entities from the many side. Otherwise loading all needed entities will result in more interactions with the database.

Accessing and modifying lazy relations outside of a stateless session bean only works in case the web container and EJB container are executed in the same JVM. The distribution of presentation and business components into different JVMs forces the serialization of the persistent entities. Because the entities are no more accessible per reference, all needed relations have to be preloaded before serialization. Using an extended EntityManager through @Remote interfaces is not beneficial and should be avoided; the lazy-loading problem still persists and the developer has to preload all relations in advance.

The transparency of relation fetching, change tracking, and simple save and undo mechanisms makes the usage of the extended EntityManager especially interesting for domain-driven, object-oriented applications. In this particular case, the entities would consists of the state and behavior. A method of a single entity could change the state on the entire graph of dependent objects. Because at least the root entity remains managed between method calls, all changes will be transparently flushed to the database.

The entities can be treated as fully fledged, well encapsulated, domain objects with real behavior. You can work with the objects transparently, without worrying too much about persistency. Because the graph remains attached, there is no need for synchronization and merging. This greatly reduces the total amount of infrastructural methods and boilerplate code.

Accessing EJB

Until now I covered the DI mechanisms inside the EJB container. Most enterprise applications, however, come with more or less rich presentation layers, which have to access the business logic. The Dependency Injection of EJB and resources is available outside the EJB container as well. The following technologies listed are able to use Dependency Injection directly:

- **Servlet:** Servlets, Servlet filters, event listeners
- **JSP:** Tag handlers, tag library, event listeners

- **JSF:** Scoped managed beans
- **JAX-WS:** Service endpoints, handlers
- **Java EE Platform:** Main class, login callback handler (of the application client)
- **JAX-RS:** Root resource classes, providers
- **EJB:** Beans, interceptors

Nevertheless, the usage of session beans is not limited to the specifications listed above. Any non-Java EE frameworks are able to access the session beans using the traditional lookup mechanism. Frameworks such as Google Guice, Wicket, Struts, Tapestry, and many others could just rely on a utility class (formerly `ServiceLocator`, a Bean Locator pattern that I will cover in Chapter 5) which performs the lookup internally and returns a reference to an EJB.

The EJB 3.1 specification introduced the notion of global JNDI naming. The container uses the following syntax to generate a global JNDI name and register a session bean with it:

```
java:global[/<app-name>]/<module-name>/<bean-name>#<fully-
qualified-interface-name>
```

Every deployed session bean can be conveniently accessed using the naming scheme above via `InitialContext#lookup`.

Session beans are accessible for standard as well as non-standard frameworks and Java EE extensions. Only frameworks included in the Java EE umbrella, however, are able to access the EJBs via Dependency Injection out of the box.

Servlets are the foundation of nearly all popular Java web frameworks available today. Accessing to EJB from Servlets works the same as access between EJBs. The reference to a `@Local` or `@Remote` session bean can be easily injected using the `@EJB` annotation.

```
public class HelloServlet extends HttpServlet {

  @EJB
  private HelloBean helloBean;
 protected void doGet(HttpServletRequest request, HttpServletResponse
response)
    throws ServletException, IOException {
  }
```

The session beans can be either deployed to an independent ejb-jar module or packaged with the Servlet in a web archive (war). The simplest possible solution would be the injection of a stateless session bean with no-interface view. Servlets are stateless, pooled components, so the Dependency Injection here is only limited to the stateless session beans. The injection of a stateful session bean into a Servlet would make it shareable across different browsers. Even worse, the stateful session bean would be accessed concurrently, which is not allowed and would result in the exception `javax.ejb.ConcurrentAccessException`.

```
@Stateless
public class HelloBean{

    public String sayHello(String message) {
```

```
        String retVal = "Echo from bean: " + message;
        return retVal;
    }
}
```

Similarly all kinds of session beans can be injected directly into the JSF backing beans. Even the injection of stateful session beans into session-scoped backing beans is supported. The Dependency Injection is identical to the Servlet example above: the annotation @EJB has to be used also in this case. Access to a stateful session bean with EXTENDED EntityManager from a session-scoped backing bean allows access to attached entities. An attached entity can be bound to a JSF view declaratively. This not only minimizes the round trips, but makes the external session bean interfaces very lean.

The JAX-WS and JAX-RS APIs are mainly stateless, so only Dependency Injection of stateless session beans is suitable in this case. Also in these cases it works using the same principle.

Although most of the presentation components such as Servlets, backing beans and others are not thread-safe, the Dependency Injection of a stateless session bean solves the problem as well. The container will manage the concurrency and transactions for you. Parallel calls will be dispatched to different stateless session bean, thread-safe instances.

So instead of using, for example, EntityManager directly, it is always worth to wrap it with a stateless session bean and use injection to access it.

Summary

Configuration by Exception together with Dependency Injection radically simplified the programming model. Extensive XML deployment descriptors as well as the whole factory/lookup infrastructure became superfluous. EJB 3 components come with suitable defaults and do not have to be configured. The same is true for the DI—if there is only one choice, you don't have to configure it.

In addition, the programming model became surprisingly clean—you can deploy a POJO as a session bean applying only the @Stateless or @Stateful annotations. No realization of API interfaces or other framework dependencies are required any more.

This fact alone eliminated already the need for patterns such as Service Locator or Business Delegate. I will discuss the more appropriate Java EE patterns and best practices in the following chapters.

3

Rethinking the Business Tier

Core J2EE patterns continue to be popular among Java developers. Most patterns, however, are solutions to problems that have been addressed in Java EE. The continued use of some of these patterns only leads to inefficient and hard-to-maintain applications.

Another problem with J2EE applications are unrealistic, non-functional requirements and assumptions. Especially flexibility, decoupling from particular services and resources, or extensibility were misinterpreted and led to over-engineered applications.

Some J2EE patterns are still valid or optional. This chapter will help you rethink the Core J2EE patterns in the context of the Java EE 5 platform.

Service Façade (Application Service)

During J2EE times, Session Façade patterns were just wrappers of entity beans or DAOs. They were motivated by the shortcoming of the spec, rather than by design best practices. The technical nature of the Session Façade patterns was the reason for their thin logic. The Application Service pattern was the use case controller or façade that coordinated multiple Session Façades. In Java EE, however, things have changed.

Problem

The original motivation for the Application Service pattern is still valid and useful for service-oriented architecture styles: "You want to centralize business logic across several business-tier components and services" (www.corej2eepatterns.com/Patterns2ndEd/ApplicationService.htm).

The access to the business logic components has to be as convenient and as consistent as possible. Only a coarse-grained API can meet the requirements, it should be understandable by domain experts.

In Java EE an explicit remote and transactional boundary is still needed. The exposure of fine-grained business logic over remote interfaces simply doesn't work. Network latency is too high for fine-grained access and it is hard to execute fine-grained methods in a transaction context over the network.

Forces

- A predefined, easy-to-consume, business API is needed.
- The state of the component after the invocation of the Service Façade should be consistent.
- The realization behind the Service Façade should be encapsulated.
- The Service Façade interface should be usable as a remote service.
- The signature of the exposed methods should be stable and remain compatible, even if the realization of the component changes.

Solution

Service Façade is a stateless (in exceptional cases also stateful) session bean with a local business interface. A remote business interface should only be provided if it is going to be used from outside the Java Virtual Machine (JVM) and not injected into a Servlet, backing bean, or other web component. This is the case with an Eclipse or NetBeans Rich Client Platform (RCP) application, for example.

The Service Façade methods are designed from the domain perspective and are therefore coarse-grained. A relation to use cases, user stories, or some other kind of specification should be identifiable at first glance. Best case scenario, the methods should be understandable for domain experts or even end users. The following example shows a double-view Service Façade with standard configuration:

```
@Stateless
@Local(BookOrderingServiceLocal.class)
@Remote(BookOrderingServiceRemote.class)
@TransactionAttribute(TransactionAttributeType.REQUIRES_NEW)
public class BookOrderingServiceBean implements BookOrderingServiceLocal {

    public void cancelOrder(String id) {
    }

    public void order(String isbn, String name) {
    }
```

The Service Façade is the boundary between the presentation and business layers. The methods of the façade are triggered by the end user. Every interaction between the user and the system is a business transaction. The transaction is either completed in its entirety or not at all.

The simplest way to realize such business transactions is to map them to technical transactions. A stateless session bean with container-managed transactions (CMTs) is perfectly suitable for that purpose. A Service Façade is therefore annotated with the `TransactionAttributeType.REQUIRES_NEW` class level. This setting is inherited by all methods. `REQUIRES_NEW` always starts a new transaction and suspends the existing one.

Although not mandatory, this approach is more explicit. Even though a Service Façade is the boundary between the presentation and business layers, it is impossible to have an existing transaction. Service Façade instances shouldn't invoke each other—it just cannot be expressed by our semantics. The presentation components invoke the Service Façade method, which starts a transaction and propagates it to the services. Each interaction is modeled as a Service Façade method. A Service Façade is defined as a boundary, so invocations between Service Façade methods are therefore excluded.

From a technical point of view, however, there is no difference between the `REQUIRES_NEW` and `REQUIRED` transaction attributes of a Service Façade—you can use either attribute. The setting `REQUIRED` either starts a new transaction (in case it does not already exist) or reuses an existing transaction. As mentioned earlier, an existing transaction cannot exist in our case.

The stateless nature of the boundary causes detachment of all JPA-entities after every method call. A Service Façade implies a service-oriented way of thinking and promotes procedural programming. The methods are actually procedures, which expect parameters and return the result per value. The parameters and results can be either Transfer Objects (TOs) or detached JPA entities.

The exposed view of the Service Façade is coarse-grained and thus of less interest for reuse. The logic is in general too complex to be implemented directly in the Service Façade. It would bloat the method implementation and lead to hard-to-maintain code.

The Service Façade is designed to act as a use case controller and coordinate independent services. This ensures that the services can remain independent of each other and can be reused in other contexts or use cases. The controlled services have to be invoked in the context of the Service Façade transaction. Only then can the requirement for consistency be fulfilled.

Rethinking

Application Service (Service Façade) used to be a mandatory part of every J2EE application. It was used to isolate the presentation tier from the business tier. The parameters of the Application Service were either primitives or Data Transfer Objects (DTOs). Entity beans were not detachable, so it wasn't an option to work with entity beans as parameters or return values. The remote or local view of the Application Service as well as the realization were dependent on the EJB 2.x API. The separation between the technical infrastructure and the business logic was not given, so in most cases the Application Service was just a delegate to a plain old Java object (POJO) which implemented the valuable business logic. This separation is no longer necessary, because the Service Façade is a clean POJO that only depends on a few annotations.

The distinction between a pure controller and service is blurred as well. In J2EE, the Application Service tended to play the controller role only and coordinated existing services. This wasn't beneficial for simple, CRUD-like use cases where the Application Service only delegates all invocations to a Session Façade with exactly the same signature. The Application Service was a wrapper, with virtually no added value. A common excuse for such architectures was the future-proof and scalability requirements. However, in most cases this constellation wasn't touched until the end of the application lifecycle.

Service Façade is no longer the only choice in Java EE. The clean separation between technology and business realization allows the implementation of domain-driven approaches directly with session beans and JPA entities. Such object-oriented systems are stateful and require fine-grained interaction between the presentation and the business logic. The gateway can be used to implement this principle as well; it is, however, the exact opposite of the Service Façade. From the view of the Service Façade the gateway could even be considered as an anti-pattern.

With the introduction of EJB 3.0 the local and remote homes became optional and should no longer be used. With EJB 3.1 even the Business Interface is no longer mandatory, so you can use directly the bean implementation (the no-interface view).

The Service Façade is comprised of a local business interface and its implementation; it is a common stateless session bean. It is not recommended to use a no-interface view, because it makes testing and mocking harder. All methods are transactional—they start a new transaction on every invocation.

Conventions

- Service Façade resides in a component that is realized as a Java package with a domain-specific name, for example, `ordermgmt`.

- The realization of the façade (business interface and the bean implementation) resides in a subpackage with the name *facade* or *boundary*, for example, `ordermgmt.facade` or `ordermgmt.boundary`.

- The business interface is named after business concepts, without the obligatory local or remote suffix, for example, `OrderService` and `OrderServiceBean`.

- It is not required to use the term *facade* in the name of the bean—it's redundant. For identification purposes you could use a `@ServiceFacade` annotation.
- The Service Façade always starts a new transaction; it is not possible to participate in a transaction in progress. It is deployed with the `REQUIRES_NEW` transaction attribute.

Participants and Responsibilities

In Java EE, the Service Façade became more pragmatic. Its main responsibility is still the composition of independent and reusable services, but for simple use cases it can directly realize business logic without delegating to other participants. Figure 1shows use cases of the Service Façade.

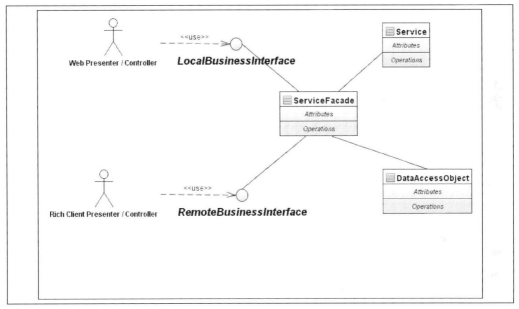

Figure 1. *Service Façade with its participants*

In more complex scenarios a Service Façade coordinates some services or DAOs. The remote business interface should be used by remote clients only. Wherever possible, the local interface should be accessed instead. Especially web frameworks such as Wicket, JSF, or Struts should rely on the local interface only.

Strategies

This section discusses the specific variants and Service Façade configurations. Dependent on your needs a Service Façade can be scaled from a simple CRUD Facade, which realizes generic data management operations, to a full-blown asynchronous SOA strategy.

CRUD Façade

A CRUD façade is nothing else than an exposed, transactional DAO. From a purist's point of view, a CRUD use case has to be realized by a service façade that delegates all calls to a DAO. In case of CRUD, however, even a dedicated DAO is already an example of overengineering. A CRUD façade is a service façade with the functionality of a DAO, or a DAO with the metadata attributes of a Service Façade.

For the sake of simplicity a CRUD façade can be deployed with a no-interface view as well. All other strategies are deployed with a local or remote business interface. Especially in the case of a generic data source for the Wicket, Web Beans, or JSF models, there is no need for an interface. The `EntityManager` in the CRUD façade can be easily mocked-out if necessary.

Dual-View Façade

In most cases, the Service Façade is accessed from web components directly and thus in process. Although most application servers recognize this co-location and get rid of the remote infrastructure to access the EJB directly, the EJB container is required by the spec to copy all parameters and return values. Unnecessary copying of all parameters and return values can become quite expensive—the performance impact is dependent on the parameter. Primitive types have no impact; the impact of copying of a complex graph of interconnected value objects can be massive. The following example illustrates the per-reference versus per-value semantics.

```
public class LocalVsValueTest extends HttpServlet {

    @EJB
    private BookOrderingServiceLocal bookOrderingServiceLocal;
    @EJB
    private BookOrderingServiceRemote bookOrderingServiceRemote;

    protected void processRequest(HttpServletRequest request,
HttpServletResponse response)  throws ServletException, IOException {
        ParameterTest tst = new ParameterTest(42);
        Object local = bookOrderingServiceLocal.referenceTest(tst);
        Object remote = bookOrderingServiceRemote.referenceTest(tst);
        out.println("The same reference (local service)?: " + (tst == local));
        out.println("The same reference (remote service)?: " + (tst == remote));
    }
}
```

Both views are injected into a Servlet. In both cases an object is passed as parameter and returned without any processing:

```
public Object referenceTest(Object reference) {
    return reference;
    }
```

Exactly the same method is exposed twice: over the remote and local interfaces. The output is not really surprising. The same reference is returned from the local business interface and a copy in the remote case.

```
The same reference (local service)?: true
The same reference (remote service)?: false
```

This is how every EJB container should behave. Most of the containers, however, provide proprietary extensions to return a reference even in the remote case. For that purpose often an application server–specific deployment descriptor has to be provided. Glassfish uses the `<pass-by-reference>true</pass-by-reference>` tag in the proprietary `sun-ejb-jar.xml` file to activate this optimization.

The façade's remote interface is exposed to external clients, so it has to remain stable during the lifecycle. On the other hand, not all methods need to be exposed remotely; some of them are only dedicated for internal use such as workflow engines, web applications, or message-driven beans.

The above requirement could be solved easily in traditional object-oriented programming. A class could expose the public methods to external clients as a formalized contract and dedicate the package private or protected methods to its friends. You can approach this requirement similarly with a Service Façade. Its remote business view could be exposed to the external clients with high stability requirements, whereas the local view could be extended on demand in a more pragmatic manner. The local business interface extends the remote interface, which makes maintenance easy. It is enough to declare the additional functionality in the local interface—all methods will be inherited from the remote method (see Figure 2).

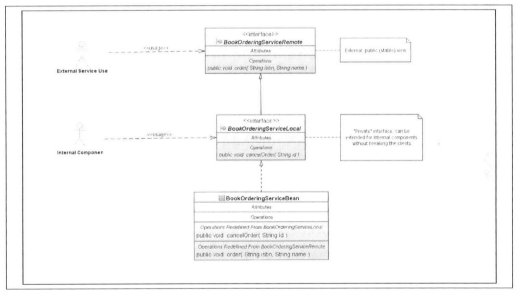

Figure 2. The dual-view Service Façade.

The session bean has to implement all methods anyway. At the beginning, the local interface is probably empty and implicitly inherits all methods from the remote business interface. As the implementation evolves, the internal view of the session bean can incrementally be extended without breaking the public view. Both interfaces can be easily injected to their consumers. The local view is only available for the consumers inside the same JVM, but is not limited to be used by web frameworks only. It can be exposed via a RESTFul interface, JMS, or any other kind of adapter.

SOA Façade

The SOA Façade, compared to the other strategies, is asynchronous in nature and has rich metadata. In an SOA-world, services are expected to be autonomous and independent of each other as well as technology agnostic. These two facts already speak against the use of distributed transactions (2PC). A transactional and consistent serial invocation of different services is therefore impossible. The solution to this challenge is asynchronous messaging, fire-and-forget style. The asynchronous communication implies that the error resolution and consistency are the responsibility of the message consumer not the producer.

At the implementation level, you have to omit the return value. All methods are `void`. This in turn makes a Service Façade especially interesting as a JMS consumer. The incoming messages are consumed by a message-driven bean and transformed into the Service Façade parameters. The following example shows a message-driven bean as an asynchronous adapter.

```
@MessageDriven(mappedName = "jms/ServiceFacade", activationConfig = {
@ActivationConfigProperty(propertyName = "acknowledgeMode", propertyValue =
"Auto-acknowledge"),
@ActivationConfigProperty(propertyName = "destinationType", propertyValue =
"javax.jms.Queue")
    })
public class BookMessageConsumerBean implements MessageListener {

    @EJB
    private BookOrderingServiceLocal bookOrderingServiceLocal;

    public void onMessage(Message msg) {
        if(msg instanceof ObjectMessage){
            try {
            ObjectMessage objectMessage = (ObjectMessage) msg;
                Serializable payload = objectMessage.getObject();
                if (payload instanceof OrderVO) {
                    OrderVO orderVO = (OrderVO) payload;
                    String name = orderVO.getName();
                    String isbn = orderVO.getIsbn();
                  this.bookOrderingServiceLocal.order(isbn, name);
                } else {
                  handleError("Payload is not a OrderVO", payload);
                }
            } catch (JMSException ex) {
             throw new IllegalStateException("…: " + message,ex);
            }
        }else{
    handleError("Message is not of type ObjectMessage",message);
        }
}
```

The message-driven bean is already transactional; the EJB container starts a transaction before the `onMessage` method. This becomes a problem, because the Service Façade also starts a new transaction—it is usually deployed with the `TransactionAttributeType.REQUIRES_NEW` level. Java EE does not support nested transactions, so the message-driven bean transaction will succeed, regardless of whether the Service Façade's transaction was rolled back or not.

Success for a message-driven bean means removal of the message from the `Destination`. This leads to nasty errors; the business logic can fail and cause a rollback of the active transaction in the Service Façade and the message-driven bean will not recognize this failure. A rollback can be caused by the invocation of `SessionContext#setRollbackOnly` without even throwing an exception. Although the transaction fails in the Service Façade, the message will be consumed anyway. It silently disappears from the destination. Such a case could have a severe impact, especially in case the message was intended to be delivered reliably. The client relies on the guaranteed delivery of the message, which actually happens, but the message gets lost between the consumer and the business logic.

The issue above can be fixed easily with the `TransactionAttributeType.REQUIRED` attribute or be made even more explicit with the `MANDATORY` type on the Service Façade. The transaction started in the message-driven bean will then be propagated to the Service Façade. A possible rollback will prevent the message to be acknowledged—it will return to the destination and be redelivered after a configurable period of time (in most cases immediately). This in turn can lead to indefinite delivery attempts, which can be fixed counting the redelivery failures and moving the `Message` to an error queue after a certain number of attempts, or setting up the JMS provider.

Wrapping a Service Façade with a message-driven bean is a common way to invoke synchronous methods asynchronously (see Service Activator). The problem described above has nothing to do with JMS, but with transactional messaging. The Service Façade has to reuse the propagated transaction rather than starting a new one.

The fire-and-forget communication style is only one aspect of an SOA. In the first place, rich meta data and explicit contracts make the distinction between enterprise application integration (EAI) architecture and real SOA. The additional description of the contract (so called meta data) can be used for more or less pragmatic purposes. The main problem with fire-and-forget messaging is the complex error handling and many necessary type checks. The decoupling does not come for free.

Some of the type checks are crosscutting functionality and can be factored out easily into a reusable interceptor. The expected type information has to be passed to the interceptor from the contract, which can be done with a custom annotation:

```
@Target({ElementType.METHOD,ElementType.TYPE})
@Retention(RetentionPolicy.RUNTIME)
@Documented
public @interface ExpectedMessageType {
    Class<? extends Message> value();
}
```

Because a message-driven bean consists of only one method, `onMessage`, the annotation can be declared on the class level as well as the method itself. The only attribute of the `ExpectedMessageType` is the value with the type `Class`. It is intended to specify the expected type:

```
@ExpectedMessageType(ObjectMessage.class)
public void onMessage(Message message) {}
```

This meta information is leveraged by the `MessageTypeCheckInterceptor` interceptor.

```
public class MessageTypeCheckInterceptor {

    @AroundInvoke
    public Object audit(InvocationContext ic) throws Exception{
        Method method = ic.getMethod();
        if("onMessage".equals(method.getName())){
ExpectedMessageType messageType =
method.getAnnotation(ExpectedMessageType.class);
            Class type = messageType.value();
            Object messageParameter = ic.getParameters()[0];
    if(!type.isAssignableFrom(messageParameter.getClass())){
                escalateError(type,messageParameter);
            }
        }
                return ic.proceed();
    }
```

The interceptor is intended to be used with message-driven beans, so it only turns active for the method onMessage. It searches for the annotation, fetches the expected type, and compares it with the actual message type. In case it matches, the onMessage method will be invoked; otherwise the error will be escalated. Escalation does not mean just throwing an exception—the error has to be reported to some ticketing or emergency management system. From the interceptor point of view, it would suffice to publish the error via a dead letter or back-out queue. The consumption of the message, as well as the actual escalation, goes beyond the scope of the book and is proprietary in general.

The requirement for escalation of such messages is given for all fire-and-forget architectures and SOAs in particular. The centralization of proper error handling in an interceptor makes not only the code cleaner, it also minimizes the probability of errors. Furthermore, a centralized error-handling aspect can be easily maintained and configured.

The same idea of contract enrichment with metadata cannot only be applied to message-driven beans, but also to the Service Façade itself. Additional custom annotations on a class, method, and even parameter level could enrich the Service Façade and provide necessary information for monitoring, validation, or exception handling.

An @NotNull annotation on the parameter level could provide a hint for the interceptor for not-null checks:

```
@Interceptors(PreconditionInterceptor.class)
public class BookOrderingServiceBean implements BookOrderingServiceLocal {

    public void order(@NotNull String isbn, String name) {
        System.out.println("order ISBN: " + isbn + " name: " + name);
    }
}
```

The interceptor searches for parameters, checks for the not-null condition, and processes possible errors.

```
public class PreconditionInterceptor {
```

```
    @AroundInvoke
    public Object checkParameters(InvocationContext invocationContext) throws
Exception{
        List<String> invalidParameters = invalidParameters(invocationContext);
        if(!invalidParameters.isEmpty()){
            Method method = invocationContext.getMethod();
            escalateError(method,invalidParameters);
            throw new IllegalArgumentException("The contract of the method: " +
method + " was violated!");
        }else{
            return invocationContext.proceed();
        }
    }

    private List<String> invalidParameters(InvocationContext context){
        List<String> invalidParameters = new ArrayList<String>();
        Annotation[][] parameterAnnotations =
context.getMethod().getParameterAnnotations();
        for (int i=0;i<parameterAnnotations.length;i++) {
            for (Annotation annotation : parameterAnnotations[i]) {
                if(annotation instanceof NotNull){
                    Object value = context.getParameters()[i];
                    if(value == null){
                    Class parameterType =    context.getMethod().getParameterTypes()
[i];
            invalidParameters.add(i+ " parameter of type " +
parameterType.getName() + " is null!");
                    }
                }
            }
        }
        return invalidParameters;
    }

    private void escalateError(Method method,List<String> invalidParameters) {
                        //escalate errors
    }
}
```

The way error handling is realized, depends on the SOA infrastructure and its requirements. In case of validation errors it is sufficient to throw an exception, whereby the violation of Service Level Agreements (SLAs) such as performance contracts should be escalated to an emergency management infrastructure.

Another example of cross-cutting checks is, for example, the @MaxTime annotation, which defines the maximum invocation time. An interceptor could use this additional information, compare it with measured time, and report slow methods.

Lightweight Asynchronous Façade

From a conceptual point of view, a lightweight asynchronous façade is an SOA façade with pure EJB 3.1 without JMS. EJB 3.1 introduced an easy way to invoke session bean methods asynchronously. It is sufficient to declare methods as `@Asynchronous`; they will be invoked in a background thread. However, this approach has some limitations regarding the return value. Only `void` and `java.util.concurrent.Future` types are allowed. The result value of an asynchronous invocation is available to the client by returning a `Future<V>` object for which the `get()` and `get(long timeout, TimeUnit unit)` methods return the result value. A concrete `Future<V>` implementation called `javax.ejb.AsyncResult<V>` is provided by the container. `AsyncResult<V>` has a constructor that takes the result value as a parameter. The following example uses `@Asynchronous` methods in EJB 3.1:

```
@Asynchronous
@Stateless
public class BookOrderingServiceBean implements BookOrderingService {

    public Future<OrderVO> order(String isbn, String name) {
        OrderVO orderVO = ...
        return new AsyncResult<OrderVO>(orderVO);
    }

    public void cancelOrder(String id) {

    }
}
```

The built-in support for asynchronous processing is not only easier and cleaner compared to the JMS way, but it also allows bidirectional communication. Request-response communication style is much harder to implement using messaging. You would need an input queue, output queue, and at least three independent transactions. Furthermore, the initiator of the communication will have to wait for the response and block. The question is, how long to wait for a response? A timeout is not the guarantee for failure; it could occur just after a successful completion of the transaction. Such an error is hard to handle.

Also, from the management and monitoring perspective, is the `@Asynchronous` way comparable to JMS. The method is executed in the background thread, which in turn will come in general (it isn't covered by the spec) from a thread pool managed and monitored by the server.

The lightweight asynchronous façade is a viable alternative for a service-oriented way of exposing EJB functionality. Furthermore asynchronous EJB 3.1 methods are more appropriate for the implementation of asynchronous behavior, without typical SOA requirements.

Messaging and JMS in particular, provide looser coupling, but are harder to develop and maintain. Especially robust error handling is challenging and requires additional infrastructure-like error queues and even emergency management systems.

It is the developer's responsibility to ensure not only the correct type of the `javax.jms.Message`, but also its content. Both problems simply do not exist in case of `@Asynchronous` methods. The compiler checks the method signature for you.

In J2EE, JMS was often used just for asynchronous execution of synchronous methods. There was no other way to invoke session beans in a background thread. EJB 3.1 introduced an elegant way to solve the background execution without relying on messaging.

The `Future` even allows the cancellation of the current task with the method `boolean cancel(boolean mayInterruptIfRunning)`. The EJB, in turn, is able to check a cancellation request with the invocation of `SessionContext#isCancelled()`. Such a cancellation protocol is not available for JMS and is hard to implement on top of it as well.

Multichannel Façade

The Service Façade methods can be exposed easily via local and remote business interfaces with almost no effort. The local methods are available only for in-process clients, whereas the remote interfaces are accessible for other JVMs via RMI-IIOP as well. With additional meta data, Service Façade methods can be exposed via the Web Service Description Language (WSDL) and SOAP in particular. The following snippet demonstrates the exposure of a Service Façade as a WSDL/SOAP:

```
@Stateless
@Local(BookOrderingServiceLocal.class)
@Remote(BookOrderingServiceRemote.class)
@TransactionAttribute(TransactionAttributeType.REQUIRES_NEW)
@WebService
public class BookOrderingServiceBean implements BookOrderingServiceLocal {

    public void order(String isbn, @WebParam(name="orderName") String name) {
        System.out.println("order ISBN: " + isbn + " name: " + name);
    }
```

The Web Service annotations (JSR-181) allow the customization of the WSDL signature such as parameter names or method names, or even exclude particular methods from the WSDL completely.

The protocols described thus far are very well integrated with the EJB 3.1 spec. In the practice, there is still a need for the exposure of methods to non-Java clients in a more pragmatic and compatible fashion as is the case with SOAP.

RESTFul Web services (JSR-311) are just one option—and they are part of the Java EE 6 specification. RESTFul Web Services, however, is a standalone API which is not as tightly integrated with EJB 3.0 as JSR-181.EJB 3.1 can not only be injected into a JAX-RS resource, but can even expose itself as a REST resource and be addressed directly. A resource class is going to be uniquely addressed by a URL (order, in our case); its methods are associated with `@GET`, `@POST`, `@PUT`, `@DELETE`, and are invoked respectively.

```
import javax.ws.rs.ProduceMime;
import javax.ws.rs.ConsumeMime;
import javax.ws.rs.PUT;
import javax.ws.rs.Path;
import javax.ws.rs.GET;
import javax.ws.rs.PathParam;
import javax.ws.rs.QueryParam;

@Path("orders")
public class OrderRestAdapter {
```

```
@EJB
private BookOrderingService orderingService;

@GET
@ProduceMime("application/xml")
@Path("{orderId}/")
public OrderDTO getOrder(@PathParam("orderId") Integer orderId) {
    Order found = this.orderingService.find(orderId);
    OrderDTO orderDTO = new OrderDTO(found);
    return orderDTO;
}

@PUT
@ConsumeMime("application/xml")
public void placeOrder(OrderDTO orderDTO) {
```

```
this.orderingService.placeOrder(orderDTO.getOrder());
    }
}
```

The JSR-311 provider cares about the marshaling of the parameters and return values in a variety of formats. The most common formats are `text/plain`, `application/xml`, and `application/json`. A RESTFul client only relies on plain HTTP and the data format. Actually a RESTFul interface is far more robust and technology independent compared to SOAP and even the WS-* suite. HTTP didn't changed for years, and the parameters and return values are just plain payload and are as robust as the application's design.

The class `OrderRestAdapter` is enriched with some `javax.ws.rs` annotations, which are necessary for the exposure of a RESTFul interface. In addition, it is a typical adapter; it cares about the conversion of the `Order` entity into XML format. For that purpose a Java Annotation for XML Binding (JAXB) annotated DTO is used:

```
@XmlRootElement
public class OrderDTO {

    private Order order;

    public OrderDTO() {
        this.order = new Order();
    }

    public OrderDTO(Order order) {
        this.order = order;
    }

    @XmlElement
    public Integer getIsbn() {
        return this.order.getIsbn();
    }

    public void setIsbn(Integer isbn) {
```

```
        this.order.setIsbn(isbn);
    }
```

The `OrderDTO` delegates all invocations to the Order entity and exposes itself for JAXB serialization and de-serialization.

The popular open source project Hessian (http://hessian.caucho.com/) is a binary web service protocol. It is based on Servlets and is very fast and scalable. Bindings for different languages are already available. The integration with a Service Façade is very similar to RESTFul services. A protocol adapter takes the responsibility for the conversion of parameters and return values. It delegates the Service Façade via the local business interface, which remains protocol agnostic.

The key for success in multichannel scenarios is the decoration of a protocol-independent Service Façade with protocol-specific adaptors. The Service Façade remains largely technology neutral and consequently can be reused in different scenarios and protocols. With the emerge of Java FX, Flex, Air and Ajax, multichannel Service Façades become an interesting strategy for solving the interoperability problem.

Most of the protocols are not transactional, so there is a huge difference between JMS, RESTFul or Hessian integration. A message-driven bean starts the transaction before the invocation of the Service Façade, which is clearly not the case in RESTFul and Hessian scenarios. Thus the Service Façade can be still deployed with the `TransactionAttributeType.REQUIRES_NEW` attribute. The transaction will be started as the adapter invokes the façade, accordingly a rolled back transaction in the Service Façade will not cause a redelivery of a SOAP message or REST request.

IIOP Façade

IIOP Façade is a specific case of the Multichannel Façade. It exposes its remote view in a CORBA / IIOP compliant way. EJB 2 components were exposed via CORBA / IIOP per default. This is still the case with EJB 3, but only with RemoteHome and Remote views, so some additional work is required. Before I expose the interface in CORBA-compliant way, I should clarify the motivation first.

CORBA seems to have a bad reputation in the enterprise, it is said to be heavyweight. Even more interesting is the fact that CORBA / IIOP currently seems to get traction in embedded devices. Furthermore, CORBA is already widely deployed; bindings for many different languages are widely available. Clients written in other languages such as C++ can communicate easily with the IIOP Service Façade directly, without additional libraries or frameworks. Although it might sound somehow esoteric, direct IIOP communication between legacy clients and EJBs is often the simplest and most robust solution.

More likely is the requirement for efficient communication with .NET clients. Although .NET clients do not support IIOP directly, open source frameworks such as .NET-IIOP (http://iiop-net.sourceforge.net/) enable fast (times faster than SOAP) bridge between both platforms.

To make a Service Façade IIOP compatible, an EJB 2 Remote Home interface has to be provided:

```
public interface IIOPServiceFacadeHome extends EJBHome{
```

```
    public IIOPServiceFacadeRemote create() throws
CreateException,RemoteException;
}
```

It is basically the factory of the Remote Interface `IIOPServiceFacadeRemote`. It isn't the remote business interface, but the old EJB 2 style one:

```
public interface IIOPServiceFacadeRemote extends EJBObject{
    public String order(String isbn,String name) throws RemoteException;
}
```

The Bean class is marked as `@Stateless` and declares `IIOPServiceFacadeHome` with the `@RemoteHome` annotation. The remote interface does not have to be declared, it is just derived from the `IIOPServiceFacadeHome` factory method return type, as shown in the following IIOP-compatible EJB 3 snippet:

```
@Stateless
@RemoteHome(IIOPServiceFacadeHome.class)
public class IIOPServiceFacadeBean {
    @EJB
    private BookOrderingServiceLocal serviceLocal;

    public String order(String isbn,String name){
        this.serviceLocal.order(isbn, name);
        return "Book with isbn: " + isbn + " was ordered";
    }
}
```

`IIOPServiceFacadeBean` is still an EJB 3 stateless session bean, so that Dependency Injection remains available. Either the real Service Façade, or a Service could be injected. In case you have only to expose the functionality of the Service Façade via IIOP exclusively, an indirection of this kind is not needed.

For test purposes, the façade is invoked from an RMI-IIOP client using the plain JDK-ORB. No application server–specific JAR is required, as shown in this example

```
import com.abien.patterns.business.iiopsf.IIOPServiceFacadeHome;
import com.abien.patterns.business.iiopsf.IIOPServiceFacadeRemote;
import javax.naming.Context;
import javax.naming.InitialContext;
import javax.rmi.PortableRemoteObject;

public class CorbaClient {

  public static void main(String[] args) throws Exception{

    System.setProperty("org.omg.CORBA.ORBInitialPort","3700");
    System.setProperty("org.omg.CORBA.ORBInitialHost","localhost");
    System.setProperty(Context.INITIAL_CONTEXT_FACTORY,
"com.sun.jndi.cosnaming.CNCtxFactory");
        Context context = new InitialContext();
        Object object =
context.lookup("...business.iiopsf.IIOPServiceFacadeHome");
```

```
        IIOPServiceFacadeHome facadeHome = (IIOPServiceFacadeHome)
PortableRemoteObject.narrow(object, IIOPServiceFacadeHome.class);
        IIOPServiceFacadeRemote remote = facadeHome.create();
        String status = remote.order("12X","Java EE 6");
        System.out.println("Order status: " + status);
    }
}
```

The first attempt will end with a `NullPointerException`. It is caused by the lack of stubs. They can be created easily with the JDK `rmic` tool.

```
rmic -classpath [PATH_TO_EJB_API];[CLASS_FILES] -iiop
com.abien.patterns.business.iiopsf.IIOPServiceFacadeHome
```

```
rmic -classpath [PATH_TO_EJB_API];[CLASS_FILES] -iiop
com.abien.patterns.business.iiopsf.IIOPServiceFacadeRemote
```

JDK lacks of support for dynamic IIOP stub generation, what makes this step necessary. The IIOP-compatible view comes with some additional overhead and makes the Service Façade less clean. Even considering the additional overhead and ugliness a IIOP Service Façade could be the easiest possible solution for communication with non-Java, and especially C++ and .net clients.

Testing

Regardless on the strategy you choose, Service Façade exposes coarse-grained use cases and thus business functionality. It is the boundary between the presentation and business logic. Hence, it is often used as a separation strategy to build independent design and developer teams.

A Service Façade encapsulates the realization of the component and exposes a public API to its clients. High-quality unit tests for the public methods of a Service Façade are absolutely mandatory, whereby extensive tests of the artifacts behind the façade are optional in the overall context.

In EJB 3.0 support for embeddable EJB containers did not exist—so the bootstrapping had to be performed manually. Because EJB 3.0 and JPA entities are POJOs, it was rather painless. With few additional lines of code not only the injection of other beans (just an additional line of code) but of the `EntityManager` is possible.

The short initialization routine can be encapsulated easily in a base, abstract class. It takes the responsibility for the initialization of the `EntityManager`, as well as the `EntityTransaction`:

```
public class AbstractPersistenceTest {
    protected EntityManager em;
    protected EntityTransaction et;

    public void setUp() {
        em = Persistence.createEntityManagerFactory("[PU_NAME]").
                createEntityManager();
        et = em.getTransaction();
    }
```

}

Both protected fields are inherited by the concrete unit test classes:

```
public class BookOrderingServiceBeanTest extends AbstractPersistenceTest{

    private BookOrderingServiceBean serviceBean;

    @Before
    public void initDependencyInjection(){
        super.setUp();
        this.serviceBean.em = em;
        this.serviceBean.deliveryService = new DeliveryServiceBean();
        this.serviceBean = new BookOrderingServiceBean();
    }

    @Test
    public void testOrder() {
        et.begin();
        String isbn = "42";
        String name = "Rethinking The Patterns";
        this.serviceBean.order(isbn, name);
        et.rollback();
    }
}
```

The concrete unit test just initializes the Service Façade and tests its methods. Needed resources can be mocked out easily using frameworks such as jmock (http://jmock.org), easymock (www.easymock.org/), or mockito (http://mockito.org/)—depending on the Service Façade complexity.

Unit Tests are nice but totally unrealistic. The purpose of a unit test is to test the isolated functionality of a single unit such as a class. The entire environment is going to be emulated. A test suite is executed in sequential manner.

In a typical enterprise context a Service Façade will be executed in a massive parallel and multi-user environment. The unit tests, however, can be easily misused for load testing. Commercial as well as open source tools such as jmeter (http://jakarta.apache.org/jmeter) provide scripting infrastructure, where existing Java code can be executed in hundreds of threads, emulating concurrent users. Load tests should be performed at least once a week—you will be surprised how many synchronization issues, bottlenecks, deadlocks, memory leaks, and configuration problems will be found during the tests. Early tests help you not only to ensure the consistency of the system, but to gather the experience of its behavior under heavy load. Such tests do not have to be realistic—instead they should generate as much load as possible and try to break the system, without think times, network throttling and so on.

Documentation

Well-written documentation is as important as good unit tests. Especially the intensions, examples and usage hints are useful for the Service Façade users. The technical responsibility can be written once in, for example, a wiki and be only reused in different components or even applications. It should contain the responsibility, transaction management, and strategy. In the actual project it is sufficient just to refer to the concept—without repeating the already described facts.

In UML, the entire façade with its participants can be documented with a single interface as shown in Figure 3.

Figure 3. Service Façade in UML class diagram.

The interface represents its public view; the actual implementation is not that interesting. The stereotype <<Service Facade>> makes it clear, that the interface is the proxy for the Service Façade.

At the source level, the Service Façade pattern can be documented with a custom annotation. The following example uses a marker annotation to tag the façade:

```
@Stateless
@Remote(DocumentedServiceFacade.class)
@ServiceFacade(responsibility="Marker annotation
example",documentationLink="http://blog.adam-bien.com")
public class DocumentedServiceFacadeBean implements DocumentedServiceFacade {}
```

An annotation has some important advantages over JavaDoc—the meta data remains in byte code and is accessible via reflection. The so persisted documentation can even be leveraged during the build process or with static analysis tools.

```
@Target(ElementType.TYPE)
@Retention(RetentionPolicy.RUNTIME)
@Documented
public @interface ServiceFacade {
    /**
     * A pointer to existing documentation,
     * user story or use case.
     */
    String documentationLink() default "";
    /**
     * The  essential intension and responsibility of the
     * Service Facade
     */
    String responsibility();
}
```

In the example above the documentationLink attribute is optional, the responsibility is not. An annotation can even force the developer to provide some essential information. As we already discussed in the SOA Façade strategy such annotation can have even more formalized meaning and provide additional meta data which can be consumed by an interceptor.

Consequences

- **Consistency:** All methods are transactional. The transaction is propagated to all artifacts invoked in the scope of a Service Façade. A Service Façade ensures consistency.

- **Encapsulation:** A Service Façade decouples (depending on the strategy) more or less the client from the components behind the facade.

- **Performance:** A façade makes an interface coarser. This is important for remote communication. Several local invocations are bundled to few remote ones.

- **Usability:** The methods of a Service Façade should make sense even for a domain expert. Instead of invoking a bunch of accessors (getters / setters), Service Façade methods are more fluent.

- **Team building:** Service Façade is a hard interface between the business and the presentation. Therefore it is a natural boundary between user interface and back-end teams.

- **Testability:** A Service Façade has to be deployed with unit, integration, and, most importantly, load tests.

- **Crosscutting:** A Service Façade is the single point of entry. All communication is routed through the façade. Therefore it is a superb place for the implementation of crosscutting concerns such as monitoring, auditing, or precondition checks.

- **Decoupling:** Independent, fine-grained, services are coordinated by the Service Façade and can remain independent and reusable in other context.

Related Patterns

Application Service (J2EE), Session Façade (J2EE), Gateway (Java EE), Service (Java EE), DAO (J2EE / Java EE), DTO (J2EE / Java EE).

Service (Session Façade)

The original context of a Session Façade (SF) was defined in the Core J2EE pattern as following:

> "Enterprise beans encapsulate business logic and business data and expose their interfaces, and thus the complexity of the distributed services, to the client tier" [http://java.sun.com/blueprints/corej2eepatterns/Patterns/SessionFacade.html].

The context changed in Java EE quite a bit. A Service is rather procedural and realizes activities or subprocesses. In an object-oriented, domain-driven context, a Service realizes cross-cutting, domain object−independent logic. In an SOA a Service plays the main role and implements the actual business logic.

Problem

The original intention of the Session Façade was to wrap entity beans and encapsulate fine-grained interactions with the business objects:

> "In a multitiered Java 2 Platform, Enterprise Edition (J2EE) application environment, the following problems arise:
>
> * Tight coupling, which leads to direct dependence between clients and business objects;
>
> * Too many method invocations between client and server, leading to network performance problems;
>
> * Lack of a uniform client access strategy, exposing business objects to misuse.
>
> [...]

> "However, direct interaction between the client and the business objects leads to tight coupling between the two, and such tight coupling makes the client directly dependent on the implementation of the business objects. Direct dependence means that the client must represent and implement the complex interactions regarding business object lookups and creations, and must manage the relationships between the participating business objects as well as understand the responsibility of transaction demarcation…

> [...]

> "Tight coupling between objects also results when objects manage their relationship within themselves. Often, it is not clear where the relationship is managed. This leads to complex relationships between business objects and rigidity in the application. Such lack of flexibility makes the application less manageable when changes are required.

> [...]

> "A problem also arises when a client interacts directly with the business objects. Since the business objects are directly exposed to the clients, there is no unified strategy for accessing the business objects. Without such a uniform client access strategy, the business objects are exposed to clients and may reduce consistent usage…" [http://java.sun.com/blueprints/corej2eepatterns/Patterns/SessionFacade.html].

The initial responsibility of a Session Façade was the management of persistence relations between entity beans. It was in the CMP 1.1 time frame and is totally out of date. In the CMP 2.x era, a Session Façade was mainly responsible for management of a single entity type. It implemented the merging and creation of domain objects directly. The execution of dynamic queries—was often delegated to a DAO.

These requirements are completely outdated as well. Entity beans are no more remote accessible, the JPA is powerful enough for most of the use cases and container-managed relations have been available for several years. Nevertheless a Service (the new name for the Session Façade) is still usable, with slightly modified responsibilities. Instead of fixing infrastructural shortcomings, the main purpose of a Service is making the realization of the business logic more maintainable and reusable.

The key element of SOA is a Service. In practice, however, services are too fine grained, to be remotely (SOA implies the distribution) accessible. On the other hand, a visible SOA service is too coarse grained, to be realized in single method. A common approach is to decompose the functionality of an SOA Service into several technical Services (this pattern) and expose them via a Service Façade.

Forces

- Services should be independent of each other.

- The granularity of a Service is finer than of a Service Façade.

- The Services are not accessible and even visible from outside the business tier.

- A Service should be not accessible from an external JVM. A remote Service invocation doesn't make sense and should be avoided.

- A Service is aimed to be reused from other component or Service Façade.

- The execution of a Service should be always consistent. Its methods should either have no side effects (be idempotent), or be able to be invoked in a transactional context.

Solution

As mentioned earlier, a Service is a product of decomposition. Therefore it is not even visible for the clients and only accessible through a Service Façade. A client may be interested in ordering products, but absolutely not interested in the reuse of the shipping logic, availability and address checks, customer relationship management, or tax computations. A Service Façade exposes the actually interesting functionality and coordinates independent Services. The Service Façade already provides transactions, state management, remoting, and other cross-cutting functionality.

The services can be developed without the consideration of cross-cutting concerns and independently of each other. Actually the services must not rely on the existence of certain aspects such as transactions or remoting. For this reason a Service is always local and comes with the TransactionAttributeType.MANDATORY transaction attribute:

```
@Stateless
@Local(DeliveryService.class)
@TransactionAttribute(TransactionAttributeType.MANDATORY)
public class DeliveryServiceBean implements DeliveryService {
```

}

A Service can be deployed either with a dedicated local business interface or with no-interface view. The choice depends on the complexity of the Service Façades. An explicit business interface makes mocking of the Service possible and unit testing easier.

The Service idiom realizes a part of the overall Service Façades functionality. Reusable and independent parts of the Service Façade are factored out into Services. The Services are coordinated by the Service Façade and located behind it. They actually comprise an internal component layer, which can be named after the pattern. The component itself is mapped to a package with a domain-specific name, for example, `ordermgmt`, the layer service resides inside the component (for example, `ordermgmt.service` or `ordermgmt.control`) alongside the other layers such as `ordermgmt.facade` or `ordermgmt.domain`.

A Service is just a stateless session bean with well-defined responsibility. It comes with local or no-interface view and the `MANDATORY` transaction attribute. With such configuration is it impossible for external clients to invoke a Service without going through a Service Façade.

A Service has to run in the scope of an existing transaction. Regardless of how many Services are executed in the transactional scope, the whole invocation remains consistent. All participating Services access resources in the same transaction. A Service uses Dependency Injection to acquire needed resources—transactional resources will be automatically enlisted in the current transaction by the container. This means, for example, for JDBC that all Services invoked in the context of the Service Façade will share a single JDBC connection (and transaction).

Services can be decorated with interceptors. The functionality of a Service interceptor, however, should be related to the Service and not intersect with the responsibilities of the Service Façade.

EJB 3.1 has still the reputation of being too heavyweight. The question often asked is, whether a Service should be implemented as POJO or a stateless session bean. The performance overhead between a POJO and a stateless session bean is negligible (about 3% on Glassfish v2). The benefits of a stateless session bean in respect to monitoring, transactions, concurrency, and Dependency Injection are huge.

There is no reason for a premature optimization, especially considering the code reduction caused by the use of session beans. A session bean can be replaced easily with a POJO at any time with almost no additional overhead. Only the already existing container services have to be provided during that migration.

Conventions

- A Service is a local, stateless session bean.
- Service resides in a component which is realized as Java-package with domain-specific name e.g. `ordermgmt`.
- The realization of the service (business interface and the bean implementation) resides in a subpackage with the name *service* or *control*, for example, `ordermgmt.service` or `ordermgmt.control`. This makes the automatic verification of the architecture easier.

- The business interface is named after business concepts, without the obligatory local or remote suffix e.g. `OrderService` and `OrderServiceBean`.

- It is not required to use the term "Service" in the name of the bean—its redundant. For identification purposes you could use a `@Service` annotation.

- The Service is always invoked in the context of an existing transaction. It is deployed with the `Mandatory` transaction attribute.

Rethinking

The Service pattern has nothing in common with the J2EE Session Façade. The main purpose of the Session Façade was the access simplification to entity beans and making the granularity coarser. In contrast, the Java EE 5/6 Service emphasizes the domain-specific services and is actually independent on the Java EE infrastructure.

A Service itself is even optional. For simple use cases a Service Façade and Service can collapse, in which case the functionality of the Service moves to the Service Façade. Likewise, functionality from Service Façades with too many responsibilities can be factored out into newly introduced Services. The design should scale in both directions.

Participants and Responsibilities

A Service is always executed in the context of a Service Façade or gateway. It relies on the existence of transactions, security, remoting and other cross-cutting concerns. A Service implements business logic and can use all available resources for its realization. Legacy resources can be wrapped in an explicit DAO, which can be considered as a specific kind of a Service. Access to standardized and well-integrated resources such as JPA does not have to be further encapsulated. Premature encapsulation could result in many delegate invocations and layers without any additional value.

Strategies

A Service is a hidden, or encapsulated, Service Façade without the cross-cutting functionality, which is required for the exposure. Thus, the strategies of the Service Façade SOA Service Façade and Lightweight Asynchronous Service Façade can be applied directly to a Service. The protocol-related strategies, however, are not applicable at all. A Service is not capable to handle remote calls.

Stateless Session Bean Strategy

Using stateless session beans is the default way to build Services. The business logic is implemented as a stateless session bean with a local business interface or no-interface view only. All methods are deployed with the `TransactionAttributeType.MANDATORY` transaction setting.

The Service can (and should) use Dependency Injection to acquire back-end resources; it enjoys concurrency and transaction control and can be monitored out of the box. The benefits simply outweigh the two main shortcomings: dependency on the EJB API caused by the use of EJB 3 annotations and potential performance penalty caused by the container overhead. The dependency caused by annotations is minimal and can even be completely removed using deployment descriptors. Although all annotations and dependencies on the EJB 3 API would be removed from the application code, you shouldn't underestimate the XML plumbing. Writing XML is labor-intensive and brittle. The dependency on the EJB technology is really low—the annotation can be removed easily in case the EJBs turn out to be not appropriate for your needs.

Surprisingly the EJB container overhead turns out to be really low. In case of the Glassfish v2ur2 application server, the difference between a pure POJO and a stateless session bean is only a few milliseconds or about 3%. In the relation to distribution, database access or invocation of legacy resources, the overhead caused by the EJB infrastructure is absolutely insignificant.

POJO Strategy

Developers often wonder whether a Service should be implemented as a stateless session bean or a POJO. In the context of Java EE 5+, POJOs simply require you to write more code comparing them to EJB 3.1. This additional effort has to be justified somehow. A possible reason is the integration of already existing POJOs, without having source code available. They could be integrated using XML, but this comes with some relatively high amount of effort and the violation of the DRY principle. The fully qualified class (as well as the interface) name has to be defined in the deployment descriptor. This information, however, already exists in Java code and makes refactoring harder.

To demonstrate this approach, inject the Swing `javax.swing.table.TableModel` class as a local business interface into the `LegacyTestBean` class and use the `javax.swing.table.DefaultTableModel` as the bean class. Use the `beanName` as logical reference; you could even get rid of this completely and use the fully qualified name. The following snippet demonstrates the injection of a Swing Table model into an EJB 3:

```
import javax.swing.table.TableModel;

@Stateless
public class LegacyTestBean implements LegacyTest {
    @EJB(beanName="Table")
    TableModel tableModel;

    public String accessTable(){
        return "Row count: " + tableModel.getRowCount();
    }

}
```

In the deployment descriptor, it is sufficient to refer to the reference with the value of the `beanName`. Also, the type of the bean, the business interface, and the implementation of the class has to be specified. The following snippet demonstrates the declaration of the `DefaultTableModel` as a Stateless Session Bean in `ejb-jar.xml`:

```
<ejb-jar>
 <enterprise-beans>
  <session>
   <ejb-name>Table</ejb-name>
    <business-local>javax.swing.table.TableModel</business-local>
```

```
    <ejb-class>javax.swing.table.DefaultTableModel</ejb-class>
    <session-type>Stateless</session-type>
  </session>
 </enterprise-beans>
</ejb-jar>
```

The descriptor, however, is complete. Other beans can still be deployed using plain annotations only.

It is sometimes more pragmatic just to reuse the legacy class as a POJO, instantiating it with the new operator. This is especially true for stateless utility classes, especially with static methods, without any access to transactional resources such as databases or JMS.

The EJB container is not aware of pure POJOs. It is neither able to handle their lifecycles nor to monitor them. Be aware of this fact when choosing this strategy for green field projects.

DAO Hybrid

Separation of Concerns was the driving force for the hard separation between Services and DAOs. The JPA EntityManager is actually a DAO, or has at least all of its characteristics. There is no real need to encapsulate it further with a dedicated DAO.

The construction and execution of named queries, however, is relatively labor intensive and can result in lot of plumbing code, so it is a good idea to encapsulate named queries in a dedicated place. This task can be achieved either in a DAO or a Service, both layers at the same time are only needed in exceptional cases. In practice, the layers often collapse, because there is no need for further decoupling of the Service from EntityManager. The construction of queries and even the reuse of query logic is often project specific, but still highly reusable across services. The reuse can be easily achieved using inheritance. Instead of delegating to a DAO, a Service could just inherit from it. In that case, a Service would act as a DAO, which is actually not entirely wrong. The injection of EntityManager is available in the superclass and would be available instantly for the Service too. Because a session bean is just a bunch of cohesive methods and not an object, it is unlikely that there be a need to inherit from another class in addition. The Service could even inherit from an already existing, generic DAO class as shown in the following sample:

```
@Stateless
public class CrudServiceBean{

    @PersistenceContext
    protected EntityManager em;

    public <T> T create(T t) {
        this.em.persist(t);
        this.em.flush();
        this.em.refresh(t);
        return t;
    }
//remaining methods
}
```
In that case, the CrudServiceBean class, as well as the Service
(DAOServiceHybridBean) with DAO capabilities, would be deployed as session
beans and available in the JNDI tree. The injected EntityManager has to be

declared as protected or exposed with a getter. Otherwise it will not be accessible in the concrete Service, which is required for the implementation of specific queries. Here's the code for the DAO service:

```
@Stateless
public class DAOServiceHybridBean extends CrudServiceBean{
    @Override
    public void create(String isbn,String name){
        create(new Book(isbn,name)); //inherited
    }
}
```

With this strategy the Service implementation can be greatly simplified and is actually reduced to the minimum. All the plumbing code is factored out in the `CrudServiceBean` and is easily accessible from the Service. No delegation and injection of additional beans is required.

This strategy is especially efficient and maintainable in concrete projects, with project-specific queries. Domain-specific filters, role-dependent `where` statements, and other context-dependent behaviors can be encapsulated in the `CrudServiceBean` superclass and be consistently reused across different Services.

Testing

Testing of Services is identical to testing the Service Façades. The testing techniques described earlier can be applied to a Service. Services are optional, so their usage already implies additional added value and non-trivial implementation. It is therefore a good idea to provide unit tests for a Service as well, however it is more a suggestion, than a hard requirement.

Documentation

Documenting a Service is almost identical to documenting the Service Façade. In UML class diagrams, Services can be emphasized with the <<Service>> annotation. It is sufficient to model them as a class without the interface—the interface doesn't provide any additional information.

The <<Service>> stereotype is the placeholder of the session bean configuration and structure such as state management, distribution, or transaction handling. Marking a class with the stereotype <<Service>> makes it explicit, that it is expanded into a local, stateless session bean with the MANDATORY transaction attribute. It becomes clear that all associations to other services will be mapped to Dependency Injection of their interface, and their relationship to entities will result in the injection of the EntityManager.

The pragmatic use of custom stereotypes formalizes the model and even allows the generation of the entire infrastructure. The obvious infrastructure can even be generated with template engines such as Velocity or Freemarker. The use of generators or sophisticated Model Driven Architecture (MDA) tools is not always beneficial. From a development point of view, Java EE is lean enough to be manually coded. A generator, on the other hand, ensures consistent naming conventions, patterns and layering which can significantly increase the maintainability. This becomes especially interesting for outsourcing projects with many external partners involved.

Consequences

- **Reuse:** Services encourage internal reuse of fine-grained logic. They can be shared between components and Service Façades.

- **Consistency:** A service is hidden behind a façade and always executed in the context of already existing transaction.

- **Testability:** Services can be easily mocked out, which simplifies the testing of the Service Façade. Services are POJOs, so they can be tested easily as well.

- **Complexity:** Not all use cases are complex enough to justify the introduction of an additional Service layer. The enforcement of Services can result in empty (that is, delegate) Services or Service Façades. CRUD use cases can be easily realized with a Service Façade only.

- **Service orientation:** A service already implies a service-oriented approach, which results in procedural business logic. Process- or workflow-driven use cases can be easily realized with tasks (services), operating on resources (entities). In domain-driven applications, services should only realize cross-cutting concerns, otherwise the design will not be DRY.

Related Patterns

Application Service (J2EE), Session Façade (J2EE), Gateway (Java EE), Service (Java EE), DAO (J2EE / Java EE), DTO (J2EE / Java EE).

A Service is coordinated by Service Façades or gateways; it invokes DAOs and is able to produce DTOs.

Persistent Domain Object (Business Object)

The original problem description in J2EE Core Patterns was short and sound: "You have a conceptual domain model with business logic and relationship" [www.corej2eepatterns.com/Patterns2ndEd/BusinessObject.htm].

Even in the original description of the Business Object J2EE Pattern, the realization of the conceptual model with procedural approaches was considered as dangerous with regard to bloating code duplication spread over different modules and therefore hard to maintain.

At that time, however, the realization of object-oriented and persistent Business Objects wasn't possible with standard J2EE technologies. Only additional extensions such as Java Data Objects (JDO) or later open source frameworks such as Hibernate were able to manage the persistence of object-oriented entities transparently.

Problem

The vast majority of J2EE applications were build in the procedural way. The business logic was decomposed into tasks and resources, which were mapped into Services and anemic, persistent entities. Such a procedural approach works surprisingly well until type-specific behavior for domain objects has to be realized.

The attempt to realize object-oriented algorithms with procedural techniques ends up in many `instanceof` checks or lengthy `if` statements. Such type checks are required, because the domain objects are anemic in the procedural world, so that inheritance doesn't really pay off. Even in case inheritance was used for designing the domain model, the most powerful feature, polymorphic behavior, wasn't leveraged at all. Anemic domain model forces the developer to implement the type checks outside the entities—that is, in Services or Service Façades.

The anemic structures (these are not objects by definition) have to expose their internal states to the outside world. Otherwise it wouldn't be accessible to the Services and Service Façades any more. The exposure of an internal state is realized with field accessors (getters and setters), that is with a lot of plumbing.

All the shortcomings mentioned here are caused by the lack of object orientation in the persistence layer in most J2EE and Java EE applications.

Forces

- Your business logic is complex.
- The validation rules are domain object related and sophisticated.
- The conceptual model can be derived from the requirements and mapped to domain objects.
- The domain objects have to be persisted in a relational database (it's the common case).
- The use cases, user stories, or other specification documents already describe the target domain in an object-oriented way. The relation between the behavior and the data can be derived from the specification.

- It is a green field project, or at least the existing database was designed in a way that allows the use of JPA. That is, the tables and columns are reasonably named and the database is not overly normalized.

Solution

The solution is surprisingly simple: Model your application with real objects and don't care about the persistence at the beginning. *Real objects* means cohesive classes with encapsulated state, related behavior, and inheritance. Just put business logic into the domain objects and use inheritance were appropriate. JPA turns out to be really flexible in mapping rich domain objects into relational tables. The more complex logic you have to realize, the easier object-oriented persistence can be maintained and developed.

Anemic domain models do not have any behavior by definition, so it has to be provided somewhere else. Usually the behavior is realized in Services (stateless session beans), which access and manipulate the state of anemic objects. The Services need to access the entities state, so it is entirely publicized. This is achieved with getters and setters, which expose every single attribute to the outside world. It is not a huge problem in general, but this approach results in a lot of plumbing and obfuscates the essential business logic.

The real problem is that if statements needed to differentiate between the entity types. Such checks are needed to realize type-dependent behavior in a procedural way. Every introduction of a new subclass, or even change of the existing business logic requires to find, enhance, and test the type checks. The computation of shipping costs dependent on weight and the OrderItem type would look like this in a procedural world:

```
@Stateless
public class ShipmentService {
  public final static int BASIC_COST = 5;

  @PersistenceContext
  private EntityManager em;

    public int getShippingCosts(int loadId) {
       Load load = em.find(Load.class, loadId);
       return computeShippingCost(load);
    }

   int computeShippingCost(Load load){
       int shippingCosts = 0;
       int weight = 0;
       int defaultCost = 0;
       for (OrderItem orderItem : load.getOrderItems()) {
           LoadType loadType = orderItem.getLoadType();
           weight = orderItem.getWeight();
           defaultCost = weight * 5;
           switch (loadType) {
               case BULKY:
                   shippingCosts += (defaultCost + 5);
                   break;
```

```
                  case LIGHTWEIGHT:
                      shippingCosts += (defaultCost - 1);
                      break;
                  case STANDARD:
                      shippingCosts += (defaultCost);
                      break;
                  default:
                  throw new IllegalStateException("Unknown type: " + loadType);
              }
          }
          return shippingCosts;
      }
}
```

The entire logic resides, as expected, in a Service or Service Façade and consists mainly of the type checks. The Service has to differentiate between the different types to apply type-dependent computation algorithms. The same logic can be expressed with only a fraction of code in an object-oriented way. Even a Service is no longer needed—the logic is implemented in the domain object itself. The following snippet shows polymorphic business logic inside a domain object, without type checks:

```
@Entity
public class Load {

    @OneToMany(cascade = CascadeType.ALL)
    private List<OrderItem> orderItems;
    @Id
    private Long id;

    protected Load() {
        this.orderItems = new ArrayList<OrderItem>();
    }


    public int getShippingCosts() {
        int shippingCosts = 0;
        for (OrderItem orderItem : orderItems) {
            shippingCosts += orderItem.getShippingCost();
        }
        return shippingCosts;
    }
//...
}
```

The computation of the total costs is realized inside a rich domain object, the Persistent Domain Object (PDO), and not inside a Service. This not only reduces the total amount of code, but it makes the code also easier to understand and maintain. The actual computation of type-specific costs is performed in the concrete subclasses, which makes it a lot easier to be tested separately:

```
@Entity
public class BulkyItem extends OrderItem{
```

```
    public BulkyItem() {
    }

    public BulkyItem(int weight) {
        super(weight);
    }

    @Override
    public int getShippingCost() {
        return super.getShippingCost() + 5;
    }
}
```

The computation of the shipping cost of a `BulkyItem` can be changed, without touching the remaining classes. Also, a new subclass can be introduced without affecting the computation of the total costs in the class `Load`.

The creation of a PDO graph is easier and more intuitive, comparing it to the traditional getter/setter-driven approach. Instead of creating the anemic objects separately and wiring them together afterwards, you can take a concise object-oriented approach as shown in the following snippet:

```
Load load = new Load();
OrderItem standard = new OrderItem();
standard.setLoadType(LoadType.STANDARD);
standard.setWeight(5);
load.getOrderItems().add(standard);
OrderItem light = new OrderItem();
light.setLoadType(LoadType.LIGHTWEIGHT);
light.setWeight(1);
load.getOrderItems().add(light);
OrderItem bulky = new OrderItem();
bulky.setLoadType(LoadType.BULKY);
bulky.setWeight(1);
load.getOrderItems().add(bulky);
```

The Builder pattern allows the construction of the `Load` object with the specific `OrderItems` in a convenient way. As shown in the following example, the method chaining saves some superfluous lines of code and allows autocompletion support in common IDEs:

```
Load build = new Load.Builder().
    withStandardItem(5).
    withLightweightItem(1).
    withBulkyItem(1).
    build();
```

In addition validation logic is performed in the method build, so that the creation of empty `Load` objects can be avoided. The following code demonstrates the Builder pattern realized with a static inner class inside a PDO:

```
@Entity
public class Load {
```

```java
@OneToMany(cascade = CascadeType.ALL)
private List<OrderItem> orderItems;
@Id
private Long id;

protected Load() {
    this.orderItems = new ArrayList<OrderItem>();
}

public static class Builder {

    private Load load;

    public Builder() {
        this.load = new Load();
    }

    public Builder withBulkyItem(int weight) {
        this.load.add(new BulkyItem(weight));
        return this;
    }

    public Builder withStandardItem(int weight) {
        this.load.add(new StandardItem(weight));
        return this;
    }

    public Builder withLightweightItem(int weight) {
        this.load.add(new LightweightItem(weight));
        return this;
    }

    public Load build() {
        if (load.orderItems.size() == 0) {
            throw new IllegalStateException("...");
        }
        return this.load;
    }
}

void add(OrderItem item) {
    this.orderItems.add(item);

}

public int getShippingCosts() {
    int shippingCosts = 0;
    for (OrderItem orderItem : orderItems) {
        shippingCosts += orderItem.getShippingCost();
    }
    return shippingCosts;
}
```

```java
    public OrderItem lightest(){
      if(this.orderItems == null || this.orderItems.size() == 0)
          return null;
      Collections.sort(this.orderItems, new WeightComparator());
      return this.orderItems.iterator().next();
    }

    public OrderItem heaviest(){
      if(this.orderItems == null || this.orderItems.size() == 0)
          return null;
      Collections.sort(this.orderItems, new WeightComparator());
      Collections.reverse(orderItems);
      return this.orderItems.iterator().next();
    }

    public OrderItem dropHeaviest(){
        OrderItem heaviest = heaviest();
        if(heaviest != null)
            drop(heaviest);
        return heaviest;
    }

    public OrderItem dropLightest(){
        OrderItem lightest = lightest();
        if(lightest != null)
            drop(lightest);
        return lightest;
    }

    public Load drop(OrderItem orderItem){
        this.orderItems.remove(orderItem);
        return this;
    }
    public Long getId() {
        return id;
    }

    public int getNumberOfOrderItems(){
        return this.orderItems.size();
    }
}
```

The Builder pattern is implemented as a static inner class, which creates the `Load` object and provides methods with fluent names (for example, `withBulkyItem`). Each method creates a corresponding subclass of `OrderItem`, adds it to the load, and returns the Builder instance itself. This allows the construction of the `Load` with convenient method chaining.

Up to this point, the logic was limited to the construction and the computation of the shipping costs. Even more interesting is the realization of non-idempotent methods. The method `dropHeaviest` removes the heaviest `OrderItem` instance from the `Load` instance.

Nothing exciting about that, but you have to keep in mind that the PDOs are persistent entities. Every change to the state, and even relations, will be synchronized automatically with the persistence at the end of the transaction. Just imagine an object-oriented implementation of the subversion client with JPA. A change of a versioned file has to be propagated to all packages until the project root is reached. The entire path is marked as changed. An SVN commit on the project level causes a recursive descending of all changed folders until all changed files are committed as well. To implement such a cascading algorithm in an object-oriented way is straightforward, whereas a procedural approach is error prone and hard to maintain.

Conventions

- PDOs are JPA entities with emphasis on domain logic and not the technology.

- PDOs reside in a component that is realized as a Java package with a domain-specific name, for example, `ordermgmt`.

- The PDO resides in a subpackage (layer) with the name `domain` or `entity`, for example, `ordermgmt.domain` or `ordermgmt.entity`. This makes the automatic verification of the architecture easier.

- The name of the domain object is derived from the target domain.

- Getters and setters are not obligatory—they should be used only in justified cases.

- The methods are not only accessors, but they model behavior which also changes the state of the domain objects.

- All methods are named in a fluent way.

- It is not required to use the acronym PDO in the name of the entity. For identification purposes you could use a `@PDO` annotation.

Rethinking

The J2EE CMP persistence didn't support inheritance or polymorphic queries. The anemic domain object approach was the only viable and reasonable solution. The J2EE patterns were designed with those restrictions in mind. Even the introduction of alternative solutions such as JDO or Hibernate didn't improve the situation—most of the domain objects were still anemic.

Dumb entities and procedural session beans were the only best practice for J2EE. Although the procedural approach can be surprisingly efficient for simplistic, data-driven use cases, a more complicated logic can be hardly expressed with persistent structures.

Java EE 5, together with JPA, introduced inheritance and polymorphic queries to the persistence layer. JPA entities are just annotated Java classes with only insignificant restrictions, so object-oriented approaches and patterns can be applied to persistence layer.

It's time to rethink the way how complex logic is going to be developed. The persistence layer should consist of self-contained domain objects with clear responsibilities and an encapsulated state and behavior. The persistence is a cross-cutting concern and should not have any impact on design and not in particular on the amount of logic residing in domain objects. Only the remaining cross-cutting and often procedural logic should be implemented in a Service.

Actually the Persistent Domain Objects become a best practice and the Anemic Domain Model an anti-pattern, at least in more ambitious projects.

Participants and Responsibilities

The PDO plays the most important role in a domain-driven architecture. It represents a concept from the target domain. Its responsibility is to express and implement the business logic as simple and explicit as possible. The PDO's state is persisted to the database by the `EntityManager`.

A PDO is not an active artifact. It has to be created and maintained by a Service, Service Façade or Gateway. A Service implements a cross-cutting functionality such as archiving, reports, or exposure of the functionality of back-end systems, whereby a Gateway helps the PDO to expose its functionality directly to the presentation.

Strategies

Regardless which strategy you are choosing, the PDO business methods should always be executed in an attached state. Only then do you get the benefits of transparent state synchronization and even delta computations performed by the `EntityManager`. Most of the JPA providers synchronize the JPA entities with the persistent store smartly—only changed entities, relations, and even attributes are flushed to the database.

It only works for changes performed on an attached entity. If you transfer a PDO across the network, it becomes serialized and detached. The `EntityManager` loses its link to the serialized PDO. You will have to merge your changes manually—which either leads to complex computation of the delta between the origin and actual state, or finer operations on the remote Service Façades.

PDOs should always be accessed per reference, which actually implies the execution of the presentation layer and the PDOs in the same JVM. This in-process execution is very natural for the web clients, where the whole EAR is executed in the same JVM anyway, but rather esoteric for rich clients. The same effect in a rich client environment requires an in-process execution of the `EntityManager` within the presentation layer. A rich Internet application turns into a fat client. It might sounds strange, but frameworks such as Adobe AIR or even Google Gears follow the same strategy. They even come with a local database to allow offline capabilities.

DSL / Test / Domain Driven

The only force in this strategy is the domain of the business logic and nothing else. The PDOs are developed with respect to the test-first approach—the main concern is the usability and therefore the fluent interface. The state is entirely encapsulated, property accessors are rarely used. The intensive use of method chaining, Builder patterns, and inner classes is typical for this strategy. The information needed by a PDO is transformed and provided manually.

Because a PDO with a DSL-like interface cannot adhere to conventions (unlike JavaBeans), it makes a DSL PDO less interesting for visual components with declarative data binding as is known in the JSR-295 (Beans Binding), or already mature and heavily used in JSF.

Fat PDO

PDOs are real objects with state and behavior. The persistence capabilities are provided by a session bean. A Gateway, Service, or Service Façade use an injected `EntityManager` to persist the root entity initially. From this point you can manipulate the state of the root as well as the related entities, and all changes will be automatically flushed to the database by the `EntityManager`. This works only as long as you do not need to access the database directly from PDOs. Injection of `EntityManager` into persistent entities is not supported.

A PDO is a real object and can thus perform any arbitrary operation on its state as well as manipulate its child objects or create new entities. Especially the persistence creation of entities that are not directly related to the current graph of objects is not possible. You will have to either associate the newly created entity with an already attached object or invoke `EntityManager#persist`. The `EntityManager` is not available in PDOs and the association between the newly created object and graph of entities only to persist it may not be desired. A far more elegant way would be a Dependency Injection of `EntityManager` into a PDO. Unfortunately it isn't supported in JPA, so a workaround is required.

The `Load` PDO is created by the `Builder` inner class, but the creation is usually not persistent. You either have to persist the `Load` instance in the session bean or pass the `EntityManager` to the Builder. The first case only works for simpler cases; the latter cannot be solved without additional work. The following code demonstrates accessing an `EntityManager` with a static method in a PDO:

```
import static ...persistenceutils.ThreadLocalEntityManager.*;

@Entity
public class Load {

    @OneToMany(cascade = CascadeType.ALL)
    private List<OrderItem> orderItems;

    @Id
    @GeneratedValue
    private Long id;

    protected Load() {
        this.orderItems = new ArrayList<OrderItem>();
    }

    public static class Builder {

        private Load load;

        public Builder() {
            this.load = new Load();
        }

        public Builder withBulkyItem(int weight) {
            this.load.add(new BulkyItem(weight));
            return this;
        }
```

```
    //...some methods omitted

    public Load build() {
      if (load.orderItems.size() == 0) {
      throw new IllegalStateException("Cannot create Load...");
      }
        em().persist(this.load);
        return this.load;
    }
  }
  public static Load find(long id) {
      return em().find(Load.class, id);
  }
//...some methods omitted
```

The client accesses the PDOs not directly but via the Service Façade, which starts a new transaction. A transaction is associated with the current thread of execution by the application server. If you manage to associate an EntityManager instance with the current thread, the PDO could get easily access to the transactional EntityManager instance and use it for queries or for persisting detached entities. The EntityManager participates in the current transaction; even better, all other session beans (for example, Service) that are enlisted in the same transaction get injected by the same instance of the EntityManager. All the transaction participants will have access to the same EntityManager and its transactional cache. All participants will see the same transactional state which prevents lost updates in a transaction.

The earliest possible point to get a reference to the EntityManager is in the interceptor. Although an interceptor wraps a session bean in its entirety, it still participates in its transaction. The session bean has to declare only the interceptor at the class level—so every business method is wrapped, as the following example demonstrates:

```
@Stateless
@Interceptors(EntityManagerInjector.class)
@TransactionAttribute(TransactionAttributeType.REQUIRES_NEW)
public class ShipmentServiceBean implements ShipmentService {

    public Load createBulkyItem(int weight){
        return new Load.Builder().withBulkyItem(weight).build();
    }

    public Load find(long id) {
        return Load.find(id);
    }
}
```

The interceptor EntityManagerInjector uses the injected EntityManager and passes it to the utility class ThreadLocalEntityManager using its associateWithThread method:

```
import static ...persistenceutils.ThreadLocalEntityManager.*;
public class EntityManagerInjector {
```

```
    @PersistenceContext
    private EntityManager em;

    @AroundInvoke
public Object associate...(InvocationContext ic) throws Exception {
        associateWithThread(em); //statically imported method
        try {
            return ic.proceed();
        } finally {
            cleanupThread();
        }
    }
}
```

The `ThreadLocalEntityManager` is simple as well. It only wraps and provides convenient access to the `java.lang.ThreadLocal`. This class does the actual work and implements the association between the current thread and the referenced object (in this case the `EntityManager`). The `ThreadLocal` utility keeps the `EntityManager` available in the current thread:

```
import javax.persistence.EntityManager;

public class ThreadLocalEntityManager {

    private static final ThreadLocal<EntityManager> THREAD_WITH_EM = new
ThreadLocal<EntityManager>();

    private ThreadLocalEntityManager() {}

    public static void associateWithThread(EntityManager em) {
        THREAD_WITH_EM.set(em);
    }

    public static EntityManager em() {
        return THREAD_WITH_EM.get();
    }

    public static void cleanupThread(){
        THREAD_WITH_EM.remove();
    }
}
```

The `ThreadLocalEntityManager` and `EntityManagerInjector` are use case-independent artifacts and can be reused in different projects.

This approach works well with Services and Service Façades, which are accessed each time before any PDO interaction. Gateways are more problematic, because a presentation tier component only communicates at the beginning with the stateful session bean, and then uses PDOs directly without any intermediary layer. In this case, you should move the interception one level up, for example, to the Servlet's `javax.servlet.Filter`. You could reuse the `EntityManagerInjector` code and replace the `context.proceed()` invocation with `FilterChain#doFilter()`.

Data Bound PDO

Data Bound PDO is a pragmatic variant of the PDO. It is a tradeoff between the fluent interface or purely domain-driven approach and a procedural DTO. A data-bound PDO comes with property accessors, which are intended for automatic synchronization with the presentation layer components. All data binding frameworks rely at least on JavaBeans conventions. Native clients such as Eclipse data binding or even JSR-295 expect the proper usage of `java.beans.PropertyChangeSupport` and the notification of `java.beans.PropertyChangeListeners` interested in state changes.

The procedural-style accessors are intended for reflective and not manual use. Manually crafted code should still rely on the object-oriented view and not fine-grained property access. Property accessors in general bypass cross-attribute checks and sophisticated validations. Therefore they are actually counter-productive within the PDO context.

Accessors are not mandatory for declarative data binding. The binding between a UI component and the source is performed declaratively with EL expressions (strings) and thus cannot be type-safe:

```
Binding binding =
Bindings.createAutoBinding(AutoBinding.UpdateStrategy.READ_WRITE, this,
ELProperty.create("${order.name}"), txtName, BeanProperty.create("text"));
bindingGroup.addBinding(binding);
```

The expression `${order.name}` results in the navigation `[form].getOrder().setName()/getName()` from the view through the PDO to the property `name`. The binding expression cannot be checked by the compiler and misspellings will result in runtime errors.

The existence of explicit property accessors does not improve the situation. The IDE support such as code completion is not used, because the accessors are not invoked in a programmatic way, but through reflection. The main advantage of type-safe accessors—the use of IDE support (for example, autocompletion) is not used. The only reason for their existence is the reflective access by a data binding framework, which used to be declaratively configured and not manually coded.

The PDO state, however, can be manipulated directly via reflection without the accessors. The reflection API allows direct access to even private attributes with relatively little effort. The PDOs can remain concise, without the need to implement the ugly getters and setters. The whole access mechanism can be easily encapsulated in a utility class. The following example demonstrates reflective access to private PDO members:

```
public class FieldAccess {

    public static Object get(Object obj, String fieldName) {
        try {
            return getField(obj, fieldName).get(obj);
        } catch (IllegalAccessException e) {
            throw new IllegalStateException("...: " + fieldName, e);
        }
    }
```

```
    public static void set(Object obj, String fieldName, Object value) {
        try {
            getField(obj, fieldName).set(obj, value);
        } catch (IllegalAccessException e) {
            throw new IllegalStateException("...: " + fieldName, e);
        }
    }

    static Field getField(Object obj, String fieldName) {
        try {
            Field field = obj.getClass().getDeclaredField(fieldName);
            field.setAccessible(true);
            return field;
        } catch (NoSuchFieldException e) {
            throw new IllegalStateException("...", e);
        }
    }
}
```

The class `FieldAccess` provides the access to private fields with static utility methods. This is nice, because they can be statically imported:

```
@Entity
@Table(name="DB_ORDER_ITEM")
public class OrderItem {

    @Id
    @GeneratedValue
    private Long id;

    private int weight;

    @Enumerated(EnumType.STRING)
    private LoadType loadType;

    public OrderItem(Long id, int weight, LoadType loadType) {
        this.id = id;
        this.weight = weight;
        this.loadType = loadType;
    }
}
```

The use is straightforward. The methods `get()` and `set()` do expect the instance of the object and the name of the attribute:

```
        OrderItem item = new OrderItem(LONG_VALUE, 2, LoadType.BULKY);
        Long id = (Long) get(item, "id");
        set(item, "id",21);
        id = (Long) get(item, "id");
```

The invocation of the traditional accessor, `item.getId()`, is equivalent to `FieldAccess.get(item,"id")`. The property names could be derived using UI conventions. The UI components could be either annotated with the property names or, even better, the names can be computed from the component names. This approach reduces code duplication and plumbing, but still doesn't violate the encapsulation. Most of the available tools, however, do not support such binding visually, but it is still interesting for meta data-driven applications.

Testing

PDOs are annotated classes and can be tested as common POJOs. For the business logic tests you will not even have to mock out or bootstrap the EntityManager. The instances needed to perform the test can be easily created in the @Before or @BeforeClass methods and used in the actual test methods. The following example demonstrates a PDO business logic test without involving the EntityManager:

```
public class LoadTest {

    @Test(expected=IllegalStateException.class)
    public void empty(){
        Load build = new Load.Builder().build();
    }

    @Test
    public void mixedLoad(){
        Load load = new Load.Builder().
                withStandardItem(5).
                withLightweightItem(1).
                withBulkyItem(1).
                build();
        int actual = load.getShippingCosts();
        int expected = (5*5) + (5-1) + (1*5+5);
        assertEquals(expected,actual);
    }
    @Test
    public void heaviest(){
        Load load = new Load.Builder().
                withStandardItem(5).
                withLightweightItem(1).
                withBulkyItem(1).
                build();
        OrderItem heaviest = load.heaviest();
        assertNotNull(heaviest);
        assertEquals(5,heaviest.getWeight());
        assertTrue(heaviest instanceof StandardItem);
    }
//...
}
```

PDOs are non-trivial by definition; they were designed to reflect concepts from the target domain. Unit tests of PDOs are essentially important for the overall quality of the system. In addition, you are forced to use the PDOs via the public API (which forces you to think outside the box). Unit testing turns out to be a good usability check for the PDO's interface fluency—any inconveniences will be exposed to you during the tests. Good PDOs are easy to test as well—it's good quality assurance.

The JPA persistence can be used for testing with only little effort. Only the `EntityManager` has to be created using the `Persistence` and the `EntityManagerFactory`, as shown in the following PDO tests:

```
public class LoadTestWithPersistence {

    private EntityManager em;
    private EntityTransaction et;

    @Before
    public void setUp() throws Exception {
        this.em = Persistence.createEntityManagerFactory("test").
createEntityManager();
        this.et = this.em.getTransaction();
    }

    @Test
    public void mixedLoad(){
        Load load = new Load.Builder().
                withStandardItem(5).
                withLightweightItem(1).
                withBulkyItem(1).
                build();
        int actual = load.getShippingCosts();
        int expected = (5*5) + (5-1) + (1*5+5);
        assertEquals(expected,actual);
        this.et.begin();
        this.em.persist(load);
        this.et.commit();
        this.em.clear();
        Long id = load.getId();
        this.et.begin();
        Load found = this.em.find(Load.class, id);
        this.et.commit();
        assertEquals(expected,found.getShippingCosts());
        assertEquals(load.getNumberOfOrderItems(),found.getNumberOfOrderItems())
;
        //...
    }
//...
}
```

The local unit tests could even have integrational character. At least rudimentary tests with an `EntityManager` are useful to find OR mapping problems. In more complex applications, unit tests without persistence become increasingly bloated; in fact, the creation of the test fixture may be really complex. In such cases, a local test database can make it much easier to populate the test data once and reuse it for several test runs.

Documentation

The focus on the business logic and not technology is the key to success. Especially the naming of the PDO itself, as well as its methods is essential. Ambiguous naming should be prevented even in the early iterations. A wiki turns out to be a good documentation tool and pragmatic interface between the developers and domain experts. A two-column table (with Name and Essential Responsibility headers) is good enough to document the essential responsibilities and clarify ambiguous names.

PDOs represent key concepts, or essential entities of the target domain. It is useful to visualize the PDOs as well as their relations between each other. UML class diagrams are perfectly suitable for this purpose. For the documentation of PDOs only a fraction of the UML capabilities is sufficient. In fact, most of the UML features and especially generic stereotypes and tagged values are not well suited to document the essential responsibility and context of a PDO. Instead of relying on the built-in, generic stereotypes and tagged values, introduce a custom, unambiguous stereotype <<PDO>> (see Figure 4).

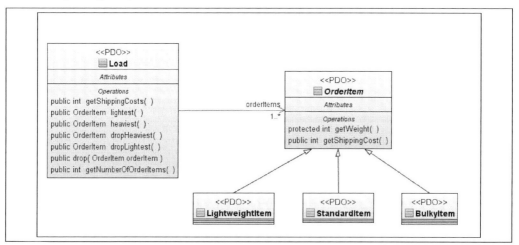

Figure 4. Persistence Domain Object in UML

The PDOs are modeled as classes, only public methods are visualized. Encapsulated fields and utility methods are not interesting for overview diagrams, because they only obfuscate the essential responsibilities and shouldn't be visible.

The same principle should be applied to JavaDoc. It is frankly not possible to document private attributes and accessors, especially of a PDO, without repeating the already existing truth in source code. On the other hand, at least the essential responsibility of the PDO should be documented on the class level. The documentation should be written following the DRY principle as well—it is better to existing reference wiki pages, instead of repeating the context in JavaDoc again. The following best practices are especially important for the documentation of a PDO:

- Document the background knowledge and the intention and not the result.

- Try to capture the concepts in a central place (for example, a wiki) and provide a reference to the contents.

- Document obvious facts with marker tags (annotations such as @PDO); don't describe them over and over again (follow the DRY principle).

- Include in your documentation samples, how-tos and so on (source code rules).

- Don't allow default JavaDoc comments generated by the IDE.

- Sometimes, providing no comment at all, is the best comment. Try to minimize the amount of documentation and describe only the key concepts.

Consequences

- **Usability:** The whole idea behind PDO is improving the maintainability of complex logic by providing an easy-to-use API, a so-called fluent interface. The PDO API is clean, concise, and should be transparent to domain experts and not just developers. There is only a fraction of code needed to interact with a PDO when compared to the anemic or procedural approaches.

- **Domain expertise:** The most important prerequisite to build maintainable PDOs is to have profound domain knowledge. The domain concepts should be reflected directly in the PDO. Ideally a domain expert should understand the business logic just looking at the PDO code—the fluent interface becomes a domain-specific language (DSL).

- **Core essential responsibilities:** A PDO has to reflect only the key concepts and should not realize the cross-cutting aspects. A PDO can be used potentially by a variety of different applications and clients. Client-specific needs and requirements should be reflected in, for example, Services and not in the implementation of the PDO. Otherwise a PDO may result in a monolithic, not cohesive, set of unrelated states and methods. It becomes the main challenge to keep a PDO clean and concise. This can be achieved only with continuous refactoring and testing.

- **Testability:** PDOs are just annotated Java classes. They can be unit tested inside, as well as, outside the EJB container. Furthermore their functionality can be tested in attached or detached state.

- **Tool support:** The IDE support for building PDOs is superb. Code completion, refactoring, and debugging work really well. Some IDEs come with support for code completion and syntax highlighting of JPA QL queries, generation of `persistence.xml` and so on. The object-oriented variant of PDOs is harder to use with data binding frameworks such as value binding in JSF or beans binding. The internal state, however, can be exposed as accessors in addition to be compatible with such frameworks.

- **Extensibility:** PDOs can be easily extended using object-oriented mechanisms and inheritance in particular. JPA supports inheritance and polymorphic queries so it fits well with the PDO idea.

- **Data transfer capabilities:** A PDO can be easily transferred between layers, even remotely as detached objects. The only requirement is the implementation of the `java.io.Serializable` interface. However, a PDO contains a significant amount of business logic, which can be invoked in a detached state as well. This can lead to state changes in the entire graph. Such changes are hard to synchronize with the server's state and often require the computation of change sets or even keeping the origin state of the objects separately (for example, SDO). For that purpose PDOs are not passed in a detached state between layers in general.

Related Patterns

Composite Entity (J2EE), Domain Store (J2EE), Business Object (J2EE), Data Transfer Object (J2EE / Java EE):

A PDO is managed by a Gateway and directly exposed to the presentation tier. Services or Service Façades provide cross-cutting, PDO-independent aspects and can access PDOs as well.

Gateway

PDOs are already consistent, encapsulated objects with hidden state. There is no need for further encapsulation—they can be directly exposed to the presentation. A Gateway provides an entry point to the root PDOs. A Gateway could be even considered as an anti-Service Façade—in fact its responsibilities are inverted.

Problem

PDOs are passive artifacts. It is not possible to access them directly without an execution context. Another problem is the stateless nature of most Java EE applications. After a method invocation of a transaction boundary (for example, a stateless session bean), all JPA-entities (PDOs) become detached. The client loses its state. This forces you to transport the entire context back and forth between the client and the server, which leads to the following problems:

- Heavily interconnected PDOs become hard to merge. Even for fine-grained changes, the whole graph of objects has to be transported back to server. It is not always possible to merge the graph automatically and even consistently.

- Because the transport of the context becomes too expensive and the merging functionality on the server side increasingly complex, transaction boundary (for example, Service Façade) is extended with additional methods to manage each particular excerpt of the entire graph. This results in the explosion of hard-to-maintain methods (aka God Façades), lots of redundancies, and procedural code.

- Dependent PDOs cannot be lazily loaded in a detached state and thus in the presentation tier. The server has to know in advance, which subgraph of interconnected objects has to be transported to the client. Dedicated methods (for example, `getCustomerWithAddress()`) are introduced to overcome the problem.

- Every change of the client's state has to be merged with the server.

- For some business logic, such as additional queries, a PDO may require access to the `EntityManager`. The `EntityManager`, however, is only available on the server and not the client.

Forces

- PDOs are accessible locally, per reference.

- PDOs are already well encapsulated; there is no need for further layering and abstraction.

- Your application owns the database, so it can be changed on demand.

- Changes performed in the user interface are likely to affect the database. It is likely, that an additional UI-control will cause the enhancement of the corresponding table with additional columns accordingly.

- The application is interactive. The validation logic is non-trivial and depends on an object's state. For example, whether the dragging of an additional `Load` to a `TransportVehicle` is enabled could not only be dependent on the particular `Vehicle` type, but also on its current load level. The drop action would change the current state of the `Vehicle`, which in turn would change its validation rules.

- Users decide when their changes are stored and when not. The business logic cannot be expressed in service-oriented manner, with self-contained, atomic and independent services.

Solution

The solution is very simple. Create a perfect anti Service Façade. Instead of cleanly encapsulating the PDOs, try to expose PDOs as conveniently for the UI as possible to the adjacent layer. Allow the user to modify the PDOs directly without any indirection.

The described approach above actually contradicts the common J2EE principles, according to which encapsulation is the only way to achieve maintainability. This is only true for perfect abstractions and encapsulations, which are very hard to find in enterprise projects.

The inverse strategy works even better in some use cases—just get rid of any layer (which in all likelihood is leaky anyway according to Joel Spolsky's Law of Leaky Abstractions [www.joelonsoftware.com/articles/LeakyAbstractions.html]) and expose the business logic directly to the presentation tier. Every change in the structure of the persistence layer would be immediately visible in the user interface—this makes the implementation of feature requests really easy.

Your presentation is coupled to the particular implementation of the business logic, but the concrete implementation is already encapsulated. JPA abstracts from the particular provider, and EJBs are nothing else than annotated POJOs. In other words, the technology is pretty well hidden already. The concrete state and implementation of domain-specific logic is well encapsulated too —it's the main responsibility of the PDOs.

Another challenge is the implementation of a consistent and concise transaction handling. Usually the transaction handling is straightforward: a transaction is started and committed before and after every invocation of the Service Façade (the boundary) method. This strategy works well, because the entire implementation of the business logic resides behind the Service Façade and is executed atomically.

The Gateway, however, exposes the PDOs directly to the presentation, so it loses the control over the PDOs and transactions in particular. Furthermore the user is allowed to access and modify the PDOs directly, which makes centralized transaction management with a stateless Service Façade impossible. You can modify the detached PDOs directly and a Gateway is lacking of fine grained `merge` methods.

The solution to the problem is the introduction of state on the server side. A stateful Gateway can keep the PDOs attached with an `EntityManager` declared as `PersistenceContext.EXTENDED`. The `EntityManager` needs a transaction only as a trigger to flush the changes to the database, which can be started by a method that overrides the class default. The following examples shows a stateful Gateway implementation:

```
@Stateful
@TransactionAttribute(TransactionAttributeType.NOT_SUPPORTED)
@Local(OrderGateway.class)
public class OrderGatewayBean implements OrderGateway{
```

```
@PersistenceContext(type=PersistenceContextType.EXTENDED)
EntityManager em;

private Load current;

public Load find(long id){
    this.current = this.em.find(Load.class, id);
    return this.current;
}

public Load getCurrent() {
    return current;
}

public void create(Load load){
    this.em.persist(load);
    this.current = load;
}

public void remove(long id){
    Load ref = this.em.getReference(Load.class, id);
    this.em.remove(ref);
}

@TransactionAttribute(TransactionAttributeType.REQUIRES_NEW)
public void save(){
    //nothing to do
}

public void update(){
    this.em.refresh(this.current);
}

@Remove
public void closeGate(){

}
}
```

The implementation of the gateway is simple. It is a stateful session bean with EXTENDED EntityManager. All incoming transactions are going to be suspended with TransactionAttributeType.NOT_SUPPORTED on the class level. This is actually only possible with an EXTENDED EntityManager, which can be injected only into a stateful session bean. An EntityManager with default configuration injected to a stateless session bean would throw the exception javax.persistence.TransactionRequiredException in most of its methods invoked without an active transaction.

The method save() overrides the class default with the REQUIRES_NEW transaction attribute which forces the container to start a new transaction. This, in turn, causes the EntityManager to flush all attached entities into the database and eventually to send the commit to the database.

Since the Gateway is stateful, it can maintain a client-specific state, which is also a reference to a PDO. You cache the root PDO `Load` and make it so easier accessible to the Gateway clients. The reference to the `Load` PDO is maintained in the `find` and `create` methods. The method `merge` is not needed, because there are no detached PDOs to attach. All changed PDOs will be automatically synchronized with the database at the end of the transaction.

The Gateway is stateful, so there is a 1:1 relationship between the client and the Gateway. This can be achieved only by injecting the Gateway to a stateful web component. If you are using JSF, you can set up this relationship by injecting the Gateway into a session-scoped backing bean:

```
<managed-bean>
    <managed-bean-name>SessionBean1</managed-bean-name>
    <managed-bean-class>…..SessionBean1</managed-bean-class>
    <managed-bean-scope>session</managed-bean-scope>
</managed-bean>
```

The web container stores a session-scoped backing bean in the `javax.servlet.http.HttpSession` so that the relationship between the user session (an open browser window) and the Gateway instance is properly maintained. You only have to inject the session bean into a session-scoped backing bean using the `@EJB` annotation:

```
public class SessionBean1 {
    @EJB
    private OrderGateway orderGateway;
```

The Gateway can claim a significant amount of memory. The total amount depends on the number of attached entities inside a user session. It might become a problem in applications with many concurrent sessions, so you should free the resources as soon as possible. The lifecycle of the Gateway is directly dependent on the lifecycle of the `HttpSession`. The destruction of the `HttpSession` should cause the immediate destruction of the Gateway. This can be easily achieved by overriding the `destroy` method of the backing bean and invoking an annotated `@Remove` method:

```
@Override
public void destroy() {
    //closeGateway is annotated with @Remove
    this.orderGateway.closeGateway();
}
```

In the popular web framework Wicket, you could look up the Gateway session bean in your custom session object. A little bit trickier is the initial set up in a plain Servlet environment. You would have to search for the Gateway in the `HttpSession` first. In case the search was not successful, you will further search for it in `InitialContext` and then store it in the `HttpSession`.

A rich client such as a Swing / SWT application would be the most natural way to use Gateway, because the entire application already represents the user session. Unfortunately a RIA is already distributed by definition, so that all PDOs become automatically detached (because of serialization), after every call. This fact makes the use of a classical Gateway far less interesting to RIA clients. In a fat client configuration a Gateway is still an interesting option for RIAs.

Conventions

- A Gateway resides in a component which is realized as a Java package with a domain-specific name, for example, `ordermgmt`.

- The Gateway resides in a subpackage (layer) with the name *facade* or *boundary,* for example, `ordermgmt.facade` or `ordermgmt.boundary`. This makes the automatic verification of the architecture easier. The Gateway resides in the same subpackage as a Service Façade.

- A Gateway is often named after the cached root entity; it is not necessary to keep the name Gateway.

- A Gateway is a local, stateful session bean with the `NOT_SUPPORTED` or event `NEVER` transaction attribute on class level.

- Dedicated, mostly empty, methods are starting a new transaction with the `REQUIRES_NEW` configuration and flush the transient state to the database.

- Gateway is deployed with a single local business interface in general. The no-interface view optimization is possible, but then the dynamic proxy pattern wouldn't work anymore in unmanaged environments such as RIAs.

Rethinking

The idea of a Gateway became possible only recently with the introduction of Java EE 5. In a J2EE world such a pattern wouldn't make any sense, because the lack of inheritance and detaching capabilities in CMP 2.0 persistence.

The attempt to introduce such a pattern in today's enterprise projects would probably be met with resistance. In the past years, one of the important measurement points of a scalable architecture is the degree of coupling and the amount of layers. Such a metric applied to a Gateway pattern would result in rather poor results. A Gateway neither tries to encapsulate the PDOs nor to introduce another layer. The opposite is true: a Gateway is the glue between layers, because it attempts to make access to the domain objects as easy as possible.

A Gateway is the manifestation of the "Leaky Abstraction" principle, which is defined as following:

> "From the perspective of Spoelsky's Law of Leaky Abstractions, all non-trivial abstractions resist complete implementation by their very nature. Consequently, implementation details will always leak through, regardless of how well-conceived, and no matter how rigorously they attempt to faithfully represent the abstraction. Sometimes the leaks are minor, other times they are significant, but they will always be present, because there is no such thing as a perfect implementation of an abstraction..." [http://en.wikipedia.org/wiki/Leaky_abstraction].

Regardless of how hard you will try to encapsulate a non-trivial implementation, it will always be leaky. It is therefore smarter to directly expose an already well-designed entity, instead of trying to further encapsulate it. This is especially true for UI-driven projects. The customer drives the requirements from the UI perspective, so that the realization of a feature will affect the presentation tier first. Such changes are not local to the presentation and will hit the adjacent layers as well. The leakier the boundary between layers, the more beneficial the effects the introduction of Gateway will have on your architecture.

Participants and Responsibilities

A Gateway exposes PDOs directly to the presentation layer. The most important participant is the PDO or an anemic domain object and the UI itself. The Gateway is just an intermediary and provides only the execution context for the PDOs. A Gateway is responsible for:

- Keeping the `EntityManager` open between method calls, so that the already known PDOs do not become detached.

- Providing as convenient and direct an exposure of PDOs as possible.

- Providing a defined synchronization point (the method `save`) and optional undo method (`EntityManager#refresh`).

- Per-reference (local) access to the PDOs. This requires you to run the EJB container in the same JVM as your web container. It is the default setting of the most application servers.

- Implementing the cross-cutting operations and especially query methods.

A Gateway, however, depends on some PDO qualities as well:

- PDOs should be designed to be directly accessed in the presentation. Their functionality should be well encapsulated.

- The public PDO methods should always leave the domain object in a consistent state. This can be hardly achieved with plain getters and setters.

The presentation tier has to be able to keep, or at least determine, the user's state. Your web framework should be capable to keep the reference to the Gateway associated with the user's session. This is already given in JSF, can be easily achieved with Wicket, and is a little bit harder with plain Servlets.

Strategies

The in-process execution of the Gateway pattern is common in all strategies. It is also crucial for the notion of transparent persistence. The stateful nature is typical for all strategies and allows keeping all PDOs attached for the length of the conversation.

Server-Side Gateway

This is the most common strategy. The Gateway is deployed as a stateful session bean and is accessed by the web container *per reference*. The Java Context and Dependency Injection Contract aka WebBeans specification (JSR-299), or its popular implementation, JBoss Seam, can be considered as a Gateway pattern on steroids. The WebBeans specification is the integration layer between JSF and EJB 3 and simplifies the access to JPA entities making the backing bean superfluous.

In addition, WebBeans provides several conversations (similar to subsessions) inside a `HttpSession`. WebBeans becomes especially interesting for scenarios with many independent subdialogs and complex wizards. Both WebBeans and Seam are stateful frameworks and are based on stateful session beans or even longer conversations such as business processes. The same is true for the Gateway pattern, but it provides only a subset of the WebBeans functionality. On the other hand, its realization is straightforward.

If you are using a Gateway on the server only, you can omit the business interface. The Gateway bean could be directly injected into the JSF backing bean or the Wicket WebPage. Keep in mind, that this approach will make testing, especially mocking, harder and swapping the implementation becomes impossible.

RIA Gateway

A Gateway is just a POJO so it is not limited to server use. It can also be started in the context of a RIA. It is directly executed in client's VM. Frankly, this would turn a thin RIA into a fat client. All the layers would be executed at the client side, so it is a fat client by definition. Fat client may sound no more up to date to you, but keep in mind that several popular frameworks are already converging into this direction.

Adobe AIR is a client runtime that can be compared to applets or a WebStart application but is Flash based. The AIR runtime (and the AIR applications you build) also comes with an embedded database. Even more interesting is Google Gears. This in-browser installed AJAX framework comes with an embedded database, A Gears application accesses the database from JavaScript. It is nothing else than an even more aggressive form of a fat client. (In general, just avoid to use the term *fat client* in meetings, sessions, and architectural descriptions. It is good neither for your project nor your career.)

A Gateway can either access an embedded database or a remote database. It is only dependent on the configuration of the JDBC driver in the persistence. Java DB (AKA Derby DB) has been included with the JDK since version 1.6. If you switch to the `EmbeddedDriver`, the `jdbc.url` will not refer to a host name, but to a path in the local file system. The following snippet shows the `persistence.xml` configuration for local bootstrapping with an embedded Derby DB:

```
<persistence-unit name="test" transaction-type="RESOURCE_LOCAL">

<provider>...essentials.PersistenceProvider</provider>
      <class>...business.gateway.domain.Load</class>
    <!-- remaining entities -->
    <exclude-unlisted-classes>true</exclude-unlisted-classes>
  <properties>
<property name="toplink.jdbc.url" value="jdbc:derby:./sample;create=true"/>
    <property name="toplink.jdbc.driver"
value="org.apache.derby.jdbc.EmbeddedDriver"/>
  </properties>
</persistence-unit>
```

To access the remote database, you will only have to change the driver and the `jdbc.url` again:

```
<property name="toplink.jdbc.url" value="jdbc:derby://localhost:1527/sample"/>
<property name="toplink.jdbc.driver"
value="org.apache.derby.jdbc.ClientDriver"/>
```

The Dependency Injection of the `EntityManager` is not automatically given outside the container. It has to be provided either by you (injecting it manually) or by the embeddable EJB 3.1 container. The bootstrapping of an EJB 3.1 embeddable container is straightforward:

```
javax.ejb.EJBContainer ec = EJBContainer.createEJBContainer();
javax.naming.Context ctx =  javax.ejb.EJBContainer.getContext();
OrderGateway orderGateway =
(OrderGateway)ctx.lookup("java:global/gateway/OrderGateway");
```

EJB 3.0, however, did not support a standardized way to bootstrap the EJB container outside the application server. Because a session bean is a POJO, it can be instantiated and used as any other Java class. It is basically the same approach as instantiating the bean in the `@Before` method in your unit test:

```
this.em = Persistence.createEntityManagerFactory("test").createEntityManager();
this.et = this.em.getTransaction();
this.gateway = new OrderGatewayBean();
this.gateway.em = this.em;
```

Bootstrapping the `EntityManager`, instantiating the Gateway, and injecting the references is a repetitive task. Gateway comes already with some well-known constraints and conventions. It is required to have a parameterless (default) constructor and has a field with the `EntityManager` type annotated with `@PersistenceContext` annotation. Furthermore it is a stateful sesssion bean, so its lifecycle is well defined as well:

- `newInstance()` (invocation of default constructor)
- Dependency injection (if any)
- `PostConstruct` callbacks (if any)
- `Init` method, or ejbCreate<METHOD> (if any)

In general, a Gateway has neither a `PostConstruct` nor a `ejbCreate` method. In most cases, it is sufficient to perform the first two steps of the lifecycle to simulate the required container's lifecycle. Both steps can be easily extracted into a generic factory class. The whole lifecycle can be even further automated with reflection. We know that the `OrderGatewayBean` implements the local business interface with consistent naming conventions. Following conventions, the name of the interface would be `OrderGateway`—without the `Bean` ending. This information is used to derive the bean implementation from the local business interface passed as a parameter to the factory method. The following example shows the `BeanLocator` generic factory and injector:

```
public class BeanLocator {

    public final static String SUFFIX = "Bean";
    public static final String UNIT_NAME = "test";
    private static BeanLocator instance = null;
    private EntityManager em;
    private EntityTransaction et;

    private BeanLocator() {
```

```
            EntityManagerFactory emf =
Persistence.createEntityManagerFactory(UNIT_NAME);
        this.em = emf.createEntityManager();
        this.et = this.em.getTransaction();
    }

    public final static synchronized BeanLocator locator() {
        if (instance == null) {
            instance = new BeanLocator();
        }
        return instance;
    }

    public <T> T createAndInject(Class<T> beanInterface) {
        String beanName = beanInterface.getName();
        beanName += "Bean";
        try {
            Class clazz = Class.forName(beanName);
            Object newInstance = clazz.newInstance();
            injectIntoField(newInstance, PersistenceContext.class, this.em);
            ...
    }
```

The business interface, passed as a parameter, is used to find the name of its implementation (the bean class) and it sets the method's return type as well. The `BeanLocator` is a singleton, the `EntityManager` is created in its private method once. The classic `getInstance()` method was renamed to `locator()` to make it more fluent:

```
OrderGateway g = locator().createAndInject(OrderGateway.class);
```

The creation is straighforward; more interesting is the injection of the `EntityManager` into the Gateway. The field might actually have private visibility which is actually not a big issue for reflection:

```
public static void injectIntoField(Object obj,Class anno,Object value){
        try {
            Field field = getField(obj, anno);
            if(field != null)
                    field.set(obj, value);
        } catch (IllegalAccessException ex) {
        throw new IllegalStateException("Error accessing attribute " +ex, ex);
        }
    }

    public static Field getField(Object obj, Class anno) {
    Field[] declaredFields = obj.getClass().getDeclaredFields();
            for (Field field : declaredFields) {
                if(field.getAnnotation(anno) != null){
                    field.setAccessible(true);
                    return field;
                }
            }
        return null;
```

```
    }
```

You enumerate through all fields and ask for the declaration of the @PersistenceContext annotation. You set the found Field to be accessible, which allows access to even private members. Finally, the value of the Field will be overridden with the current EntityManager instance. Using only a few lines of code, you are able not only to instantiate the Gateway but also to inject the EntityManager into its private member. And there were no changes to the existing OrderGatewayBean needed.

A remaining challenge is the realization of the transaction management. The container is responsible for the interpretation of the annotations in conjunction with defaults and manages the transactions for you. This functionality is not available outside the (< EJB 3.1) container, so you also have to control transactions. The creation of the Gateway is encapsulated in a factory, so you could use the decorator pattern, or even aspects, to manage the transactions. The introduction of an entire aspect-oriented framework just to decorate a method is overkill. It would introduce additional complexity, make the deployment of the libraries necessary, and require the use of special compilers or specific classloaders or Java agents.

OrderGateway with its business interface is a perfect candidate to be decorated with a dynamic proxy. Dynamic proxy is part of JDK and has been available since version 1.3. It doesn't require any additional libraries and can be considered a subset of a fully fledged AOP framework. For our purposes it is good enough. The JVM is able to create instances for a given interface on the fly. You only have to pass a specific implementation of an InvocationHandler which will be invoked by the JVM:

```
Class clazz = Class.forName(beanName);
Object ins = clazz.newInstance();
injectIntoField(ins, PersistenceContext.class, this.em);
return withTransactions(ins,beanInterface,this.em, this.et);
```

Fortunately, the dynamic proxy works with reflection, so you are able to provide a generic and DRY solution. In the following example, the dynamic proxy utility decorates an interface with the transaction aspect:

```
import java.lang.reflect.Proxy;
import javax.persistence.EntityManager;
import javax.persistence.EntityTransaction;

public class Decorator {

 public static <T> T withTransactions(Object target,Class<T> view, EntityManager
em,EntityTransaction et) {
      Class allInterfaces[] = new Class[]{view};
                              TransactionHandler handler = new
TransactionHandler(target,em,et);
      ClassLoader cl = target.getClass().getClassLoader();
      return (T)Proxy.newProxyInstance(cl,allInterfaces,handler);
   }
}
```

The `java.lang.reflect.Proxy.newProxyInstance` method requires a `ClassLoader` instance, all interfaces that have to be intercepted, and the actual handler. The delegation requires few lines of code and has nothing to do with the actual `BeanLocator`, so you can factor it out into a standalone `Decorator` utility class.

The crux of the matter is the `TransactionHandler` implementation. It realizes the `InvocationHandler`, which forces you to implement the `invoke` method. This method represents an *around* aspect—the origin method is fully wrapped, so you can provide additional functionality before and after its execution. The following example demonstrates the implementation of the transaction aspect with dynamic proxy:

```
public class TransactionHandler implements InvocationHandler {

    private EntityManager em = null;
    private EntityTransaction et = null;
    private Object target = null;

    public TransactionHandler(Object target, EntityManager em,
EntityTransaction et) {
        this.et = et;
        this.em = em;
        this.target = target;
    }

    public Object invoke(Object proxy, Method method, Object parameters[])
            throws Throwable {
        Object retVal;
        Method targetMethod = null;
        boolean transactional = false;
        try {
            targetMethod = getMethodForTarget(method,
method.getParameterTypes());
            transactional = isTransactional(targetMethod);
            if (transactional) {
                this.et.begin();
            }
            retVal = targetMethod.invoke(target, parameters);
            if (transactional) {
                this.et.commit();
            }
        } catch (InvocationTargetException e) {
            if (transactional) {
                this.et.rollback();
            }
            throw e.getTargetException();
        } catch (Exception e) {
            throw new RuntimeException("unexpected invocation exception: " ...);
        }
        return retVal;
    }

    private boolean isTransactional(Method targetMethod) {
```

```
        TransactionAttribute annotation =
targetMethod.getAnnotation(TransactionAttribute.class);
        if (annotation != null) {
            TransactionAttributeType value = annotation.value();
            if (value.equals(TransactionAttributeType.REQUIRES_NEW)) {
                return true;
            }
        }
        return false;
    }
  //... some methods omitted
}
```

It is only required to start transactions for methods annotated with declared the
`TransactionAttributeType.REQUIRES_NEW` annotation. All other methods would
inherit the `NOT_SUPPORTED` class annotation, so you only invoke the target (the Gateway
instance) without proxying it.

The correct implementation should suspend and resume the incoming transaction. However, this
transaction is neither needed nor even possible in our scenario—Gateway is directly accessed by
the UI and the UI must not control transactions. You could, however, easily implement all
`TransactionAttributeTypes` with a dynamic proxy, but it is not relevant for a Gateway
implementation.

With two classes and some utility methods, you are able to start the Gateway outside the
container. The Gateway does not have to be modified, it can even be deployed inside the origin
`ejb-jar.jar` to the client. This ensures strict separation between the Gateway and its
presentation tier.

Hybrid Gateway

Regardless how well your customer receives the RIA, it would be grossly negligent to tightly
couple the Gateway with a concrete presentation framework. Chances are that your customer will
insist in the near future to expose a subset of your rich client functionality to the web. The
Gateway is an EJB 3, so it should be deployable to the server. A carefully designed and deployed
RIA Gateway has this ability already.

The Hybrid Gateway is tested on the client and server, so it can be deployed in parallel to both
environments. This is more common than you might think. Deploying the Gateway directly to the
client solves a lot of problems, but it makes the exposure of reusable services to the outside world
nearly impossible. A server-side deployment makes the exposure of existing functionality via
REST, SOAP, RMI or IIOP relatively easy. You only have to encapsulate the fine-grained
Gateway with a Service Façade, which would increase the granularity of the services and makes
them remote capable.

Testing

A Gateway should not contain any complex business logic. It can be used, however, as a
convenient entry point to the PDOs under test. A Gateway can be easily instantiated in the unit

test. Actually there is no difference between the execution in the RIA or unit test context. You could even use the `BeanLocator` for bootstrapping as shown in the following example:

```
public class EmbeddableContainerTest {

    private OrderGateway gateway;
    private EntityManager em;
    private EntityTransaction et;

    @Before
    public void initPersistence(){
        EntityManagerFactory emf =
Persistence.createEntityManagerFactory("test");
        this.em = emf.createEntityManager();
        this.et = this.em.getTransaction();
        this.gateway = locator().createAndInject(OrderGateway.class);
    }

    @Test
    public void createAndSave(){
        Load load = new Load.Builder().withBulkyItem(1).build();
        this.gateway.create(load);
        Long loadId = load.getId();
        Load current = this.gateway.getCurrent();
        assertSame(load,current);

        Load found = this.em.find(Load.class, loadId);
        assertNull(found);

        this.gateway.save();

        found = this.em.find(Load.class, loadId);
        assertNotNull(found);
    }
}
```

Regardless of how trivial a Gateway implementation really is, a unit test should always be written for it. Gateway is a central entry point to the domain logic. PDOs are non-trivial by nature, so possible mapping errors such as inconsistent transaction or state management can cause serious problems in latter iterations. Such problems can be easily spotted in the early iterations, even before the integration tests.

Gateway is stateful, so load and robustness tests are especially important. Every user has a Gateway instance, which in turn is associated with an `EntityManager`. Each `EntityManager` instance maintains its own JPA entity cache. The `EntityManager` injection is configured as `PersistenceContext.EXTENDED`, so the cache is not cleared after every transaction.

All PDOs remain attached, in extreme cases for the length of the session. The size of PDOs in memory is hard to estimate in advance, but can be easily measured during a load test. Such tests do not have to be realistic, more important is testing the behavior of the system under heavy load.

Such tests should be performed as early as possible. This gives you enough time to migrate to a stateless architecture in case the scalability of the system does not satisfy your expectations.

Documentation

Because Gateway does not contain sophisticated business logic in general, there is no need to document every occurrence of a Gateway in your project. It is more important to document the concept behind a Gateway once, and then only point to the already existing documentation. A lean, tutorial-like documentation with some sample code is perfectly suitable for that purpose. It is also unnecessary to document a Gateway in a UML diagram. It only provides an execution and session context for the PDOs. Just keep the diagrams concise and emphasize the essential business logic, that is, the PDOs.

Consequences

- **Scalability:** Gateway is a stateful component. All PDOs are cached in the user session. The scalability of this pattern is highly dependent on the cache size and the length of the session. This pattern doesn't scale as good as a stateless, service-based architecture in general. However, it is absolutely sufficient for most applications. The actual scalability is hard to estimate but easy to verify with brute-force load tests.

- **Performance:** When the user needs frequent access to the same data, a stateful architecture could provide better performance. The PDOs will be loaded only once for the entire session and can be locally accessed *per reference*.

- **Consistency:** Cached PDOs can become stale. The bigger the session and the more users access the same database, the more likely are lost updates and other interferences between cached objects. The introduction of the Gateway pattern automatically implies the use of optimistic lock strategies. A well defined strategy for handling the `javax.persistence.OptimisticLockException` should be defined and tested in early iterations.

- **Testability:** A Gateway is not only easy to test, it also further simplifies testing PDOs.

- **Maintainability:** In non-trivial, problem-solving applications, a Gateway can greatly improve the maintainability. It simplifies the architecture and makes the intermediary layers superfluous. This is especially true in projects, where the database is under your control and your customer thinks in UI forms. On the other hand, Gateway can significantly increase the complexity of a service-oriented application with many external services. In that case, PDOs will only represent a subset of the entire business logic. The interfaces to the external systems operate with DTOs, which are detached per definition. Furthermore, the direct exposure of the internal, not well-encapsulated state and behavior (DTOs and fine-grained services) together with encapsulated and attached PDOs makes the development of the presentation logic more complex and the architecture brittle.

- **Productivity:** PDOs are directly exposed to the presentation tier. They are even available for declarative data binding (for example, in JSF), or can be directly manipulated in the presenter (AKA controller). Every extension in the domain logic is immediately available in the presentation.

- **Ease of use:** After you get the idea of always attached objects and transaction triggered synchronization, the development becomes surprisingly easy. Issues such as lazy loading, synchronization of complex object graphs, or computation of change sets simply do not exist.

Related Patterns

Composite Entity (J2EE), Domain Store (J2EE), Business Object (J2EE), Data Transfer Object (J2EE / Java EE), Service Façade (J2EE / Java EE), Service (J2EE / Java EE):

A Gateway exposes PDOs to the presentation logic. It has opposite capabilities to a Service Façade. It is actually an inversion of a Service Façade and any SOA-like approaches.

Fluid Logic

Java is a static language with emphasis on its strong typing. Java is well suitable for the implementation of well-defined, stable business logic. Algorithms that often change require recompilation and even redeployment of the whole application.

Problem

Strong typing and the static nature of Java are features and drawbacks at the same time. For integration purposes, dynamic languages such as JavaScript, Ruby, or Python are better suitable and more efficient. With Java it is hardly possible to evaluate or interpret business logic at runtime. You could use tools such as ANTLR (www.antlr.org) to build your own domain-specific language (DSL), which would be evaluated or interpreted at runtime. You shouldn't underestimate the effort it takes to design, test, document, and deploy a custom DSL.

Forces

- You want to execute parts of the business logic dynamically.

- Algorithms that often change have to be isolated and loaded dynamically—without affecting the rest of the application.

- The affected code changes structurally—compilation at deployment time is not sufficient.

- The realization of a custom interpreter is too expensive and too hard to maintain.

- You are searching for a standard way to integrate scripting components with your Java EE environment.

Solution

The problem has been solved since Java 6 Standard Edition. JSR-223 (Scripting for the Java Platform) is a thin and pragmatic API that allows interaction with more than 100 scripting languages. You can even pass Java objects that become available to the script as parameter to the ScriptEngine. The initialization of the ScriptEngine takes only a few lines of code. The script can be executed in managed and unmanaged environments as well. Even the same class can be used outside the container and be deployed as a stateless session bean without any change. The following example demonstrates how to embed JavaScript for dynamic formula evaluation:

```
import javax.annotation.PostConstruct;
import javax.ejb.Stateless;
import javax.script.Bindings;
import javax.script.ScriptContext;
import javax.script.ScriptEngine;
import javax.script.ScriptEngineManager;

@Stateless
public class Calculator {
    private static final String ENGINE_NAME = "JavaScript";
   /* On Mac OS X AppleScriptEngine instead of JavaScript is available
    private static final String ENGINE_NAME = "AppleScriptEngine";
    */
    private ScriptEngine scriptEngine = null;
```

```java
    private final static double FIVE = 5;

    @PostConstruct
    public void initScripting() {
        ScriptEngineManager engineManager = new ScriptEngineManager();
        this.scriptEngine = engineManager.getEngineByName(ENGINE_NAME);
        if (this.scriptEngine == null) {
            throw new IllegalStateException("Cannot create... " + ENGINE_NAME);
        }
    }

    public Object calculate(String formula) {
        Object retVal = null;
        try {
            Bindings binding = this.scriptEngine.createBindings();
            binding.put("FIVE", FIVE);
            this.scriptEngine.setBindings(binding, ScriptContext.GLOBAL_SCOPE);
            retVal = this.scriptEngine.eval(formula);
        } catch (Exception e) {
            throw new IllegalStateException("Cannot create...: " + e, e);
        }
        return retVal;
    }
}
```

Consequently, the script is going to be executed in the context of the EJB, participates in transactions, and has access to container services. You could even pass an attached entity to the script, manipulate the state with the language of your choice, and let the `EntityManager` on the Java side synchronize the changes with the database. This allows you to use scripts for manipulation of domain objects and is especially interesting for integration purposes or mapping between incompatible object hierarchies.

The session bean (a Service in general) can be easily used outside the container without changes and is thus well suited to unit testing. You only have to execute the initialization of the scripting environment before accessing the script, as shown in the following example:

```java
public class CalculatorTest {

    private Calculator calculator;

    @Before
    public void setUp() {
        this.calculator = new Calculator();
        this.calculator.initScripting();
    }

    @Test
    public void calculate() {
        String formula = "2*2";
        Object actual = this.calculator.calculate(formula);
        assertNotNull(actual);
        assertTrue(actual instanceof Double);
```

```
        assertEquals(4.0,actual);
    }
}
```

JavaScript has been available with the JDK since version 1.6 (on Mac OS X the AppleScript). If you plan to use other scripting languages, you will have to deploy additional JARs for this purpose.

The scripting code can be loaded as a stream from any resource and is therefore location-agnostic. In the `Calculator` sample the actual script is passed as a method parameter and evaluated at runtime.

JSR-223 allows also tighter integration between Java and scripting languages. A dynamic language of your choice could even implement Java interfaces, which could be invoked from a Java class.

Conventions

Fluid Logic is a specific Service. All Service conventions and best practices are applicable to the Fluid Logic service as well. Refer to the Service section for more details.

Rethinking

Back in the J2EE 1.x days, scripting was considered to be inappropriate for an enterprise application. This prejudice became sometimes expensive—some projects even developed a custom interpreter to be able to provide scripting-like behavior.

On the other hand, dynamic languages are highly overhyped these days; they, too, have their shortcomings. The quality of static analysis, refactoring, and IDE support of scripting languages is much lower compared to plain Java. Furthermore, the lack of type safety in most languages requires you to write more unit tests.

Reasonable use of scripting has its advantages. The fluid logic is easily replaceable and can be changed in a running system without redeployment. Because the scripts are loaded dynamically, they can be stored and managed in a database or downloaded from the network.

Participants and Responsibilities

The `ScriptEngine` is the most important player. It is part of the JSR-223 API and responsible for the encapsulation of the actual execution environment (the SPI). The Java code is independent of the engine implementation.

The generic `ScriptEngine` is created by the `ScriptEngineManager`, what is comparable to the JDBC-class `java.sql.DriverManager` and its relation to the actual `java.sql.Driver`. It tries to find and instantiate an appropriate `ScriptEngine` for the given name.

The initialization of the `ScriptingEngine` and converting the actual parameters into bindings takes a few lines of code and is encapsulated in a simple POJO. In addition to the encapsulation, the POJO is a classic adapter—it exposes a more meaningful interface to the user. For its user it is just another Service, the existence of scripting is totally transparent.

Strategies

There are no limits in the scripting integration—and therefore countless strategies. The Fluid Logic pattern can be used in all tiers, layers, and components for different purposes. All the variations aim for a common goal: seamless integration between Java and scripting with the best of both worlds as result.

Testing

Testing of the scripting integration with EJB 3 is trivial; tests of the dynamic scripts may become a challenge. In addition to the actual logic the type safety has to be tested as well. If the script is the actual user input, the robustness of the solution has to be verified. Especially the resistance against malicious code (for example, invoking `System.exit(-1)`) has to be proofed.

The interpretation process is significantly slower, when compared to the execution of compiled Java code. The extensive use of scripting in your Java application may result in performance hit. You should verify the actual performance with load and stress tests early.

Documentation

Fluid Logic is a Service and should be documented as such. In addition, the reasons and intentions for the integration of dynamic languages, as well as the functionality of the script have to be explained well. Introducing new APIs and technologies always causes some friction, especially when introducing dynamic languages to hard-core Java developers. Clearly stated intentions and reasons for the integration with a scripting language may save some time and avoid long discussions.

Consequences

- **Performance:** Fluid Logic will affect your performance. The important question is whether your application will be still fast enough.
- **Robustness:** Dynamic languages are not type-safe in general. You will have to invest more effort in testing to achieve the same level or stability, as with plain Java.
- **Maintainability:** The intention of the Fluid Logic pattern is to make it easier to maintain often changing logic. Fluid Logic increases the maintainability, provided that the developers know the language. On the other hand, multi-lingual projects are harder to understand, test, and debug. The impact of scripting in your Java projects is highly dependent on the developer skills and use case.
- **Portability:** JSR-223 scripts are executed inside the JVM and are portable across JVMs and application servers.
- **Flexibility and agility:** Here shines the Fluid Logic pattern. Scripts can be modified, reloaded, and replaced at runtime—without even redeploying the application. The script does not even have to be deployed inside the EAR, WAR, or EJB-JAR and can be conveniently loaded from outside.

- **Security:** Although the scripts are executed inside the JVM and run in an environment guarded by the `SecurityManager`, introduction of scripting provides a potential and unpredictable security hole. Even though the script is not able to shut down the JVM or delete some files because of the `SecurityManager` configuration, you could still introduce a malicious script which compromises the consistency of the business logic.

Related Patterns

Fluid Logic is a flexible Service with easy-to-swap implementation. It can be used in the same context as a Service.

Paginator and Fast Lane Reader

EJB 2.1 was limited in terms of persistence. It was neither possible to iterate through a large set of entity bean instances, nor to extract and return only the interesting parts from the query result. The original Fast Lane Reader pattern was designed as a workaround for the shortcoming:

> "…Sometimes applications access data in a tabular fashion, such as when browsing a catalog or a list of names or when exporting data in batches for use elsewhere. This kind of data access is usually read-only. In such situations, using entity beans to represent persistent data incurs overhead and provides little benefit. Entity beans are best for coarse-grained access to individual business entities, and are not effective for read-only access to large quantities of tabular data.

> "The Fast Lane Reader design pattern provides a more efficient way to access tabular, read-only data. A fast lane reader component directly accesses persistent data using JDBC components, instead of using entity beans. The result is improved performance and less coding, because the component represents data in a form that is closer to how the data are used…. " [http://java.sun.com/blueprints/patterns/FastLaneReader.htm].

JPA 1.0 solves already the initial problems out-of-the-box. It provides a way to extract only the interesting attributes from an entity and allows pagination in a large amount of results. The Fast Lane Reader pattern became a best practice in Java EE for some use cases, rather than a workaround for a shortcoming of the specification.

Problem

The JPA is not able to stream objects, rather than load the entire page into memory at once. For some use cases such as exports, batches, or reports direct access to the database cursor would provide better performance.

Forces

- You have to iterate over a large amount of data.
- The data cannot be loaded at once into the client and has to be cached on the server.
- The client is interested only on some attributes of the entity.
- The data is accessed mostly in a read-only way.

Solution

There is no single solution for the problem; instead you have different strategies each with its own requirement. All the variations are realized by a stateful or stateless session bean, which implements the iteration logic or exposes the live `ResultSet`. The Fast Lane Reader pattern is a specialized Service Façade or, in more complex applications, a reusable Service.

Conventions

The Fast Lane Reader pattern is a specific form of a Service Façade or Service—the corresponding conventions can be directly applied to this pattern.

Rethinking

The `EntityManager` already provides easy-to-use iteration logic. The classic Value List Handler pattern is implemented by the `EntityManager` and therefore no longer required. Also, native SQL queries can be executed and mapped to either existing entities or returned as a list of primitives. This eliminates the need for DAOs and makes the Fast Lane Reader implementation leaner.

Participants and Responsibilities

The Fast Lane Reader pattern is used directly by the application client. In most cases the Fast Lane Reader operates directly on the `EntityManager`. There is no need to access a DAO or Service to get simplified access to the persistence—`EntityManager` is already simple enough. The Fast Lane Reader pattern can be considered as a lean and standalone Service Façade, which is accessed locally by the application client.

Strategies

The principle of all strategies is exactly the same: server-side iteration in a big collection of persistent items. Those items do not have to be PDOs; some strategies work with ResultSet and so the database directly.

Paginator and Value List Handler

If the results of a query exceed a manageable amount of entries, it becomes hard to handle in the UI. Instead of returning potentially hundreds or thousands of records, the entire result set is split into smaller chunks, the pages. They can be easily bound to UI models and directly handled by UI components.

The classic `java.util.Iterator` works similarly—it traverses a `java.util.Collection` implementation and returns a single instance for each iteration. A single instance is too fine grained for pagination purposes, but it could be easily extended to an Iterator<List<Customer>>.

A session bean can directly implement the `java.util.Iterator` interface as it business interface. The classic (JDK) `Iterator` is stateful—its implementation remembers the actual position in the collection. It is more convenient and natural to implement the iteration in a stateful way. The current index could be maintained inside the stateful session bean and do not have to be passed back and forth.

```java
@Stateful
public class CustomerQueryBean implements Iterator<List<Customer>> {

    @PersistenceContext
    private EntityManager em;

    private int index = 0;
    private int pageSize = 10;
    private boolean next = true;

    public void setPageSize(int pageSize){
        this.pageSize = pageSize;
    }
```

```java
    public List<Customer> next(){
        List<Customer> retVal = null;
        Query query = this.em.createNamedQuery(Customer.ALL);
        query.setFirstResult(getFirst());
        query.setMaxResults(pageSize);
        retVal =  query.getResultList();
        if(retVal.size()==0){
            this.next = false;
        }
        index++;
        return retVal;
    }

    private int getFirst(){
        return index * pageSize;
    }


    public boolean hasNext() {
        return this.next;
    }

    public void remove() {
        throw new UnsupportedOperationException("Operation remove ...");
    }

    @Remove
    public void close(){
        this.em.clear();
        this.em.close();
    }
}
```

The Paginator implements the `java.util.Iterator` interface; its user is only interested in the iteration logic and can rely on the Iterator's methods only. The EJB API as well as the existence of a session bean implementing the interface are totally hidden. The following example the standalone unit test of the pagination logic:

```java
public class CustomerQueryBeanTest {

    private CustomerQueryBean query;
    private CustomerMgrBean mgr;

    private EntityManager em;
    private EntityTransaction et;

    @Before
    public void initialize() throws Exception {
        this.em =
Persistence.createEntityManagerFactory("Paginator").createEntityManager();
        this.et = this.em.getTransaction();
```

```
        this.query = new CustomerQueryBean();
        this.query.em = this.em;
        this.mgr = new CustomerMgrBean();
        this.mgr.em = this.em;

        this.et.begin();
        for(int i=0;i<100;i++){
            Customer customer = new Customer();
            customer.setName("Duke: " +i);
            this.mgr.create(customer);
        }
        this.et.commit();
    }

    @Test
    public void next() {
        while(query.hasNext()){
            List<Customer> customers = query.next();
                System.out.println("Size: " + customers.size());
            for (Customer customer : customers) {
                System.out.println("Customer: " +customer);
            }
        }
    }
    @After
    public void cleanUp(){
        this.et.begin();
        this.mgr.deleteAll();
        this.et.commit();
    }
}
```

In fact, the only difference between the classic Iterator and the Paginator implementation is the page size. The `Iterator#next()` invocation returns a list of entities and not a single one. The client typically needs two nested loops to iterate over the whole result.

The Paginator implementation as a `java.util.Iterator` requires to be implemented as stateful session bean. The method `next()` extracts the current excerpt from the list and moves the cursor to the next page. There are no parameters, so it is not possible to pass the current index from outside—it has to be remembered internally. The Paginator uses the `EntityManager` with the default `PersistenceContextType.TRANSACTION` type. There is no need to keep the entities managed—they become detached after every iteration step. Changes to the entities are not reflected in the database. The behavior could be easily changed with the `PersistenceContextType.EXTENDED` configuration. With this modification you could change the state of the entities during the iteration—the `EntityManager` will flush the changes to the database at the end of the transaction for you.

Instead of storing the current index (that is, page number) inside the session bean, you could also pass it from outside. For this purpose you will have to change the Paginator signature to be able to pass the current index—and abstain from a direct `java.util.Iterator` implementation.

Page or Everything

Pagination is a common requirement in larger result lists. It is very likely, that you will be asked by your client to implement such a feature in a web or rich Internet application. Pagination in a large result set, however, is not user friendly and is rarely used. The user will probably want to see the most relevant results and then either refine the query or display a larger, but still limited, amount of entries at once. If the user is still not satisfied with the result, let him or her redefine the query.

The implementation of the Page or Everything strategy is a simplified form of the classic Paginator implementation. You do not even have to implement the `java.util.Iterator`. You only have to check whether the first page contains the entire result. If not you will ask the user to re-execute the query and return a still bounded number of objects (for example, the first thousand) or refine the query.

If you select one object more as requested, you get the check for the existence of additional pages almost for free. The following code demonstrates a sample implementation of the Page or Everything Paginator strategy.

```
@Stateless
public class CustomerQueryPageOrEverythingBean{

    @PersistenceContext
    EntityManager em;

    private static int MAX_PAGE_SIZE = 1000;

    public List<Customer> getAllCustomers(int maxResults){
        if(maxResults == -1 || maxResults > MAX_PAGE_SIZE)
            maxResults = MAX_PAGE_SIZE;
        else
            maxResults +=1;
        Query query = this.em.createNamedQuery(Customer.ALL);
        query.setMaxResults(maxResults);
        return query.getResultList();
    }
}
```

The Page or Everything Paginator is implemented as a stateless session bean—there is no need to maintain the current index or cache objects internally. The user of this modified Paginator version, however, will have to do a little more work and check whether the return value is larger as requested to indicate the existence of further pages:

```
@Test
public void getAllCustomers() {
    int pageSize = 5;
    List<Customer> all = this.query.getAllCustomers(pageSize);
    assertNotNull(all);
    assertEquals(pageSize+1,all.size());
}
```

Table View

Sometimes it is required to provide an efficient way to iterate over an excerpt or even a set of related entities but return a different view to the client. This can be achieved by fetching the entities with `EntityManager` and transforming them inside a Service or Paginator. This approach is neither fast, nor easy to maintain. Especially the merging and extraction of entity data is error-prone and can become quite complex.

Another possibility is the execution of more complex native SQL statements and mapping them into existing entities or TOs. The query could become complex and the filter criteria highly repetitive. You will need the filter in all related queries that return the particular subset.

Especially in the context of pagination, where the data is mostly retrieved for read-only purposes, database views are the easier and more efficient alternative. Instead of implementing a lot of plumbing on the Java side all the work could be easily done in the database. You only have to create a SQL view—it is a part of the SQL standard and is even supported by the Derby DB shipped with Java as stated in the Apache Derby 10.0 documentation.

```
CREATE VIEW APP.V_CUSTOMER(NAME,CITY) AS SELECT NAME,CITY FROM
APP.CUSTOMER
```

For SQL queries there is no difference between views and tables, so you can easily map a JPA entity to a view transparently. The code on the Java side remains clean and simple, and you will even get better performance. There is a drawback: not all views can be updated. Whether a view is updatable highly depends on the complexity and particular database. For example, in the Derby DB all views are not updatable.

This strategy is not only applicable to the different Paginator strategies, but can be applied to all JPA entity in general. This provides additional flexibility and makes database refactorings easier.

Live Cursor and Fast Lane Reader

All described strategies so far were disconnected from the database. Although the entities remain attached to the `EntityManager`, the entire page is loaded at once into the level one cache (that is, identity `HashMap` or transactional cache).

If you are only exporting data, or want to fetch a bunch of primitives from the database as fast as possible, even the conversion of JDBC types into objects could become too much overhead.

With EJB 3 you can surpass the `EntityManager` and get access to its `java.sql.Connection` directly. The `DataSource` can be as easily injected as the `EntityManager`. The `DataSource` and `EntityManager` would even share the same `java.sql.Connection` instance, if you are accessing them in the same transaction. You will see all the changes already sent to the database from both resources. The application server, however, will commit or roll back the (single) connection at the end of the (JTA) transaction. The following FastLaneReader implementation demonstrates direct, transactional access to the `DataSource` from a session bean:

```
@Stateless
public class CustomerFastLaneReaderBean {

    @Resource(name="jdbc/sample")
```

```
DataSource ds;

public List<String> getCustomerNames(){
    List<String> allNames = new ArrayList<String>();
    Connection con = null;
    Statement stmt = null;
    ResultSet resultSet = null;
    try {
        con = ds.getConnection();
        stmt = con.createStatement();
    resultSet = stmt.executeQuery("select name from CUSTOMER");
        while (resultSet.next()) {
            String name = resultSet.getString("name");
            allNames.add(name);
        }
        return allNames;
    } catch (SQLException ex) {
        throw new RuntimeException("Cannot perform query: " +ex,ex);
    }finally{
        try {
            resultSet.close();
            stmt.close();
            con.close();
        } catch (SQLException ex) {
            //cannot handle
        }
    }
}
}
```

In production quality code you should use `PreparedStatements` instead of executing queries directly each time. `PreparedStatements` not only faster, but also more robust. They will be constructed once and reused several times. The syntactical correctness of the `PreparedStatement` will be already validated at the construction time and not at runtime first.

As mentioned earlier, you are iterating over the data in the database without converting the rows into objects. This saves time and resources and is especially interesting for high-volume, data-oriented tasks such as the creation of reports, exports, or transformations. If you do not need objects to realize table or dataset-oriented logic—direct access to the database could be even easier to implement.

In general, direct JDBC usage is an exception rather than the rule. It results in a lot of code and is error-prone and hard to maintain. If you are a SQL expert and you know what you are doing, you could even achieve better performance as with JPA.

On the other hand, working directly with `EntityManager` is fast enough for most use cases, lean, and easy to maintain.

Testing

Paginator tests are identical to DAO, Service Façade or Service tests. The logic of each variant is easily unit testable. Its especially recommended to test the iteration logic intensively—even small errors can be hard to find during integration tests. Some Paginator strategies are stateful, so they should be load and stress tested for potential bottlenecks, memory leaks, and scalability issues.

Documentation

From an architectural point of view, a Paginator is a specific Service Façade. It can be documented as such, using the `<<ServiceFaçade>>` stereotype or the `<<Paginator>>` stereotype depending on whether the iteration is an exception or a common approach in your project. It should be documented once (for example, in a wiki) which strategy is used, with project-specific requirements. After doing so, there is no further need to repeat the intentions and mechanics of a Paginator in JavaDoc. It is enough to reference the wiki entry or other another pragmatically written document.

Consequences

- **Performance:** In general, the performance is better when using the Paginator instead of returning a huge result set at once. You can achieve the best performance with the Fast Lane Reader pattern.

- **Scalability:** Stateful Paginator implementations have to maintain state, which has to be replicated to other cluster nodes. This could become a bottleneck—it is highly dependent on the particular application server implementation and has to be verified with load tests.

- **Robustness:** Paginator returns chunks of a potentially huge result set to its clients and prevents them to run out of memory.

- **Consistency:** Most Paginator strategies cache at least the current page. Even the entities remain attached; they are not automatically refreshed from the database. The current page could become stale just after fetching. Paginator should always be used with optimistic locking—except in the case of read-only implementations.

- **Testability:** Paginator has no dependencies to the application server or Java EE APIs, and thus is well-suited to unit testing.

- **Portability:** Paginator is portable across application servers. Fast Lane Reader is the only strategy which uses native SQL directly and may become dependent on the particular database.

Related Patterns

Paginator uses the `EntityManager`. In rare cases, it could rely on an existing Service or DAO implementation. Paginator is used directly by its clients, for example, backing beans, RESTFul services, Servlets or Wicket pages.

Retired Patterns

Some of the popular best practices in the J2EE no longer apply to Java EE 5. Some of them became an anti-pattern. The patterns listed in this section are retired in mainstream Java EE 5 applications, but could still be interesting for special purposes or during migration from J2EE to Java EE 5.

Service Locator

Original Intention

The Service Locator was a mandatory pattern in J2EE. All registered resources and components had to be located first:

> "Service lookup and creation involves complex interfaces and network operations.
>
> [...]
>
> "Use a Service Locator object to abstract all JNDI usage and to hide the complexities of initial context creation, EJB home object lookup, and EJB object re-creation. Multiple clients can reuse the Service Locator object to reduce code complexity, provide a single point of control, and improve performance by providing a caching facility" [http://java.sun.com/blueprints/corej2eepatterns/Patterns/ServiceLocator.html].

Reasons for Retirement

- Dependency Injection is available in most Java EE components. JNDI lookups are no longer required to access other session beans or resources.
- The creation of a home interface became optional, and therefore the creation of remote and local interfaces.
- `PortableRemoteObject.narrow` is optional in EJB 3.0—the session bean can be accessed with simple `Context#lookup`.
- The complexity of the infrastructural code was greatly reduced by the EJB 3.0 specification. A Service Locator would not further reduce the complexity of the code; on the contrary, it would increase it. You should use Dependency Injection whenever possible and only in exceptional cases a generic Service Locator implementation.
- For the exceptional cases a specialized Service Locator form, the BeanLocator, can be used.

Composite Entity

Original Intention

In CMP 1.0 even relations between persistent entities had to be implemented manually. This was fixed in CMP 1.1 with the introduction of local interfaces, but wasn't really transparent. Furthermore, CMP 1.0 were remote visible, so that the granularity of the Composite Entities was of big concern as well:

> "Entity beans are not intended to represent every persistent object in the object model. Entity beans are better suited for coarse-grained persistent business objects.
>
> [...]

"Use Composite Entity to model, represent, and manage a set of interrelated persistent objects rather than representing them as individual fine-grained entity beans. A Composite Entity bean represents a graph of objects" [www.corej2eepatterns.com/Patterns2ndEd/CompositeEntity.htm].

Reasons for Retirement

- CMP 2.1 persistence didn't support relationships very well. Furthermore, CMP entities came with home interfaces which had to be used in a similar fashion as `EntityManager`. With the advent of JPA, all this overhead was gone. Implementation of relationships became natural.

- JPA entities are just domain objects, which are persistent. You can apply whatever patterns you want without any overhead.

- JPA are object oriented per default. The Composite Entity pattern in Java EE became degraded to a usual GoF Composite.

Value Object Assembler

Original Intention

In J2EE the access to persistent storage was associated with a huge ceremony. Fetching some entities from a database wasn't an easy task. The Value Object Assembler was a dedicated pattern to merge, transform or extract data from different data sources:

"In a Java 2 Platform, Enterprise Edition (J2EE) application, the server-side business components are implemented using session beans, entity beans, DAOs, and so forth. Application clients frequently need to access data that is composed from multiple objects.

[...]

"Use a Transfer Object Assembler to build the required model or submodel. The Transfer Object Assembler uses Transfer Objects to retrieve data from various business objects and other objects that define the model or part of the model" [http://java.sun.com/blueprints/corej2eepatterns/Patterns/TransferObjectAssembler.html].

Reasons for Retirement

- Even the `EntityManager` implements a part of the origin intention of the Value Object Assembler: it is able to return a submodel from a graph of interconnected entities.

- Creation of submodels and conversion of attached entities into Transfer Objects is a responsibility of the Service Façade or Service. There is no need to introduce a specific component or pattern to implement the conversion.

- In the majority of all use cases, you could even get rid of using dedicated Transfer Objects and pass detached and even attached entities between layers or tiers.

Business Delegate

Original Intention

J2EE clients were directly exposed to the J2EE API (EJB, JMS) and complexity (`RemoteException`, `CreateException` and more complex lookups). This fact was reflected in the origin intention:

> "A multi-tiered, distributed system requires remote method invocations to send and receive data across tiers. Clients are exposed to the complexity of dealing with distributed components.

> [...]

> "Use a Business Delegate to reduce coupling between presentation-tier clients and business services. The Business Delegate hides the underlying implementation details of the business service, such as lookup and access details of the EJB architecture" [http://java.sun.com/blueprints/corej2eepatterns/Patterns/BusinessDelegate.html].

Reasons for Retirement

- The majority of all EJB 2.1 exceptions were checked. The EJB client had to catch, or at least know, the exceptions and became polluted with the EJB 2.1 API. The separation between business logic and infrastructural code was not given. Business Delegate fixed this issue. With EJB 3.0 all checked exceptions are optional—the business interface is identical to the external Business Delegate interface.

- Business Delegate used Service Locator to fetch the home interface and created the local or remote interface internally. EJB-related exceptions were converted to neutral system exceptions. In EJB 3.0, home interfaces became optional; the business interfaces can be fetched directly from JNDI.

- Business Delegates were used to decouple the business logic from the presentation as well. This is no longer necessary, because business interfaces can be directly injected into most of the presentation components.

Domain Store

Original Intention

CMP J2EE wasn't transparent and caused lots of plumbing. The Domain Store pattern was designed to fix this problem:

> "Use a Domain Store to transparently persist an object model. Unlike J2EE's container-managed persistence and bean-managed persistence, which include persistence support code in the object model, Domain Store's persistence mechanism is separate from the object model" [www.corej2eepatterns.com/Patterns2ndEd/DomainStore.htm].

Reasons for Retirement

`EntityManager` can be considered as a standardized implementation of the Domain Store pattern. It is the Domain Store pattern.

Value List Handler

Original Intention

CMP didn't provided any semantics for data iteration or detachment. The Value List Handler pattern was introduced to fix this limitation:

> "Use a Value List Handler to control the search, cache the results, and provide the results to the client in a result set whose size and traversal meets the client's requirements" [http://java.sun.com/blueprints/corej2eepatterns/Patterns/ValueListHandler.html].

Reasons for Retirement

- CMP 2.1 could not be detached. Value List Handler was responsible for the conversion of CMP instances into Transfer Objects. Since the introduction of JPA the entities can be easily detached without additional effort.

- The implementation of the Value List Handler is rather trivial. It is the implementation of the classic Iterator pattern.

- Value List Handler became a strategy of the Paginator pattern.

4

Rethinking the Integration Tier

System integrators working on Java EE projects have to deal with lots of legacy and incompatible code. Unfortunately the chances to start a totally green field project in the enterprise are extremely low. In addition to Enterprise Information Systems (EIS) and Legacy Hosts, system integrators are confronted with J2EE applications, .NET applications, and Web 2.0 logic available through REST or scripting.

The realization of the integration logic makes the difference between Java EE and J2EE. In J2EE, the integration logic is mainly factory and POJO based. In Java EE 5 and 6 all the factories and infrastructural code can be replaced with pure EJB 3 components. The patterns are more pragmatic and practical. The dream of totally decoupled tiers and implementation independence is no more the driving force. The experience shows that the integration tier of an already deployed system does not change too frequently.

In other words, there is no need to provide an (often leaky) abstraction for possible future changes. Existing services are in general only abstracted with a lean adaptation layer and are not entirely encapsulated. This allows for a more natural and efficient interaction between the business and the integration layers and lowers the development costs. The components of the integration layer can be injected into the services of the business tier, sometimes even exposed directly to the presentation components. It mainly depends on the complexity of your application.

The boundary between the integration and business layers begins to blur as well. The Data Access Object (DAO) and Transfer Object (TO) patterns can be classified as belonging to either layer. The responsibility of the DAO has a slightly more integrational character. The same is true for a TO. A TO is often used in the business tier to implement client-specific views or projections of domain objects. In most cases, however, a TO is introduced to map incompatible data sources such as WebServices, XML sources, stored procedures, or even native code to easier manageable Java classes.

This chapter discusses integration approaches for problematic or even Java EE incompatible resources. Beyond the discussion of plain resource integration, I will also explain the integration of legacy J2EE components.

Data Access Object

The original context of a Data Access Object (DAO) is defined in the Core J2EE pattern catalog:

> "Access to data varies depending on the source of the data. Access to persistent storage, such as to a database, varies greatly depending on the type of storage (relational databases, object-oriented databases, flat files, and so forth) and the vendor implementation" [http://java.sun.com/blueprints/corej2eepatterns/Patterns/DataAccessObject.html].

The motivation for this pattern was the decoupling of the business logic from the concrete realization of the data store mechanisms. This is no longer the main motivation for the majority of current applications.

Problem

The real problem of this pattern is its overuse. The idea of decoupling from the database, and even its vendor, is neither realistic nor, in most cases, necessary. In enterprise applications a particular type of database is rarely replaced with another one. An application that uses a SQL database will hardly ever be ported to another storage type such as LDAP, object databases, or even flat files.

Looking back to past projects, even switching database vendors has happened only in rare cases. Customers tend to stick with one relational database vendor for the life cycle of their applications. Databases tend to live longer than an application. Decoupling from a database seems to be a strange strategy, considering the average database lifetime, it would be more appropriate to worry about the coupling between the database and the application and not vice versa.

An introduction of another layer of abstraction or encapsulation causes additional development and maintenance effort. A complete abstraction of the underlying data store is only possible for simplistic use cases and therefore leaky. These days, it is hard to justify the DAO pattern with the original intention.

J2EE had another problem: the insufficient power of CMP 2.0. The standard persistence mechanism was not powerful enough for sophisticated use cases.

The limited EJB-QL query capabilities, no access to native SQL, and the lack of dynamic queries forced the developers to access the database using plain JDBC. It was a good idea to encapsulate database access behind a replaceable and mockable implementation.

Most of the CMP 2.x applications today are hybrids of CMP 2.x and the DAO pattern. DAOs were used for sophisticated queries and the CMP 2.x for updates of business objects.

Nonetheless, enterprise applications still need to encapsulate legacy resources. This requirement, however, is an exception rather than the rule. JPA 1.0 introduced the `EntityManager` interface, a perfect DAO implementation that hides not only the JPA providers, but even translates abstract JPA queries into database-specific SQL queries.

Forces

- You have to access a legacy (that is, JPA incompatible) data source or resource.
- You have to keep the data access abstraction testable and mockable.
- You want to decouple the proprietary implementation of the resource access from the rest of the application.

- Your application is service oriented: the business logic and the data access are separated.

- You have to deal with non-standard, legacy data sources.

- Your queries are too complex; you want to maintain them in a dedicated place.

Solution

Use a stateless session bean with a dedicated, local business interface to abstract and encapsulate the interactions with the data store. A no-interface view session bean can be used as well; the realization, however, is harder to replace then. The additional `@Local` interface allows easy replacement of the bean implementation and thus provides additional flexibility. A business interface simplifies the testing of the DAO outside of the container. A DAO pattern is reduced in a Java EE 5 environment to an interface and a class, with some EJB-specific annotations.

The session bean is not only responsible for accessing and transforming the data, but for resource and connection handling as well. The needed resources (for example, `javax.persistence.EntityManager` or `javax.sql.DataSource`) should preferably be injected; it drastically reduces the amount of code. The container takes care about concurrency, resource management, and transaction enlistment of the injected resources. Resource-specific details such as the name of a stored procedure or the in/out parameters have to be fully encapsulated and not exposed to the clients.

The introduction of an additional factory is not needed. It would only increase the complexity and amount of infrastructural code. The local view of this bean can easily be injected to other services with standard mechanisms,—no custom infrastructure is required.

The DAO Session Bean is annotated with `@TransactionAttribute(TransactionAttributeType.MANDATORY)`, so all DAO methods can be invoked only in an already existing transaction. The transaction is going to be started by services that use the DAO to access the persistence. Because the main goal of the DAO is the strict separation of persistence details and business logic, a DAO has to be invoked from a business logic component and not directly from the presentation. An attempt to invoke a DAO directly from the presentation tier is the first indication that it is probably superfluous. A Service, or even Service Façade, would probably do a better job in this case.

Rethinking

In an EJB 3/Java EE 5 environment you don't have to use the low-level JDBC to access the database any more. You can use the generic, yet powerful JPA query language as well as native SQL to fetch not only the persistent objects, but also Data Transfer Objects and even primitive data types from the database. It is even possible to execute update and delete statements without using the low-level JDBC API. The JPA comes with the `EntityManager`, which provides generic data access functionality. Access couldn't be simpler. The `EntityManager` can be directly injected to any Session Bean:

```
@Stateless
@TransactionAttribute(TransactionAttributeType.MANDATORY)
public class BookServiceBean implements BookService {
    @PersistenceContext
```

```
private EntityManager em;
```

The `EntityManager` is already an interface; its realization belongs to the JPA Service Provider Interface (SPI) and can be declaratively swapped without changing the code:

```
<persistence …
  <persistence-unit name="book" transaction-type="JTA">
    <provider>org.eclipse.persistence.jpa.PersistenceProvider</provider>
…
```

`EntityManager` methods are very similar to the classical DAO implementations (CRUD), except for the extensive use of Java 5 SE generics (http://java.sun.com/j2se/1.5.0/docs/guide/language/generics.html) (Java 5 SE and so generics were not available at the J2EE time).

The `EntityManager` is already an abstraction and encapsulation, so —further decoupling is not necessary and would be even counterproductive. The abstraction from the service provider is leaky, as every other abstraction, but the situation will definitely not improve with an additional layer of indirection.

The `EntityManager` can be considered as a generic implementation of the DAO pattern. It can be used as a DAO and be injected to existing services. Heavy use of JPA query language, however, would blur the expressiveness of the business logic. The creation of queries can be easily factored out into dedicated query builders—or utility classes. The services could inherit the query logic from an abstract class as well.

In Java EE, the DAO pattern is optional and no longer the only way to access the data store. `EntityManager` as an abstraction is sufficient for most in-house software projects. In product development, however, a dedicated DAO as an additional layer of abstraction could be necessary. Nonetheless, the introduction of such a layer without clear requirement is always suspicions and should be justified with hard requirements.

In short, in Java EE 6, a dedicated DAO is an exception rather than the rule. The DAO can often be replaced with an `EntityManager` injected into a Service.

Conventions

The concrete implementation of the `CrudService` interface is going to be injected into the client (for example, a Service) by the container. The DI made the DAO factory superfluous. All DAO strategies are only comprised of a business interface and its bean implementation (a session bean). This structure is valid for all DAO strategies and variations. Further simplification with a no-interface session bean is not suitable. A direct injection of the DAO implementation makes testing outside the container harder and replacement of the implementation nearly impossible. Figure 1 illustrates the structure of the DAO pattern.

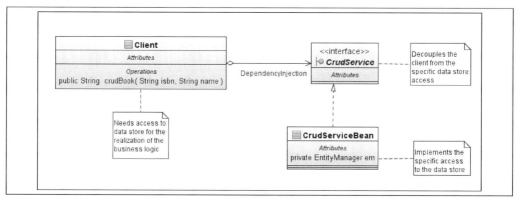

Figure 1. The Structure of the DAO pattern

A generic DAO is deployed once and reused from various components. Therefore it should be placed in a generic package, for example:

```
...[application_name].integration.dataservices
```

Domain-specific DAOs should reside in the related business component, for example:

```
[application_name].book.dataservices
```

or shorter:

```
[application_name].book.ds
```

Participants and Responsibilities

- **Client:** The DAO client is generally implemented as a (stateless or stateful) session bean that accesses the DAO functionality. It uses the DAO to get convenient access to the data store. The client uses the DAO in the context of its business logic realization, so the DAO is always invoked in the context of an active transaction. The DAO is injected into the client by the container. The Client is independent of the specific realization of the data store access.

- **DAO:** A DAO is implemented as a stateless session bean and responsible for encapsulation of proprietary APIs and technologies. This includes the transformation of proprietary exceptions—even chained ones. A DAO provides convenient, high-level access to the data store. It raises the level of abstraction. For the sake of convenience and decoupling, the main responsibility of a DAO is resource management and conversion between technology-specific data representation, into higher-level domain objects. Access to standard Java EE resources and their management is greatly simplified by the container, in case a session bean is used for the implementation. In case JPA is used as data store, the EntityManager takes the responsibility of the data conversion, connection handling, and transaction enlistment.

- **Data Store:** Data Store is a fully integrated (like JPA), standardized (like JDBC, JCA), or proprietary resource that has to be accessed for data access. JPA access comes already with Java EE—additional encapsulation is rarely needed. It is always a good idea, however, to use DAOs to encapsulate proprietary data access and decouple the domain logic from proprietary technology.

Strategies

All the strategies aim for the same goal: simplification of data access and pragmatic decoupling from the concrete data store. Dependent on the project-specific needs, this generic requirement can be met by different implementations efficiently.

Generic DAO

The signature of the `EntityManager` methods is already generic. The result methods of the `javax.persistence.Query` cannot be type-safe, because they have to materialize an object from a given row set of unknown type. These methods return a single object or a `java.util.List` of objects, respectively. The user of the `Query` class will have to cast the result to a particular JPA entity anyway. The DAO implementation returns only the raw list of objects,—casting remains the responsibility of the client. For all other methods the return type is inferred from the parameter where possible. This makes the usage of the generic DAO implementation more convenient.

The `CrudService` interface is not polluted with the EJB API—it is just a clean plain old Java interface (POJI). It contains not only the usual suspects (such as the `create`, `find`, `update`, and `delete` methods), but some finders as well. The following snippet shows the interface of a generic DAO:

```
public interface CrudService {
    <T> T create(T t);
     <T> T find(Object id,Class<T> type);
    <T> T update(T t);
    void delete(Object t);
  List findByNamedQuery(String queryName);
  List findByNamedQuery(String queryName,int resultLimit);
 List findByNamedQuery(String namedQueryName, Map<String,Object> parameters);
  List findByNamedQuery(String namedQueryName, Map<String,Object> parameters,int
resultLimit);
}
```

Interestingly, the `create` and `update` methods are not `void`, but have the same return type as their parameter. The reason for that is a possible modification of the JPA entity by the container. The `create` method could delegate the computation of, the technical, auto-incremented key to the `EntityManager`. The same is true for the `update` method, where the `@Version` field of a PDO may be changed in case optimistic concurrency is used. The computed id is needed to find the created entity later. In case you are working with business keys or UUIDs only, you could change the return value of the `create` method to `void`.

The updated domain entity with the fresh `@Version` has to be returned to the presentation layer and used for subsequent interactions with the `EntityManager`, otherwise any further attempt to update the entity will fail with `javax.persistence.OptimisticLockException`.

The implementation of the interface is a stateless, local session bean with `MANDATORY` transaction setting. The DAO expects to be invoked in a context of already active transaction. The

`CrudService` interface is exposed with the `@Local` annotation, this approach ensures its independence from the EJB API.

The implementation of the method `create` isn't obvious at the first glance. The passed entity is persisted first, then the `flush` method is invoked. This forces the `EntityManager` to flush its cache to the database. The state of the cached entities will be written to the database with one or more `INSERT` statements—but not committed yet. Either the database or the `EntityManager` will have to compute any technical primary key now. After the flush invocation, the entity is going to be refreshed. The state of the entity is overwritten with the state in the database. Finally, the fresh entity is returned to the caller. This strange behavior is sometimes required to force the JPA provider to update the technical key in the entity instance. The `persist`, `flush`, and `refresh` sequence further enforces the update of the `@Id` computed in the database. It is not backed by the spec, but it works with the popular providers. The following example shows a generic DAO bean implementation:

```java
@Stateless
@Local(CrudService.class)
@TransactionAttribute(TransactionAttributeType.MANDATORY)
public class CrudServiceBean implements CrudService {

    @PersistenceContext
    EntityManager em;

    public <T> T create(T t) {
        this.em.persist(t);
        this.em.flush();
        this.em.refresh(t);
        return t;
    }

    @SuppressWarnings("unchecked")
    public <T> T find(Object id, Class<T> type) {
        return (T) this.em.find(type, id);
    }

    public void delete(Object t) {
        Object ref = this.em.getReference(t.getClass(), t);
        this.em.remove(ref);
    }
    public <T> T update(T t) {
        return (T)this.em.merge(t);
    }

    public List<Object> findByNamedQuery(String namedQueryName){
        return this.em.createNamedQuery(namedQueryName).getResultList();
    }

    public List<Object> findByNamedQuery(String namedQueryName,
Map<String,Object> parameters){
        return findByNamedQuery(namedQueryName, parameters, 0);
    }
```

```
    public List<Object> findByNamedQuery(String queryName, int resultLimit) {
        return this.em.createNamedQuery(queryName).
                setMaxResults(resultLimit).
                getResultList();
    }

    public List<Object> findByNamedQuery(String namedQueryName,
Map<String,Object> parameters,int resultLimit){
        Set<Entry<String, Object>> rawParameters = parameters.entrySet();
        Query query = this.em.createNamedQuery(namedQueryName);
        if(resultLimit > 0)
            query.setMaxResults(resultLimit);
        for (Entry<String, Object> entry : rawParameters) {
            query.setParameter(entry.getKey(), entry.getValue());
        }
        return query.getResultList();
    }
}
```

The implementation of the `delete` method seems to be strange at first glance. Before the entity is going to be removed, a reference to it is fetched from the `EntityManager`. This is required by the spec—only managed entities can be removed. Obtaining an entity with the `EntityManager#getReference` method is a faster and lighter variant. You could also merge or find the entity before removing.

Both approaches are only required for detached entities. If your entity is already managed, you can remove it. Merging before removing is required for checks of the `@Version` field. Only up-to-date entities can be removed. The attempt to delete a stale entity will fail with `javax.persistence.OptimisticLockException`.

Up to this point, I've described DAO methods that are delegates on steroids. They are only wrappers of existing `EntityManager` functionality.

The implementation of the query functionality is more challenging. I concentrate on `NamedQueries` only. They are good enough for most scenarios; JPA QL injection can be avoided and the performance is better when compared to dynamic queries. The DAO implementation could easily be extended to support any, even dynamically created, JPA QL or native queries:

```
    public List findByNativeQuery(String sql, Class type) {
        return this.em.createNativeQuery(sql, type).getResultList();
    }
```

All named queries have to be named uniquely. This requirement causes problems; popular queries such as "find all" or "find by name" are defined for nearly every entity. To overcome the problem, queries should be qualified with a unique prefix followed by the actual name. The prefix can be easily derived from the entity name and defined as a final field as shown in the following example:

```
@Entity
@NamedQueries({
@NamedQuery(name=Book.ALL,query="Select b From Book b"),
```

```
@NamedQuery(name=Book.BY_NAME,query="Select b From Book b where b.name = :name")
})
public class Book implements Serializable{

    public final static String ALL = "...crud.domain.Book.ALL";
  public final static String BY_NAME = "...crud.domain.Book.BY_NAME";
```

This avoids not only naming conflicts, but increases the usability as well. The constant can be passed to the DAO, and a common pitfall, misspelling of the query name, can be avoided. A purist may argue that this approach breaks encapsulation, because the DAO client has to use constants from the entity and bypass the layering. However, the entity is also used as parameter and result. The violation of the encapsulation is intentional here—it emphasizes the DRY principle:

```
this.crudServiceBean.findByNamedQuery(Book.ALL).size()
```

Queries can have an arbitrary number of parameters, which are key-value pairs. The query parameters can be conveniently chained together with method invocation on a `Query` instance:

```
        this.em.createQuery(Entity.QUERY_NAME).
            setParameter("firstParameterName", "firstValue").
            setParameter("secondParameterName", "secondValue");
```

The `Query` class is fully encapsulated inside the DAO, so exposing the query to DAO clients would break the encapsulation. Because the DAO implementation is generic, there is no way to incorporate a fixed number of parameters into the method signature in regular way. The var-args style would work, but then the first odd array index would represent the parameter name and the parameter value, which is not convenient and error prone.

Instead, you can use a `java.util.Map<String,Object>`—it already supports the notion of type-safe key-value pairs out of the box. The construction of a `Map`, however, is not fluent. The `put` method returns the value and not the `Map` itself, which makes chaining impossible.

The utility class `QueryParameter` streamlines the construction of the `Map` instance using method chaining and a simplistic implementation of the Builder pattern. The use of the `QueryParameter` utility is fully optional; the query parameters can still be passed as `Map` if needed.

```
public class QueryParameter {

    private Map<String,Object> parameters = null;

    private QueryParameter(String name,Object value){
        this.parameters = new HashMap<String,Object>();
        this.parameters.put(name, value);
    }
    public static QueryParameter with(String name,Object value){
        return new QueryParameter(name, value);
    }
    public QueryParameter and(String name,Object value){
        this.parameters.put(name, value);
        return this;
    }
```

```
    public Map<String,Object> parameters(){
        return this.parameters;
    }
}
```

The method `with` is statically imported, which makes the construction code more readable. It returns the `QueryParameter` itself, which in turn allows further chaining with the `and` method.

```
import static com.abien.patterns.business.crud.QueryParameter.*;

@Stateless
@TransactionAttribute(TransactionAttributeType.REQUIRES_NEW)
public class DAOClient{

    @EJB
    private CrudService crudService;


public List<Book> find(String name,int numberOfPages){
    return this.crudService.findByNamedQuery(Book.BY_NAME_AND_PAGES,
                with("name",name).
                and("pages", numberOfPages).
                parameters()).
                getResultList();
    }
}
```

Neither the parameters nor the result of the query itself are type-safe. This is the due to the generic implementation of this strategy. Type safety has to be provided by the DAO client, it can easily wrap the generic methods and provide a more specific and type-safe interface.

Domain-specific DAO

Nothing prevents us to provide a type-safe DAO, which is designed to operate on a particular domain object. Such a DAO could be extended with domain-specific extensions and additional functionality such as prefetching of dependent objects, managing common relations, creating domain-specific queries on the fly, or filtering the results to match a specific user. Those extensions are application specific and cannot be generalized in a reusable pattern. A well-designed, domain-specific DAO provides added value beyond wrapping the `EntityManager` and casting its parameters and return values.

In contrast to a generic DAO, this variant has to be deployed once for an entity type, whereby one instance of a generic DAO can manage any number of different entities. In practice, these two variants are used together. The generic one is perfectly suitable for master data management and simpler CRUD use cases. A domain-specific DAO, on the other hand, realizes specific functionality. It can even access generic DAOs for reusing basic functionality.

Attached-result DAO

The attached-result DAO returns active objects that are still connected with the data store. This is the default for a DAO implemented as a stateless session bean and injected `EntityManager`. In case the DAO reuses the enclosing transaction (which is the rule), all returned entities will remain managed. Even external (e.g. performed in Services) entity modifications will still be visible after the commit of the transaction. The generic variant described so far, operates in exactly in the same way.

In the context of a transaction, the persistence should always operate in a managed or attached way. This prevents the existence of multiple copies of the same entity and possible inconsistencies such as lost updates. Especially in more ambitious projects, several developers could work on functionality behind the transaction boundary. An attached-result DAO is compatible with this idea, because it always returns the same reference to an entity for a given primary key. All transaction participants operate on the same object instances, so lost updates inside a transaction are effectively prevented.

Working with attached objects is preferred. It is, however, not always possible to achieve this quality.

Detached-result DAO

Detached-result DAO operates in the same manner as the attached-result DAO: the method results became detached. In fact the result of a method becomes a value object or Transfer Object. Disconnecting the entities from the transactional cache is not desirable in a transaction—it is often a limitation of given data store implementation.

Nevertheless, the majority of all enterprise resources are not JPA compliant. Legacy databases without JDBC driver, flat files, and even stored procedures cannot be easily accessed via a standard JPA provider. You could implement a JPA provider to enable access to an unsupported resource. The effort, however, is much higher than bypassing JPA and accessing the proprietary resource directly.

A DAO is perfect for the encapsulation of the proprietary data access, but returns DTOs or unmanaged entities to the caller. The detached-result strategy is similar to a typical J2EE 1.4 DAO. The main responsibility is the conversion between an often data set−oriented, proprietary resource and more convenient POJOs.

More common in Java EE 5 is the use of DTOs for returning a subset of a managed entity network. This is often done for optimization purposes. A `@NamedQuery` is used to search for JPA entities, but the result is mapped to transient DTOs:

```
@NamedQuery(name=Book.ALL_DTO,query="Select new
...domain.BookDTO(b.numberOfPages,b.name) From Book b")
```

For the query execution even an attached-result DAO could be used. The generic finder returns in that particular case an unmanaged DTO instead of an attached entity.

```
List<BookDTO>        dtos        =        this.crudServiceBean.
findByNamedQuery(Book.ALL_DTO);
```

In practice such hybrid DAO strategies are common. The semantic difference between returning an attached and a detached object is not obvious and can cause inconsistencies. It is a good idea to use specific naming conventions to differentiate between DTOs and real entities; the suffix DTO is good enough for that purpose.

Back-end Integration DAO

The Common Client Interface (CCI) from the Java Connector Architecture (JCA) is very similar to plain JDBC and often needed to integrate external resources. Because the resource vendor, and not the application developer, has to implement the JCA SPI, an existing JCA realization is the easiest way to interact with the back-end system.

JCA and its proprietary counterparts are neither type-safe nor convenient to use. The developer has to deal with `ResultSets`, Input/Output parameters, and many other low-level details. Exposing this low-level API to business services would pollute the code with plumbing and mix the realization of domain-specific requirements with the infrastructure. The introduction of a DAO to encapsulate the CCI or other similar APIs such as network access, generated screen scraper code, transformation between proprietary and normalized formats and so on provides a real added value.

The structure and realization of such a back-end integration DAO is nearly the same as a standard DAO, except the interface implementation (the actual bean) interacts with existing back-end services instead of accessing the database. Because it is in practice more complicated than it may seem here, the bean often delegates calls to a variety of utilities, services, APIs, or even frameworks. Although at first glance, the back-end integration DAO looks like just another interface, its implementation is a façade that interacts with vendor-specific, even generated functionality. The back-end integration DAO falls into the detached DAO category—the data fetched by such DAOs are Transfer Objects converted from proprietary data sources, which are detached by definition.

Abstract DAO

The data access logic does not always have to be realized as a standalone DAO. Session beans already support injection of `EntityManager` and have access to its functionality. Instead of delegating to a dedicated DAO, reusable data access logic can be inherited from an abstract DAO implementation as well. The DAO methods would be available immediately—without delegating and the need of injecting the DAO.

A purist may argue, that inheriting from an abstract DAO in a Service class is not clean, because a Service is not a DAO. Inheriting from generic DAO functionality streamlines the code and is pragmatic. This approach makes sense for database-driven applications, where a major portion of business logic consist of database access. In that particular case, you could even argue that a Service class is actually a DAO.

Testing

Testing of EJB 3.0 is not unlike testing POJOs. The Dependency Injection is not available, so it has to be emulated in the `@Before` method. The same is true for declarative transactions. They have to be started and committed (rolled back) manually. The `EntityTransaction` can be obtained directly from the `EntityManager`, which, in turn, is created with the bootstrapping class `Persistence` and the `EntityManagerFactory`.

It takes three additional lines of code to test the DAO outside of the container. The bootstrapping of the JPA runtime could be easily factored out in a super class or a utility class with a single static method. The following example demonstrates testing a DAO outside of the container:

```java
public class CrudServiceBeanTest {

    private EntityManager em;
    private EntityTransaction et;
    private CrudServiceBean crudServiceBean;

    @Before
    public void setUp() throws Exception {
        this.em = Persistence.createEntityManagerFactory("test").
createEntityManager();
        this.et = this.em.getTransaction();
        this.crudServiceBean = new CrudServiceBean();
        this.crudServiceBean.em = this.em;
    }
    @Test
    public void crud(){
        Book book = new Book("1", "Productive Java EE");

        this.et.begin();

        int initialSize =
this.crudServiceBean.findByNamedQuery(Book.ALL).size();

        //create
        Book created = this.crudServiceBean.create(book);
        assertNotNull(created);
        assertEquals(book.getIsbn(),created.getIsbn());
        assertEquals(book.getName(),created.getName());
        Book found = this.crudServiceBean.find(created.getIsbn(), Book.class);
        assertNotNull(found);
        assertEquals(found.getIsbn(),created.getIsbn());

        //query
        int size = this.crudServiceBean.findByNamedQuery(Book.ALL).size();
        assertEquals(initialSize+1,size);

        String newName = book.getName() + " Second Edition";
        book.setName(newName);
        //update
        Book updated = (Book) this.crudServiceBean.update(book);
        assertNotNull(updated);

        Book foundUpdated = this.crudServiceBean.find(created.getIsbn(),
Book.class);
        assertNotNull(foundUpdated);
        assertEquals(updated.getName(),foundUpdated.getName());

        //delete
```

```
        this.crudServiceBean.delete(foundUpdated);

        Book shouldntExist = this.crudServiceBean.find(created.getIsbn(),
Book.class);
        assertNull(shouldntExist);

        int zero = this.crudServiceBean.findByNamedQuery(Book.ALL).size();
        assertEquals(0,zero);

        this.et.rollback();
    }
}
```

The manual bootstrapping is no longer necessary in EJB 3.1. The initialization in the @Before method could be replaced with the bootstrapping of the embeddable container:

```
                          @Before
   public void setUp() throws Exception {
     EJBContainer container = EJBContainer.createEJBContainer();
     Context ctx = container.getContext();
    this.crudServiceBean = (CrudService)ctx.lookup("java:global/
[EJB_JAR_NAME]/CrudServiceBean");
    }
```

The creation of the container, as well as the lookup logic, can be further encapsulated in a LookupUtility class, which uses the naming conventions and the Beans interface to compute the global jndi name, perform the lookup, and return the interface in a type-safe manner. The bootstrapping code would be effectively reduced to the following:

```
   import static ..util.LookupUtility.*;

   @Before
   public void setUp() throws Exception {
       this.crudServiceBean = lookup(CrudService.class);
   }
```

Dependency injection and transaction management, for example, would be performed by the container. There is no need to reboot the container before every single @Test method. It is smarter to start it once and reuse it not only for testing a single class, but for all classes to be tested.

The EJBContainer can be transparently cached inside the LookupUtility. This is good for performance, but would also imply the reuse of already created bean instances, which could lead in turn to non-reproducible tests.

Beyond the approach described above the use of mocks is possible as well. The EntityManager is an interface, which can be implemented anonymously for the tests. The use of an embedded database such as Java DB or HSQL (better performance in memory mode) is in most cases absolutely sufficient for DAO testing.

In case you are going to use a real EntityManager and not a mock, it has to be configured differently. The EntityManager cannot use JTA transactions outside of the container and the

JDBC connection has to be configured explicitly in the `persistence.xml` file as shown in the following example (with an embedded Derby Java database):

```
<persistence version="1.0" …">
  <persistence-unit name="test" transaction-type="RESOURCE_LOCAL">
    <provider>oracle.toplink.essentials.PersistenceProvider</provider>
    <class>….business.crud.domain.Book</class>
    <exclude-unlisted-classes>true</exclude-unlisted-classes>
    <properties>
      <property name="toplink.jdbc.user" value="APP"/>
      <property name="toplink.jdbc.password" value="APP"/>
      <property name="toplink.jdbc.url"
value="jdbc:derby:./testDB;create=true"/>
                                                    <property
name="toplink.jdbc.driver" value="org.apache.derby.jdbc.EmbeddedDriver"/>
      <property name="toplink.ddl-generation" value="drop-and-create-tables"/>
    </properties>
  </persistence-unit>
</persistence>
```

This could be easily achieved just adding an additional persistence-unit with e.g. the name "test". The declaration of additional unit has a major drawback—it becomes ambiguous and has to be specified for injection in the `@PersistenceContext` annotation. Such an enhancement could even break production code.

Instead of changing the production `persistence.xml` file, it is better to provide an additional, independent one. It just has to be visible in the classpath of the test runner.

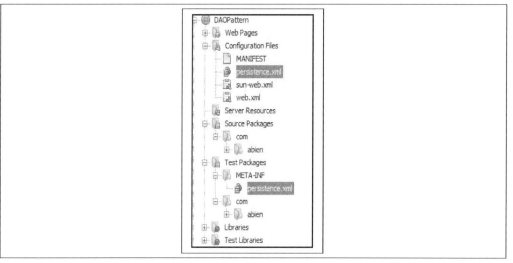

Figure 2. Different persistence.xml files for test and production.

This can be achieved creating a folder META-INF in the test source folder. The `persistence.xml` file will be included in the classpath of the test runner and is available for the persistence provider. The contents of the test folder are not deployed into production. This approach works across popular IDEs and is even easier to achieve with ANT or Maven.

Documentation

A DAO has to provide added value beyond simple CRUD operations and wrapping the `EntityManager`. This added value, has to be documented in one, easily accessible place (just like the DAO implementation details, including the transaction management attached/detached mode or the decision whether to use `@Local`, `@Remote` or no-interface view). Wikis are just perfect for this purpose. Instead of repeating the description over and over again in JavaDoc, the central documentation could be referenced from the DAO implementations. The DRY principle applies to the documentation as well. It is actually enough to mark a class as DAO. Annotations are just perfect for this purpose:

```
@Documented
@Retention(RetentionPolicy.CLASS)
@Target(ElementType.TYPE)
public @interface DAO {
}
```

Such an annotation designates a class as a DAO, which makes searching for all DAOs at build time possible. It is very useful for automatic code reviews and quality assurance. In JavaDoc only the remaining deflections or extensions from the already described principles have to be documented.

The dependencies between DAOs and their clients can be visualized in a standard UML class diagram. The DAO concept can be easily emphasized with a stereotype <<DAO>>—a natural counterpart of an annotation. Such stereotypes should be bundled in an external UML profile. Also, in this case it is not necessary to visualize all DAO methods. Only the delta from the default, such as additional methods, has to be visualized. The DAO principles can be easily expressed with a one class-icon—no need to model the interface.

Consequences

- **Additional complexity:** A DAO introduces at least two additional elements, an interface and its implementation. They have to be developed, documented, and maintained.

- **Not DRY:** The `EntityManager` already encapsulates different JPA implementations very well. It is further comparable with a generic DAO interface A CRUD DAO is just a repetition of already existing functionality. A DAO shouldn't be used just for the implementation of simple CRUD use cases or as a thin wrapper around an `EntityManager`.

- **Leaky abstraction problem:** Especially the attached-result DAO implementation is hard to be replaced with LDAP or flat file access. The introduction of a DAO, motivated by decoupling of a particular data store, is hard to achieve and will probably not pay off.

- **Encapsulation of reusable data access functionality:** The introduction of DAOs is only beneficial in case additional application-specific logic can be encapsulated in a central place. Such an approach minimizes the duplication of code and improves the maintainability. It is hard, however, to find good reuse candidates up front. In practice they are incrementally generalized and extracted in the refactoring phases.

- **Widening the scope:** A classical DAO, which encapsulates access to relational databases, became far less interesting with the introduction of JPA. Raising the level of abstraction and encapsulation of proprietary APIs provides still added value and makes the code more maintainable.

Related Patterns

The DAO pattern is a generic flavor of the Domain Store, Fast-Lane Reader, or Value List Handler patterns. A DAO is used by a Service or Service Façade. A DAO may use Generic JCA to access proprietary legacy resources.

Transfer Object and Data Transfer Object

The original description of a Data Transfer Object (DTO) or Transfer Object (TO) defined in the Core J2EE patterns catalog emphasizes the decoupling from the Entity Beans:

> "Application clients need to exchange data with enterprise beans.

> "Java 2 Platform, Enterprise Edition (J2EE) applications implement server-side business components as session beans and entity beans. Some methods exposed by the business components return data to the client. Often, the client invokes a business object's get methods multiple times until it obtains all the attribute values…

> […]

> "Entity beans, on the other hand, are multiuser, transactional objects representing persistent data. An entity bean exposes the values of attributes by providing an accessor method (also referred to as a getter or get method) for each attribute it wishes to expose.

> "Every method call made to the business service object, be it an entity bean or a session bean, is potentially remote. Thus, in an Enterprise JavaBeans (EJB) application such remote invocations use the network layer regardless of the proximity of the client to the bean, creating a network overhead. Enterprise bean method calls may permeate the network layers of the system even if the client and the EJB container holding the entity bean are both running in the same JVM, OS, or physical machine. Some vendors may implement mechanisms to reduce this overhead by using a more direct access approach and bypassing the network.

> "As the usage of these remote methods increases, application performance can significantly degrade. Therefore, using multiple calls to get methods that return single attribute values is inefficient for obtaining data values from an enterprise bean" [http://java.sun.com/blueprints/corej2eepatterns/Patterns/TransferObject.html].

The context changed dramatically in Java EE 5—it was even inverted. The JPA persistence is only visible and usable locally. The entities do not have any remote capabilities—they are just POJOs. In contrast to CMP 2.0, they are not even active—they can be executed only in the context of a session bean.

The original motivation of hiding remote entities and exposing TOs instead is deprecated.

Problem

The origin problem statement was: "You want to transfer multiple data elements over a tier" (http://java.sun.com/blueprints/corej2eepatterns/Patterns/TransferObject.html).

This particular problem was elegantly solved in Java EE 5 with detachment of persistent entities. There is no need for the introduction of another class just for transferring the entities data. JPA entities can implement a `java.io.Serializable` interface and be transferred between tiers, even remote ones. CMP 2.x entities weren't `Serializable`, the developer was forced to copy their states to a remotely transferable structure—the Transfer Object.

In most J2EE projects this procedure was automated with XDoclet, where a factory method was generated. This method created a TO with the state of the CMP 2.0 entity. XDoclet even converted dependent entities recursively. This process isn't obviously DRY, because the TOs had exactly the same structure as the persistent entities. In that case, no real decoupling between the TOs and the entities occurs. Every change in the entities was propagated immediately to the TOs.

Because of the lack of real encapsulation, an additional layer of indirection was introduced in most J2EE projects—with manually crafted TOs. In theory, the TOs had to decouple from the persistence layer and therefore should have had a different structure. In practice they were very similar, if not identical to the generated TOs. This additional transformation took place in several layers above the actual persistence. The manual conversion between the generated TOs (or even the entity interfaces) and the manually crafted TOs was and is tedious, but provided higher decoupling.

This additional layer of abstraction was rather leaky. The most common scenario is the addition of a UI element in a form—your client just wants to have an additional text field, check box or another component included in an existing form. Such an extension requires changes in the presentation layer and the TO, which is responsible for data transport between the presentation and the business tiers. The manually written conversion has to be customized with the copy logic of the additional attribute. The data of the additional field has to be stored somehow, so the persistence as well as the actual database table have to even be extended.

The vast majority of feature requests require changes in several layers. Even in case each layer would be perfectly encapsulated, the additional information has to be transported and processed through the entire system. It seems like an introduction of a DTO, just for isolation of future changes is not a good strategy. The reverse is true, it even makes the system less maintainable and more complex.

Especially in service-oriented applications, you have several consumers who access one service instance. In this particular case, functional extensions of one particular consumer are not interesting to the others. On the contrary, extensions of the functionality must not break the interface—all methods and especially the parameters have to remain binary compatible.

A service parameter can be either represented by a TO or a detached entity. A detached entity does not provide sufficient encapsulation for database schema changes caused by a feature request of a single client. A modification of that JPA entity would break the binary compatibility of all services which use it as a parameter or return value, and thus also break the compatibility of all clients.

In Java EE, TOs are mostly used to provide consumer-specific views to the persistence layer and to keep the external interfaces stable. Although hard to build and maintain, additional decoupling is one of the major SOA impacts: once deployed, the service contract must not change.

Exposing the domain layer directly to the service consumer would make future extensions impossible. Even minor changes in the persistence layer would break the binary compatibility of the service contract. With TOs and an additional translation layer, local changes to the domain model can be hidden to some degree and don't have to break the service consumer. The translation layer, in general a dedicated EJB, has to be maintained for every consumer separately, which is expensive to develop, manage, and maintain.

The main goal of SOA is agility, which is realized with independent, self-contained services. Each service provides business value to its consumer but it has to evolve without impacting other services. It is rather simple to prevent invocations between services and avoiding direct dependencies—relations between entities make the decoupling a lot harder. The parameters of one service may point to the parameters of the other, which results in direct dependency between services caused by passed data.

In practice, it is hard to find independent persistent entities (PDOs) that are not related to entities from other components or namespaces. JPA entities are objects—direct references between them are the rule. Even in a trivial case, where a `Customer` entity points to an `Address` (1:1 relation), the `CustomerService` would be dependent on the `AddressService` (actually the component of this service). Even worse, such an approach would result in class duplication. Most tools use interface description languages such as WSDL or IDL as input to generate Java stubs. The `Address` entity would be generated twice, probably in different namespaces; in the context of the `CustomerService` and the second time as a parameter of the `AddressService`.

DTOs can easily break those hard dependencies replacing the relation with a proxy. Instead of using a hard reference, the foreign key and entity type can be used to uniquely identify the relation. The relation between the entities could be resolved on demand, loading lazily the dependent entity with a service. In this sample, the `Customer` would be loaded with the `CustomerService`, but the relation to the `Address` would be explicitly and lazily loaded with the `AddressService`. There would be no direct dependency (reference) between the two TOs.

This procedural approach requires more server roundtrips and makes the code more complicated, but decouples entities (and thus services) from each other. Even with the use of code generators the DTOs (and the services) will remain independent. This approach, however, is not a best practice and works only for few entities. Loading many entities over a web service becomes too slow for most use cases. In traditional applications, such an approach is rather esoteric and overblown. In an SOA, it is the only way to decouple independent service contracts by proxying the references between entities.

More frequently, DTOs are introduced for performance improvements of use cases with deeply interconnected entities. It is in general faster to transfer only a subset of the interconnected graph of entities, instead of the entire tree. For that purpose, even 1:1 relations could be condensed into one DTO. The DTO can be directly created by the `EntityManager` as a result of a `NamedQuery`. It's a more common Java EE use case—the DTO acts as a proxy on the client side and represents an expensive-to-construct-and-transport tree of detached entities. The DTO construction can either take place directly in the service, in an `EntityManager`, or be encapsulated in a DAO.

Forces

- You want to keep the external service binary compatible. The changes of one client should not affect the others.
- The transfer of deeply interconnected entities has to be optimized.
- Different views for a single domain model are required.
- Data of proprietary resources and information systems has to be transferred to the client.

- You have to communicate with a legacy, dataset-oriented resource with POJOs.

- You want to transport presentation tier-specific metadata for building UIs on the fly.

- The object-oriented JPA entities have to be transformed into a simplified format for transfer over RESTFul, SOAP, CORBA, or even ASCII.

Solution

The actual implementation of a DTO is trivial and didn't change since the introduction of the `java.io.Serializable` interface in JDK 1.1. It is a plain Java class that implements the `Serializable` interface, in case it has to be transferred between JVMs. The state is transported as attributes, each exposed with getter and setter accessors. The following example shows a non-serializable DTO implementation for local use:

```java
public class BookDTO {

    private int numberOfPages;
    private String name;

    public BookDTO(int numberOfPages, String name) {
        this.numberOfPages = numberOfPages;
        this.name = name;
    }

    public String getName() {
        return name;
    }

    public void setName(String name) {
        this.name = name;
    }

    public int getNumberOfPages() {
        return numberOfPages;
    }

    public void setNumberOfPages(int numberOfPages) {
        this.numberOfPages = numberOfPages;
    }
}
```

In case the DTO is going to be serialized, it could even implement the `java.io.Externalizable` interface. You will have to implement the `writeExternal` and `readExternal` methods respectively as shown in the following optimized `Externalizable` DTO implementation:

```java
public class ExternalizableBookDTO implements Externalizable{

    private int numberOfPages;
    private String name;

    public ExternalizableBookDTO(int numberOfPages, String name) {
```

```
        this.numberOfPages = numberOfPages;
        this.name = name;
    }

    /** Mandatory for Externalizable*/
    public ExternalizableBookDTO() {
    }


    //getters and setters ommitted

    public void writeExternal(ObjectOutput out) throws IOException {
        out.writeUTF(name);
        out.writeInt(numberOfPages);
    }

    public void readExternal(ObjectInput in) throws IOException,
ClassNotFoundException {
        this.name = in.readUTF();
        this.numberOfPages = in.readInt();
    }
}
```

This approach not only increases the control over the compatibility, but has positive impact on performance. The `Externalizable` representation of the object is smaller, the reconstruction happens explicitly, without heavy use of reflection as is the case in default serialization. Even in this simple case, the size of the `Externalizable` object is over 20 percent smaller (96 bytes) than the identical `Serializable` DTO (124 bytes).

The nice thing about `Externalizable` is the fact that it extends Serializable, so the optimization can be introduced afterwards. The `ObjectOutputStream` and `ObjectInputStream` accept both (actually only `Serializable`—`Externalizable` is a `Serializable` DTO), so there is no difference for your serialization infrastructure.

Although the performance gain is considerable, it is not recommended to implement the `readExternal`, `writeExternal` methods manually as a general strategy. Such an implementation is coding intensive and error prone. The serialization is based on class metadata, a perfect case for code generation. An already existing model-driven architecture (MDA) or model-driven software development (MDSD) infrastructure makes such generations more viable. Even having generators available the `Externalizable` should be used with care—its implementation requires a considerable amount of code, which has to be maintained and understood.

Rethinking

A Transfer Object doesn't require major rethinking, except the fact that it became superfluous for the majority of all use cases. JPA entities do a great job transferring data between layers, especially in a single JVM. A TO use to be common as a general best practice in J2EE to hide CMP-specific details, which is no longer necessary.

Decoupling is no longer a sufficient justification for using TOs neither. TOs are structurally very similar, if not identical, to JPA Entities and therefore not DRY. Every change driven by a feature request will not only hit the JPA entities, but in most cases TOs as well.

There are enough cases beyond encapsulation and decoupling, where TOs provide real added value such as realization of additional views to a domain model, abstracting from legacy data stores, enforcement of eager loading in heterogeneous teams or even transport of client-specific metadata.

Conventions

The structure of a TO is obvious. It is a transferable POJO that is created directly from the data store or business logic. TOs are built as JavaBeans; they are comprised of a default constructor and getters and setters for every attribute.

If the intent of introducing TOs was decoupling, TOs should be stored in a dedicated subpackage that belongs to the contract, for example, `[appname].business.customermgmt.boundary` or `[appname].business.customermgmt.boundary.to`. Otherwise it is sufficient to place the TOs near the origin of their creation, for example, in the same package as PDOs, DAOs, and so on. TOs should be easily distinguishable from attached entities (PDOs). A naming convention such as the suffix TO (for example, `CustomerTO`) should fix this issue. A TO annotation would work as well, but it is not visible in the explorer in most IDEs.

Participants and Responsibilities

The main responsibility of the TO is the highest possible decoupling and data transfer optimization. A TO can be consumed and produced by the majority of all patterns and components. In most cases it is created in a DAO as a result of a query. Services, or more often the Service Façade, may return TOs to provide client-specific views to domain objects as well.

Strategies

The default strategy for a TO is just a `Serializable` Java class that conforms to the JavaBean pattern. It comes with a default constructor and every attribute is exposed via a getter and setter pair.

Builder-style TO

A builder-style TO is a usual TO with a fluent way of construction. Because of the lack of named parameters in Java, especially TOs with many attributes become hard to create. Either constructors with a huge number of parameters or many setters have to be invoked for that purpose. The following example shows a Builder pattern with consistency checks and fluent construction:

```
public class BuilderStyleDTO implements Serializable{

    private int numberOfPages;
    private String name;

    private BuilderStyleDTO(int numberOfPages, String name) {
```

```
            this.numberOfPages = numberOfPages;
            this.name = name;
        }

    private BuilderStyleDTO() {}

    public static class Builder{
        private BuilderStyleDTO builderStyleDTO;

        Builder(){
            this.builderStyleDTO = new BuilderStyleDTO();
        }
        public Builder numberOfPages(int pages){
            if(pages < 1)
                throw new IllegalArgumentException("A book should have at least
one page");
            this.builderStyleDTO.setNumberOfPages(pages);
            return this;
        }
        public Builder name(String name){
            if(name == null)
                throw new IllegalArgumentException("A book should have a name");
            return this;
        }

        public BuilderStyleDTO build(){
            return this.builderStyleDTO;
        }
    }
// remaining getters / setters ommitted
```

The Builder pattern makes the construction of a DTO with many attributes more convenient and allows additional validation of the state at creation time.

```
    @Test
    public void construct() throws Exception {
        this.builderStyleDTO = new BuilderStyleDTO.Builder().
                name("Duke Stories").
                numberOfPages(10).
                build();
    }
```

This strategy is hard to use with data binding frameworks, because most of them (JSR-295, Eclipse Binding and JSF) rely on JavaBeans patterns and not the builder style signature.

Builder-style Immutable TO

With a Builder pattern you can prescribe the setting of certain attribute. All the mandatory attributes are declared as final—their existence is checked by the compiler.

```
public class BuilderStyleImmutableDTO implements Serializable{

    private final int numberOfPages;
    private final String name;
```

```java
    private String description;

    private BuilderStyleImmutableDTO(Builder builder) {
        this.numberOfPages = builder.numberOfPages;
        this.name = builder.name;
        this.description = builder.description;
    }


     public static class Builder{
        private final int numberOfPages;
        private final String name;
        private String description;

        public Builder(int numberOfPages, String name) {
            this.numberOfPages = numberOfPages;
            this.name = name;
        }

        public Builder description(String name){
            if(name == null)
                throw new IllegalArgumentException("Description cannot be
null");
            return this;
        }

        public BuilderStyleImmutableDTO build(){
            return new BuilderStyleImmutableDTO(this);
        }
     }

    public String getName() {
        return name;
    }

    public int getNumberOfPages() {
        return numberOfPages;
    }

    public String getDescription() {
        return description;
    }

    public void setDescription(String description) {
        this.description = description;
    }
```

The mandatory parameters come without setters—they have to be passed to the builder constructor explicitly. Only for the optional parameters the fluent builder methods are provided.

```java
    @Test
    public void construct() throws Exception {
```

```
    this.dto = new BuilderStyleImmutableDTO.
        Builder(10,"Duke Tales").
        description("Cool book about Java and Duke").
        build();
    }
```

Client-specific TO

The strategies above were just variations of a TO that is aimed to transport the raw data between tiers. This was also the main goal of the TO from J2EE times. With the advent of Java 5 SE and enums and annotations, not only data but also metadata can be easily transported with the payload. This is especially useful as an additional hint for the parameterization and even dynamic creation of UIs. In addition to the name and type of every attribute, which is accessible via reflection, an arbitrary number of additional information can be attached using annotations. For more convenient access to the metadata, it is better to annotate methods (the getters) instead of fields as shown in the following client-specific annotation:

```
@Retention(RetentionPolicy.RUNTIME)
@Target(ElementType.METHOD)
public @interface Attribute {
    String displayName() default "";
    int maxDisplayLength() default 10;
    boolean required() default false;
    String validationRegexp() default "";
    String validationMessage() default "The attribute is not valid";
}
```

The type-safe metadata can be compiled into methods (or fields). The metadata is highly presentation specific, but the client-specific DTOs were designed with client-specific requirements in mind:

```
public class ClientSpecificBookDTO implements Serializable{

    private int numberOfPages;
    private String name;

@Attribute(displayName="User Name", maxDisplayLength=20,required=true)
    public String getName() {
        return name;
    }
```

The additional metadata falls into two categories: supportive information for UI customization or creation and metadata for syntactic validation of the attributes. In both cases the metadata is conveniently accessible via reflection:

```
    public void accessAnnotations(){
     Method methods[] = ClientSpecificBookDTO.class.getMethods();
     boolean found = false;
     for (int i = 0; i < methods.length; i++) {
 Attribute metaData = methods[i].getAnnotation(Attribute.class);
   if(metaData != null){
    System.out.println("Method name: " + methods[i].getName() + " display name:
" + metaData.displayName());
```

```
                found = true;
            }
        }
```

It is always a good idea to prefer standards over home-grown solutions and frameworks. The Bean Validation Java Specification Request (JSR-303) already defines a set of annotations such as `@NotNull`, `@Min` or `@Max` to express constraints for client-side validation. Borrowing some ideas from a JSR is a good strategy. In best case a JSR becomes a standard, so you could get rid of your custom library or framework—it will become a part of the platform (SE or EE). In worst case, the JSR will die, and you end up having a proprietary, home-grown solution.

Generic DTO

The idea of reflective evaluation of the DTO is not limited to the metadata and can be even applied to the payload. A generic UI does not need statically defined, use case-dependent DTOs. It is enough to provide a reflective access to the DTOs metadata and its contents. A `java.util.Map<String,Attribute>` is a perfect structure for the transportation of dynamic payload. A raw `Map` is, however, not convenient enough. Furthermore, it is hard to enrich the payload with additional metadata and to model relations between DTOs having only a plain `Map`. A lean wrapper around the attribute and relation maps with validation logic is sufficient for this purpose. The following example shows a fluid DTO for all use cases:

```java
public class GenericDTO implements Serializable {

    private static final long serialVersionUID = 1L;
    private Map<String, Attribute> attributes = null;
    private Map<String, Set<GenericDTO>> relations = null;
    private String name = null;

    public GenericDTO(String name) {
        notNull(name, "The name of the DTO cannot be null...");
        this.attributes = new HashMap<String, Attribute>();
        this.relations = new HashMap<String, Set<GenericDTO>>();
        this.name = name;
    }

    public GenericDTO add(String name, Attribute attribute) {
        notNull(name, "Attribute name cannot be null");
        notNull(attribute, "Attribute with name: " + name + " is null!");
        this.attributes.put(name, attribute);
        return this;
    }

    public GenericDTO addString(String name, String value) {
        notNull(name, "Attribute name cannot be null");
        notNull(value, "Attribute with name: " + name + " is null!");
        this.attributes.put(name, new StringType(null,value));
        return this;
    }

//some add... methods ommitted
```

```java
    public GenericDTO remove(String name) {
        notNull(name, "Attribute name cannot be null");
        this.attributes.remove(name);
        return this;
    }

    public GenericDTO addRelation(String relationName, GenericDTO genericDTO) {
        notNull(relationName, "The name of the relation cannot be null !");
        notNull(genericDTO, "The target cannot for the relation with name " +
relationName + " be null");
        addTarget(relationName, genericDTO);
        return this;
    }

    private GenericDTO addTarget(String relationName, GenericDTO target) {
        Set<GenericDTO> targets = this.relations.get(relationName);
        if (targets == null) {
            targets = new HashSet<GenericDTO>();
            this.relations.put(relationName, targets);
        }
        targets.add(target);
        return this;
    }

    public Attribute get(String name) {
        notNull(name, "Attribute name cannot be null");
        return this.attributes.get(name);
    }

    public Set<GenericDTO> getTargets(String name) {
        notNull(name, "The name of the relation cannot be null !");
        return this.relations.get(name);
    }

    public GenericDTO getTarget(String name) {
        notNull(name, "The name of the relation cannot be null !");
        return this.relations.get(name).iterator().next();
    }

    public Iterator<String> getAttributeNames() {
        return this.attributes.keySet().iterator();
    }

    public Iterator<String> getRelationNames() {
        return this.relations.keySet().iterator();
    }

    public Iterator<Attribute> getAttributes() {
        return this.attributes.values().iterator();
    }

    public Iterator<Set<GenericDTO>> getTargets() {
```

```
            return this.relations.values().iterator();
        }

        public GenericDTO validate() throws CompositeValidationException {
            Set<Map.Entry<String, Attribute>> attributeEntries =
this.attributes.entrySet();
            Iterator<Map.Entry<String, Attribute>> attributeIterator =
attributeEntries.iterator();
            CompositeValidationException compositeValidationException = new
CompositeValidationException(this.name);
            Map.Entry<String, Attribute> entry = null;
            while (attributeIterator.hasNext()) {
                try {
                    entry = attributeIterator.next();
                    Attribute attributeEntry = entry.getValue();
                    attributeEntry.validate();
                } catch (ValidationException ex) {
                    compositeValidationException.add(entry.getKey(), ex);
                }
                //some validation errors occured
                if (!compositeValidationException.isEmpty()) {
                    throw compositeValidationException;
                }

            }
            return this;
        }

        public int getNumberOfAttributes() {
            return this.attributes.size();
        }

        public boolean isEmpty() {
            return (this.attributes.isEmpty() && this.relations.isEmpty());
        }
```

The `GenericDTO` is not type-safe but very dynamic. It allows the filtering of attributes and therefore growing and shrinking on demand. With this approach, it's trivial to send only attributes intended for a particular security role over the wire. A statically typed TO cannot provide such flexibility; all its fields have to be send anyway. You will get a problem during the interpretation of the classical TOs contents on the client side. It is impossible to distinguish between fields that are empty or should be not visible to the user without additional metadata.

The metadata does not have to be defined in annotations statically, it can also be provided on the fly. This is especially interesting for applications with content management system (CMS) functionality behind. In that case, the metadata can be even stored in a database and accessed with JPA entities.

The attributes are realized as classes with the ability to construct itself from `String`. The validation logic is implemented in the concrete attribute type. In this example, the regular expressions are used for the validation. The validation is not limited to regular expressions, but they are sufficient for the majority of all cases.

```
public interface Attribute<T> extends Serializable{

    public void validate() throws ValidationException;
    public void instantiateFromString(String content);
    public void setRegexp(String regExp);
    public void setId();
    public T getValue();
    public boolean isId();
}
```

The AbstractType is generic and provides the common infrastructure for concrete attributes. It delegates the construction to the subtypes—it is an implementation of the Template pattern, as shown in the following example:

```
public abstract class AbstractType<T> implements Attribute {
    private T t = null;
    protected String regExp;
    private String contentAsString = null;
    private boolean id = false;
    private Pattern p = null;
    private Matcher m = null;

    public AbstractType(String regExp) {
        this.setRegexp(regExp);
    }

    public void instantiateFromString(String content) {
        this.contentAsString = content;
        t = construct(content);
    }
    protected abstract T construct(String content);

    public void validate() throws ValidationException{
     if(this.regExp != null){
         m = p.matcher(this.contentAsString);
         boolean valid = m.matches();
     if(!valid){
         throw new ValidationException(this.regExp,this.contentAsString);
     }
     }
    }

    public void setRegexp(String regExp) {
        this.regExp = regExp;
        compileRegexp();
    }

    public T getValue() {
        return t;
    }
```

165

```java
    public boolean isId() {
        return this.id;
    }

    public void setId() {
        this.id = true;
    }

    private void compileRegexp() {
        if (this.regExp != null) {
            p = Pattern.compile(this.regExp);
        }
    }
}
```

Because all attributes can represent itself as a `String`, the contents can be already validated in the `AbstractType` class. It uses the compiled regular expression to validate the in a `String` serialized content.

The remaining responsibility of the concrete type is the conversion of a `String` to the payload implementing the abstract `construct` method. The following example show a generic int-attribute:

```java
public class IntType extends AbstractType<Integer>{

    public IntType(String regExp) {
        super(regExp);
    }

    public IntType(String regExp,String contentAsString) {
        super(regExp);
        this.instantiateFromString(contentAsString);
    }

    public IntType(){
        this(null);
    }
    protected Integer construct(String content) {
        return Integer.parseInt(content);
    }
}
```

The sample above implements only one flavor of the basic generic DTO idea. Before you are going to implement your own TO framework it is better to rely on existing semi standards. One popular library is the Apache `BeanUtils` library (http://commons.apache.org/beanutils/). Especially the various realizations of the `org.apache.commons.beanutils.DynaBean` interface provide similar implementations, with a map-like API.

There is also a formalized and even language-neutral realization of the generic DTO available. The JSR-235, Service Data Objects (SDO) is not only standardized by the JCP, but is maintained by the Open SOA initiative (www.osoa.org/display/Main/Service+Data+Objects+Home]). The

SDO specification describes the idea of a disconnected graph of objects with implemented change tracking. The tree of SDO TOs can be sent back and forth between the client and the service. The objects and relations can be modified; the change set will be automatically computed by the framework and can be sent back to the origin service. The SDO API emphasizes its reflective nature; everything is a `DataObject` that consists of `Properties` with their `Types`.

The generic DTO is rather an exception, than a general way of data transportation. It can be efficiently used for the implementation of master data management or generic use cases such as CRUD.

Its major drawback is the explosion of instances needed for transportation. For every attribute at least two instances are needed; one for the key and one for the value. The metadata has to be carried either, so at least one additional instance is required. In best case you will get three times more instances for every attribute, comparing the generic DTO to a statically typed TO. It doesn't have to be a real problem in practice, but you have to be aware of it.

The main advantage of a generic TO is its major drawback at the same time. The lack of typing makes its content very dynamic, but hard to develop and maintain. The IDE support is very limited; autocompletion works only for the generic DTO API and not its contents.

Testing

TOs are dumb data structures with very simple interface. Every attribute of a type-safe TO is exposed with, in most cases by the IDE-generated, getter and setter pair. Getters and setters are empty in the vast majority of all cases.

There is really no need to test dumb accessors. Despite their straightforward structure, TOs are tested in practice too heavily. The main driver is the Quality Department (QA), which prescribes a certain amount of test coverage and the fastest way to achieve good test coverage; is the generation of unit tests for getters and setters.

A generic TO is an exception from the rule. It isn't type-safe and hard to debug. At least its generic functionality has to be tested once.

```
@Test
  public void construction(){
      GenericDTO dto = null;
      String description = "description";
      String name = "name";
      String numberOfPages = "numberOfPages";
      try {
          dto = new GenericDTO("Book").
          addString(description, "Duke's Adventures").
          addString(name, "Java").
          addInt(numberOfPages, 10).
          validate();
      } catch (CompositeValidationException ex) {
          fail("Not excected " + ex);
      }
      int numberOfAttributes = dto.getNumberOfAttributes();
      assertEquals("Should be three",3,numberOfAttributes);
```

```
        assertFalse("GenericDTO isn't empty",dto.isEmpty());

        Object descriptionValue = dto.get(description).getValue();
        assertNotNull(descriptionValue);
        assertEquals("Duke's Adventures",descriptionValue);
    }
```

Furthermore the a generic DTO should be tested together with its generic controllers / models counterparts from the presentation layer. It's almost duck typing—an attribute whose name is *duck* could be a duck—it will eventually turn out after casting.

Documentation

The TO principle is straightforward. It's sufficient to describe the idea with one short example and the strategy in the wiki once and reference it from code using e.g. the @TO annotation. In addition a TO should be recognizable by its name. This can be achieved with a TO suffix, for example, BookTO.

TOs are mostly motivated by the shortcomings of the technology, and not the actual functional requirements. In addition they represent an already existing business entity. Therefore it is not recommended to capture them with an UML tool. Such diagrams would contain redundant information (violate the DRY principle) and therefore would be harder to model, understand and keep in sync with the code.

Consequences

- **Not DRY:** TOs are a replication of already existing information. They have to be kept in sync with the business entity or another representation of the concept.

- **Leaky abstractions:** A DTO was originally intended to decouple the domain objects from its users. This encapsulation or abstraction is leaky. In practice, the DTOs are maintained in parallel to the domain entities. Otherwise the changes in the business logic would not be visible for the presentation components. In most cases, the customer only wants an additional field in the form, which results in the extension of all layers back to the persistence.

- **Per-value semantics:** The original name of a TO was value object. It already implied its per-value semantics in contrast to per-reference. A TO is in fact a copy of a database record or JPA entity. This can become a problem in a transactional system. Every DAO fetches operation results in a new copy of a TO in a single transaction. This is an essential difference to the behavior of managed JPA entities. EntityManager will always return the same reference to an already known object in the same transaction. Heavy use of TOs can lead to inconsistencies and lost updates, even inside a transaction.

- **Synthetic entity:** TOs can represent a concept in DRY manner as well. Especially legacy resources and systems are not accessible via JPA, often only a dataset-oriented API (JCA, JDBC) is available. A TO can provide an object-oriented view to such systems. Then, however, it is either read-only, or every TO change has to be manually synchronized with the back-end resource.

Related Patterns

Related patterns are Data Access Object, Service Façade, and Service. They can consume and produce DTOs in addition to regular entities.

EJB 2 Integration and Migration

There is no dearth of existing J2EE applications. These legacy applications have to be migrated to EJB 3 or at least integrated with new Java EE 5/6 applications. The existing EJB 2 components are accessible from outside using the traditional JNDI lookup, with RMI (JRMP) or IIOP protocol. EJB 3 supports more efficient and intelligent ways to leverage the existing functionality.

Problem

EJB 3 is a great simplification of the EJB 2 specification and reduces redundancies. EJB 3.1 has only a fraction of the artifacts required to implement the same behavior as EJB 2.

Ironically, the EJB versions prior 3.0 were underspecified, the missing parts had to be configured in proprietary deployment descriptors. This information can get lost during the migration. It is always problematic in case of cross-vendor migration, because every vendor offered a different set of proprietary features.

Session beans and message-driven beans are not the actual problem, in worst case the proprietary pooling and caching information gets lost. More challenging, but still viable, is the migration of CMP 2.1 entities to JPA.

Forces

- The legacy EJB 2.x source code is still available.
- It is likely that you will have to extend and maintain the legacy code.
- A significant amount of new features is in the pipeline.
- Unit tests are available, or you have enough time to provide these.
- New functionality is planned to be written with EJB 3.x.

Solution

You have two viable and similar strategies to approach this problem:

- Accessing and injecting existing EJB 2.x components from EJB 3
- Migrating the EJB 2 components to EJB 3

The latter solution is in the long term the most promising one. EJB 3.1 components are lean and concise. A migration from EJB 2 to EJB 3 encourages the removal of many superfluous, infrastructural artifacts and therefore has a positive effect on the maintainability.

The usual EJB 2.x suspects such as `Home`, `LocalHome`, `Remote`, and `RemoteHome` interfaces respectively, as well as the implementation of the `SessionBean` interface and the lifecycle methods became superfluous with the advent of EJB 3.0.

More precisely: these artifacts are optional, so you can still deploy EJB 3.x beans with the EJB 2.x ballast. But you shouldn't go too far and migrate the old `ejb-jar.xml` files and especially the proprietary descriptors to EJB 3. Instead of porting the plumbing, it is easier to designate the existing EJB 2 components with few annotations without heavy refactoring. It is enough to deploy them as fully featured EJB 3. After successful migration and testing, you could remove the plumbing (home and remote interfaces). This, however, requires a little bit more of manual work, because the EJB contract will change and require the compilation of its clients as well.

To migrate an EJB 2.x to EJB 3 you will have to perform the following steps:

- Set up a Continuus Integration (CI) environment such as hudson (http://hudson.dev.java.net). This step is not mandatory but highly recommended.

- Check the existence and quality of unit tests. If they do not exist, create and execute them on the legacy code. Integrate them with CI. Use them to verify the migration.

- Delete all XML deployment descriptors.

- Annotate the EJB 2.x Bean class with the @Stateless annotation and expose its LocalHome or RemoteHome respectively:

```
@Stateless
@LocalHome(LegacyFacadeLocalHome.class)
public class LegacyFacadeBean implements SessionBean
```

- Replace lookups with Dependency Injection. The Remote or Local Home get injected, not the Remote / Local interfaces, as it is the case of EJB 3:

```
public class LegacyFacadeBean implements SessionBean {

    @EJB
    private LegacyServiceLocalHome home;
```

- Create the Remote and Local interfaces with the injected home instances as is common in EJB 2.x. This should happen at the beginning of the EJB 2 lifecycle, in the methods setSessionContext, or ejbCreate. In general, the references between the beans were resolved using the Service Locator pattern or dedicated helper methods. This approach becomes superfluous after the migration inside the container, but it nicely simplifies the process. All Service Locator occurrences or utility method invocations can be safely replaced with Dependency Injection. You can resolve the references between beans in lazily or eager way. You should code in respect to the existing strategy and modify as little code as possible.

```
    private LegacyServiceLocal lookupLegacyServiceBean() {
        try {
            return this.home.create();
        } catch (CreateException ex) {
            throw new EJBException(ex);
        }
    }
    public String getMessage() {
    return "..." + this.lookupLegacyServiceBean().getCurrentTime();
}
```

- Alternatively you could use traditional lookups instead of DI. This approach is especially useful for applications without centralized Service Locator or a consistent lookup strategy. You could reuse your existing lookup mechanism in the EJB 3 container, just by resolving the Bean references with an additional annotation. The name attribute in the @EJB annotation has to correspond with the java:comp/env lookup name. For the

following sample, the lookup name would be
`java:comp/env/ejb/LegacyServiceLocal`:

```
@EJB(name = "ejb/LegacyServiceLocal", beanInterface =
LegacyServiceLocalHome.class)
public class LegacyFacadeBean implements SessionBean {
```

- It is very likely, that the code will compile, deploy, and even work. You should, however, re-execute the load and stress tests. The migration can only be considered as successful in case these tests pass.

- After successful execution of integration and load tests, you could consider to incrementally remove the superfluous Home and Remote interfaces and refactor the components into true EJB 3. This step is optional, but highly recommended. It increases the risk of migration, because you will have to remove lots of code and introduce the business interface or the no-interface view.

Only the bean implementation was touched. The Local and Remote Home as well as Local and Remote interfaces remain unchanged. This is essential because this will not break the existing clients.

The CMP 2.x persistence is harder to migrate, but a systematic migration is still possible. To migrate CMP 2.x persistence follow these steps:

- Search for common patterns. Sometimes CMP 2.x entities implemented a business interface. It was an interface that exposed the accessors as well as the relations in a clean way. Realize this interface with a JPA entity and you are done.

- XDoclet [http://xdoclet.sourceforge.net] generated home, local interface, deployment descriptors as well as TOs. TOs are actually interesting, because they were used as actual parameters and return value of the CMP 2.x consumers (session beans). This TO is a concrete class with accessors, as well as methods for relation management and can be directly migrated to a JPA entity. Remove all superfluous bookkeeping metadata (internal collections, methods and so on) and use the TO as JPA entity candidate.

- For the migration to JPA, the necessary metadata has to be provided as annotations or `orm.xml` configuration. The existing `ejb-jar.xml` and vendor-specific deployment descriptors provide valuable OR information. XDoclet genereted additional bookkeeping collections for removed / changed object inside the TOs, whichshould be marked as `@Transient` in the first iteration and can be safely removed after successful tests and refactoring.

- If there is neither a business interface nor XDoclet, you can port the CMP 2.x entities directly to JPA. The signature of the Local interface can be used as a hint or template for the implementation of JPA entities. The Local Home interface itself is a DAO candidate —it basically manages the CMP 2.x entity.

The migration of the persistence layer is the most challenging, but at the same time, the most rewarding task. After the migration process, the deployment descriptor, the Home and Local interfaces, the Bean class, and the generated DTO will collapse into a single JPA entity.

So far, I've described the migration of EJB 2 into EJB 3 components. But you could even deploy the EJB 2 session beans into the EJB 3 container. This only works, if you are upgrading the application server and not changing the vendor. Only then can the proprietary deployment descriptors be fully leveraged with no additional effort. Even in this case, you should always prefer migration over integration. In the long term, you will have to migrate. The migration process cleans the code and removes a lot of plumbing and repetition.

Strategies

In the case of EJB2 integration and migration, you have two strategies.

Single-vendor Migration

If you do not change the application server, the migration is likely to be painless. You could even deploy the existing components first, integrate them with the EJB 3 logic, write the tests, and refactor incrementally.

Cross-vendor Migration

EJB 2.x were underspecified, so that the really interesting information is contained in proprietary deployment descriptors. These descriptors are not portable. It is even unlikely, that the specific, proprietary features can be ported between the vendors at all. You should start with the mapping of functionality and check whether a successful EJB 2 port is actually possible.

On the other hand, the migration from 2.x to 3.x specification works well even in the cross-vendor scenario.

Consequences

- **Maintainability:** The migration from EJB 2 to 3 makes it easier to maintain your code. A radical migration will remove the plumbing completely.

- **Testability:** EJB 3 components are easy to test, even outside the container. This is not true for the EJB 2 components.

- **Deployment:** The EJB 3 build process is simpler and faster because the additional generation steps (for example, XDoclet tasks) are no more required. This shortens the build and increases significantly productivity.

- **Portability:** EJB 3 components are portable. You need neither proprietary nor standard deployment descriptors.

- **Integration capabilities:** Legacy EJB 2 components as well as migrated EJB 2 components can be easily accessed from EJB 3.

Testing

The success of the entire migration or porting process can only be measured with excessive testing. If there are no tests—the result is unpredictable. Especially important are the integration and load tests. Unit tests are self-evident, but they only test the expected behavior, which should not change during the migration or porting. Integration tests, however, might help you to uncover potential changes caused by the paradigm shift in the persistence layer. J2EE persistence works mostly with TOs, which are always a copy of the actual data, whereby the JPA persistence uses the per-reference semantics. In Java EE 5/6 you are accessing the attached JPA entities directly, so every change will be pushed back to the database at the end of the transaction.

Legacy POJO Integration

Not everything is a session bean, actually only a minority of all deployed components today are EJBs. There is an obvious need to integrate existing POJOs with your Java EE application and access them in a convenient and frictionless way.

Problem

Dependency injection only works in managed classes such as Servlets, Servlet filters, event listeners, tag handlers, tag library event listeners, scoped managed beans (JSF), service endpoints (JAX-WS), handlers (JAX-WS), root resource classes (JAX-RS), providers (JAX-RS), and, of course, in beans and interceptors itself. These managed classes are able either to look up or to inject resources or EJBs from the JNDI tree.

A legacy class is neither managed nor a resource stored in the JNDI tree. Of course, you can instantiate such a class with `new` and use it in the context of an EJB 3, but then the container services such as Dependency Injection, lifecycle, and concurrency management wouldn't be accessible.

Forces

- The integration should work without legacy code modification—it is not always available.
- The legacy class should be able to leverage the container services and participate in transactions.
- The legacy POJO has to be compliant with the EJB 3 programming restrictions.
- The legacy POJO has to be either thread-safe or be capable to be deployed as a singleton.

Solution

The solution is straightforward—the legacy POJO has to be deployed as an EJB 3. Then it could easily participate in transactions and be managed by the container. Furthermore, the POJO could be conveniently injected to an already existing session bean. The requirements for an EJB 3.0 session bean are really low: A class has to implement an interface and provide a default constructor. In the EJB 3.1 spec, the requirements are even lower: you have to provide the default constructor—no interface is required.

The only problem is the `@Stateless` annotation with which a session bean has to be designated. You will have to annotate your POJO, and this is only possible having source code and being able to recompile it. Decompilation and recompilation could work, but this is not always a viable option (just think about licensing and legal issues).

Fortunately, you can also provide the required metadata in `ejb-jar.xml`. Instead of annotating a class with `@Stateless`, you can declare it as a Bean in the deployment descriptor. Contrary to the EJB 2.X specification, it is not an all or nothing principle. You can even mix and match both approaches and use `ejb-jar.xml` just to integrate the legacy POJOs. For native EJB 3, you can still rely on pure annotations.

It is even possible to turn classes shipped with JDK into EJB 3. You only have to declare them as EJB 3 in the `ejb-jar.xml`. It is straightforward to deploy the `DefaultTableModel` as an EJB 3 and inject it into a regular session bean.

```
<ejb-jar>
    <enterprise-beans>
    <session>
       <ejb-name>Table</ejb-name>
    <business-local>javax.swing.table.TableModel</business-local>
       <ejb-class>javax.swing.table.DefaultTableModel</ejb-class>
         <session-type>Stateless</session-type>
    </session>
    </enterprise-beans>
</ejb-jar>
```

The `ejb-jar.xml` is straightforward. You only have to specify the class, the business-local interface and the session bean type (`Stateless` or `Stateful`).

```
@Stateless
public class LegacyTestBean implements LegacyTest {
    @EJB
    TableModel tableModel;

    public String accessTable(){
        return "Row count: " + tableModel.getRowCount();
    }
}
```

For the client of the legacy POJO there is no difference between a regular EJB 3 and an integrated POJO. The reference is injected in both cases. Even the convention over configuration mechanisms works as usual—if there is only one implementation of the interface, you do not even have to specify it.

The no-interface view introduced in EJB 3.1 even lets you integrate classes without interfaces. The only requirement here is the existence of an accessible default constructor.

Rethinking

In J2EE, it was not possible to deploy POJOs as EJB 2 without changing the code. Existing POJO infrastructure was treated as something incompatible and had to be wrapped with EJB 2.

EJB 3 objects are nothing but annotated POJOs, so that the option to deploy existing POJOs as EJB 3 components became not only available, but also viable. Back in the EJB 2 days, there was a common concern about the overhead associated with the container's runtime. It was the advent of many lightweight and POJO frameworks and architectures. The overhead introduced by the EJB 3 container is really low—it is actually only a lean (often dynamic, proxy-based) indirection layer between the caller and the bean. The overhead is absolutely comparable with other Dependency Injection frameworks. On Glassfish v2, the overhead of an EJB 3 comparing it to the same POJO is about 3 percent and can actually be measured (only a few milliseconds).

The synergy between Dependency Injection and convention over configuration makes a lot of infrastructural code superfluous. There is actually nothing more left to optimize or remove. Applications built with EJB 3 are leaner (in respect to code, amount of XML, and libraries) than the alternative frameworks or even pure POJOs.

In Java EE 5, you should justify why you are not deploying EJBs and are still relying on POJOs instead. It is nothing else than an inversion of argumentation.

Participants and Responsibilities

The legacy POJO implements functionality which is interesting for existing Java EE applications. The for deployment as a session bean necessary meta data is provided as an `ejb-jar.xml` descriptor. The regular EJBs can then get access to the legacy POJO via Dependency Injection. This procedure is totally transparent for the rest of the application. The POJO became an EJB without code modification.

Testing

The compiler does not check XML and particularly not the correctness of the declared types. The legacy POJO integration should be tested with integration tests to verify the injection and so on. Legacy code is always suspicious regarding thread safety and consistency, so that load and stress testing is recommended in this case. Unit tests are irrelevant in this context and only useful for the verification of the existing functionality of the legacy POJO.

Documentation

The Dependency Injection of a legacy POJO into a session bean should be documented with a short hint in JavaDoc. You should mention this strategy in tutorials and pragmatic architectural documents as well.

Consequences

- **Portability:** You do not change the legacy code—only additional meta data is provided. The legacy POJOs can be used in another context without any friction.

- **Performance:** The EJB 3 overhead is very low; on Glassfish v2 it's about 3 percent compared to a plain Java class. This comparison, however, is academic—in an enterprise context, you will have to start transactions and manage POJOs as well. In that case, you will achieve similar performance.

- **Scalability:** You often hear that EJB components scale better than POJOs because of pooling and clustering. Meanwhile the performance of JVM and garbage collection was significantly improved, so that instance pooling can even have negative impact on scalability. In general, EJBs can be considered as neutral regarding scalability. Clustering is only available through remote business interfaces and legacy POJOs are always accessed locally.

Related Patterns

EJB 2 integration is similar, however it works inversely—it replaces `ejb-jar.xml` with annotations, whereby in the legacy POJO integration, regular Java classes were introduced as session beans with `ejb-jar.xml`.

Generic JCA

The application server manages the concurrency, component lifecycle, and resource access for you. You are even not allowed to access incompatible resources or manage threads in your EJBs.

Problem

It is not possible to access legacy resources such as files, native libraries, or starting new threads from EJBs without violating the programming restrictions[1]. Even if the application with violated specification is deployable and all tests pass, the portability is still not given. The application server can become more restrictive with every new installed version, or even patch. Furthermore, commercial support often refuses to help in case your application does not conform to the specification.

If you want to access an incompatible resource within a transaction, it will be really hard to implement it from EJBs. You will have to switch to bean-managed transactions, or implement the `javax.ejb.SessionSynchronization` interface in a stateful session bean to track of the current transaction status. Access to incompatible resources, however, is still unsolved.

Forces

- You have to interact with Java EE incompatible resources.
- You need transactional access to legacy resources.
- The legacy resources cannot scale infinitely for technical and licensing reasons; you have to throttle the throughput.
- The legacy resource has to be accessible from EJBs.
- The solution should be portable across servers.
- It is required (for example, by operations) to manage and monitor the connector runtime from the administration console.

Solution

The programming restrictions apply to the EJB container only, so you could integrate the resource in a Servlet, MBean, or a JCA connector. Neither Servlets nor MBeans can control a transaction declaratively. A JCA adapter, on the other hand, can access every EJB-incompatible resource you want as well as actively participate in transactions and within a security context. Its lifecycle and connections are managed by the application server.

A JCA connector is the best possible solution—it is portable, standardized, easily accessible, and managed by the application server. The only caveat is its nature.

A JCA connector is a set of API and SPI interfaces, which have to be implemented first. This can be complex, especially if you are trying to implement all features and capabilities. On the other hand, a minimal JCA-implementation is surprisingly simple. It comprises two interfaces, four classes, and one XML file. Two classes are highly reusable; the remaining part is resource dependent.

---

[1] Chapter 21.1.2, JSR 220: Enterprise JavaBeansTM, Version 3.0, EJB Core Contracts and Requirements

You don't even have to implement the Common Client Interface (CCI). This API looks very much like JDBC, but is too abstract for the project-specific, pragmatic integrations. Instead of implementing the whole CCI API, you could provide a custom interface as well. A JCA adapter is connection-oriented, so you will have to map the idea of a connection to your resource. It can be a socket connection, a handle to a native resource, or a reference to an open file (file descriptor). EJBs are not allowed to access files, so transactional file access is perfectly suitable for a JCA implementation.

```
public interface Connection {
    public void write(String content);
    public void close();
}
```

A reference to a file maps well to the idea of connecting to a resource. The interface Connection represents a pointer to an open file. This interface does not even have to inherit from JCA-specific artifacts.

The next step is the declaration of the interface for the Connection factory. The DataSource interface is simple as well, but it has to inherit from the javax.resource.Referenceable and java.io.Serializable interfaces:

```
public interface DataSource extends Serializable, Referenceable {
    Connection getConnection();
}
```

This allows the registration of the DataSource in a JNDI context, which is required for the injection into EJBs. You are not constrained by the naming or signature of this interface. The names Connection and DataSource are absolutely arbitrary.

The whole integration logic for the file access is realized in the FileConnection implementation of the Connection interface. For the integration of more inconvenient resources you could use the Connection only as a façade and not the actual implementation of the integration logic. The following example demonstrates the implementation of the transactional file access:

```
package ...integration.genericjca;
//...other imports
import javax.resource.ResourceException;
import javax.resource.spi.ConnectionRequestInfo;
import javax.resource.spi.LocalTransaction;

public class FileConnection implements Connection, LocalTransaction{

    private String buffer;
    private FileOutputStream fileOutputStream;
    private ConnectionRequestInfo connectionRequestInfo;
    public final static String FILE_NAME = "/temp/jcafile.txt";
    private GenericManagedConnection genericManagedConnection;
    private PrintWriter out;

    public FileConnection(PrintWriter out,GenericManagedConnection
genericManagedConnection,ConnectionRequestInfo connectionRequestInfo) {
```

```java
            this.out = out;
            out.println("#FileConnection " + connectionRequestInfo + " "
+toString());
            this.genericManagedConnection = genericManagedConnection;
            this.connectionRequestInfo = connectionRequestInfo;
            this.initialize();
    }

  private void initialize(){
   try {
    this.buffer = null;
    this.fileOutputStream = new FileOutputStream(FILE_NAME,true);
   } catch (FileNotFoundException ex) {
       throw new IllegalStateException("Cannot initialize ..: " + FILE_NAME);
       }

    }

    public void write(String content) {
        out.println("#FileConnection.write " + content);
        this.buffer = content;
    }

    public void close() {
            this.genericManagedConnection.close();
    }

    public void destroy(){
        out.println("#FileConnection.cleanup");
        try {
            if(this.fileOutputStream != null)
                this.fileOutputStream.close();
          this.fileOutputStream = null;
          this.buffer = null;
         } catch (IOException ex) {
        throw new IllegalStateException("Cannot close stream: " +ex,ex);
         }
    }

    public void begin() throws ResourceException {
        out.println("#FileConnection.begin " +toString());
        this.initialize();
    }

    public void commit() throws ResourceException {
        out.println("#FileConnection.commit "  +toString());
        try {
         this.fileOutputStream.write(this.buffer.getBytes());
         this.fileOutputStream.flush();
         this.fileOutputStream.close();
        } catch (IOException ex) {
            throw new ResourceException(ex);
        }
```

```
    }

    public void rollback() throws ResourceException {
        out.println("#FileConnection.rollback  " +toString());
        this.buffer = null;
        try {
            this.fileOutputStream.close();
        } catch (IOException ex) {
            throw new ResourceException(ex);
        }

    }
}
```

The implementation of the actual business logic, the method `write`, is surprisingly simple—it stores the parameter in a field. The `FileConnection` is aimed to be transactional, so it implements the `begin`, `commit`, and `rollback` methods, which are declared in the `LocalTransaction` interface.

The constructor and the `begin` method initializes the stream and opens the file, the method `commit` writes the content of the internal buffer field (the actual buffer) to the file. The stream is closed and the buffer cleared in the method `rollback`.

The method `close` delegates the invocation to the `GenericManagedConnection`, which will be covered later. The `ConnectionRequestInfo` is only used in the `equals` and `hashCode` methods. It is a handle which is used by the application and the JCA-connector to identify the connection.

The implementation of the `DataSource` interface, `FileDataSource`, is even simpler:

```
package com.abien.patterns.integration.genericjca;

import java.io.PrintWriter;
import javax.naming.Reference;
import javax.resource.ResourceException;
import javax.resource.spi.ConnectionManager;
import javax.resource.spi.ConnectionRequestInfo;
import javax.resource.spi.ManagedConnectionFactory;

public class FileDataSource
        implements DataSource {

    private ManagedConnectionFactory mcf;
    private Reference reference;
    private ConnectionManager cm;
    private PrintWriter out;

    public FileDataSource(PrintWriter out,ManagedConnectionFactory mcf,
ConnectionManager cm) {
        out.println("#FileDataSource");
        this.mcf = mcf;
        this.cm = cm;
```

```java
            this.out = out;
    }

    public FileConnection getConnection(){
        out.println("#FileDataSource.getConnection " + this.cm + " MCF: " +
this.mcf);
        try {
            return (FileConnection) cm.allocateConnection(mcf,
getConnectionRequestInfo());
        } catch (ResourceException ex) {
            throw new RuntimeException(ex.getMessage());
        }
    }

    public void setReference(Reference reference) {
        this.reference = reference;
    }

    public Reference getReference() {
        return reference;
    }

    private ConnectionRequestInfo getConnectionRequestInfo() {
        return new ConnectionRequestInfo() {

            @Override
            public boolean equals(Object obj) {
                return true;
            }

            @Override
            public int hashCode() {
                return 1;
            }

        };
    }
}
```

The accessors to the `javax.naming.Reference` field are needed for the JNDI registration. The method `getConnection` just delegates the request for the connection to the `ConnectionManager`, which is implemented by the application server.

The anonymous implementation of the `ConnectionRequestInfo` interface overrides the `equals` and `hashCode` methods. All connections to the file are equal, you don't need any differentiation between them. In general, you could consider using user names or connector-specific tokens to differentiate between connections.

The remaining two classes are integration logic agnostic. You could reuse them for any connector implementation you want.

The GenericManagedConnection implements the ManagedConnection interface which belongs to the SPI and is used by the application server behind the scenes. The main responsibility of the GenericManagedConnection is the creation of the FileConnection and firing events with the notification about the connection status (started, committed, rolled back and closed).

```
package com.abien.patterns.integration.genericjca;

//java.util.* etc. imports omitted
import javax.resource.ResourceException;
import javax.resource.spi.LocalTransaction;
import static javax.resource.spi.ConnectionEvent.*;
import javax.resource.spi.ConnectionEvent;
import javax.resource.spi.ConnectionEventListener;
import javax.resource.spi.ConnectionRequestInfo;
import javax.resource.spi.ManagedConnection;
import javax.resource.spi.ManagedConnectionFactory;
import javax.resource.spi.ManagedConnectionMetaData;
import javax.security.auth.Subject;
import javax.transaction.xa.XAResource;

public class GenericManagedConnection
        implements ManagedConnection, LocalTransaction {

    private ManagedConnectionFactory mcf;
    private PrintWriter out;
    private FileConnection fileConnection;
    private ConnectionRequestInfo connectionRequestInfo;
    private List<ConnectionEventListener> listeners;

GenericManagedConnection(PrintWriter out,ManagedConnectionFactory mcf,
ConnectionRequestInfo connectionRequestInfo) {
        this.out = out;
        out.println("#GenericManagedConnection");
        this.mcf = mcf;
        this.connectionRequestInfo = connectionRequestInfo;
      this.listeners = new LinkedList<ConnectionEventListener>();
    }

 public Object getConnection(Subject subject, ConnectionRequestInfo
connectionRequestInfo)
          throws ResourceException {
        out.println("#GenericManagedConnection.getConnection");
        fileConnection = new FileConnection(out,this, connectionRequestInfo);
        return fileConnection;
    }

    public void destroy() {
        out.println("#GenericManagedConnection.destroy");
        this.fileConnection.destroy();
    }
```

```java
    public void cleanup() {
        out.println("#GenericManagedConnection.cleanup");
    }

    public void associateConnection(Object connection) {
        out.println("#GenericManagedConnection.associateConnection " +
connection);
        this.fileConnection = (FileConnection) connection;

    }

    public void addConnectionEventListener(ConnectionEventListener listener) {
        out.println("#GenericManagedConnection.addConnectionEventListener");
        this.listeners.add(listener);
    }

    public void removeConnectionEventListener(ConnectionEventListener listener)
{
        out.println("#GenericManagedConnection.removeConnectionEventListener");
        this.listeners.remove(listener);
    }

    public XAResource getXAResource()
            throws ResourceException {
        out.println("#GenericManagedConnection.getXAResource");
        return null;
    }

    public LocalTransaction getLocalTransaction() {
        out.println("#GenericManagedConnection.getLocalTransaction");
        return this;
    }

    public ManagedConnectionMetaData getMetaData()
            throws ResourceException {
        out.println("#GenericManagedConnection.getMetaData");
        return new ManagedConnectionMetaData() {

            public String getEISProductName()
                    throws ResourceException {
                out.println("#MyConnectionMetaData.getEISProductName");
                return "Generic JCA";
            }

            public String getEISProductVersion()
                    throws ResourceException {
                out.println("#MyConnectionMetaData.getEISProductVersion");
                return "1.0";
            }

            public int getMaxConnections()
                    throws ResourceException {
                out.println("#MyConnectionMetaData.getMaxConnections");
```

```java
                return 5;
            }

            public String getUserName()
                    throws ResourceException {
                return null;
            }
        };
    }

    public void setLogWriter(PrintWriter out)
            throws ResourceException {
        System.out.println("#GenericManagedConnection.setLogWriter");
        out = out;
    }

    public PrintWriter getLogWriter()
            throws ResourceException {
        System.out.println("#GenericManagedConnection.getLogWriter");
        return out;
    }

    @Override
    public boolean equals(Object obj) {
     //omitted
        return true;
    }

    @Override
    public int hashCode() {
    //omitted
        return hash;
    }

    public ConnectionRequestInfo getConnectionRequestInfo() {
        return connectionRequestInfo;
    }

    public void begin() throws ResourceException {
        this.fileConnection.begin();
        this.fireConnectionEvent(LOCAL_TRANSACTION_STARTED);
    }

    public void commit() throws ResourceException {
        this.fileConnection.commit();
        this.fireConnectionEvent(LOCAL_TRANSACTION_COMMITTED);
    }

    public void rollback() throws ResourceException {
        this.fileConnection.rollback();
        this.fireConnectionEvent(LOCAL_TRANSACTION_ROLLEDBACK);
    }
```

```java
    public void fireConnectionEvent(int event) {
        ConnectionEvent connnectionEvent = new ConnectionEvent(this, event);
        connnectionEvent.setConnectionHandle(this.fileConnection);
        for (ConnectionEventListener listener : this.listeners) {
            switch (event) {
                case LOCAL_TRANSACTION_STARTED:
                    listener.localTransactionStarted(connnectionEvent);
                    break;
                case LOCAL_TRANSACTION_COMMITTED:
                    listener.localTransactionCommitted(connnectionEvent);
                    break;
                case LOCAL_TRANSACTION_ROLLEDBACK:
                    listener.localTransactionRolledback(connnectionEvent);
                    break;
                case CONNECTION_CLOSED:
                    listener.connectionClosed(connnectionEvent);
                    break;
                default:
                    throw new IllegalArgumentException("Unknown event: " +
event);
            }
        }
    }

    public void close() {
        this.fireConnectionEvent(CONNECTION_CLOSED);
    }
}
```

The event notification is important. The application server is listening for these events and uses the information to free connections from the pool. Without these event notifications, your pool will go empty and block. The remaining methods are straightforward, but necessary plumbing.

The `GenericManagedConnectionFacatory` implements, in turn, the `ManagedConnectionFacatory` interface and is responsible for the creation of the `FileDataSource` and the `GenericManagedConnection` instances.

```java
package com.abien.patterns.integration.genericjca;
//java.io.* etc. imports omitted
import javax.resource.ResourceException;
import javax.resource.spi.*;
import javax.security.auth.Subject;

public class GenericManagedConnectionFactory
        implements ManagedConnectionFactory, Serializable {

    private PrintWriter out;

    public GenericManagedConnectionFactory() {
        out = new PrintWriter(System.out);
    }
```

```java
    public Object createConnectionFactory(ConnectionManager cxManager) throws
ResourceException {
        return new FileDataSource(out,this, cxManager);
    }

    public Object createConnectionFactory() throws ResourceException {
        return new FileDataSource(out,this, null);
    }

    public ManagedConnection createManagedConnection(Subject subject,
ConnectionRequestInfo info) {
        return new GenericManagedConnection(out,this, info);
    }

    public ManagedConnection matchManagedConnections(Set connectionSet, Subject
subject, ConnectionRequestInfo info)
            throws ResourceException {
    for (Iterator it = connectionSet.iterator(); it.hasNext();) {
      GenericManagedConnection gmc = (GenericManagedConnection) it.next();
  ConnectionRequestInfo connectionRequestInfo = gmc.getConnectionRequestInfo();
      if((info == null) || connectionRequestInfo.equals(info))
                return gmc;
        }
        throw new ResourceException("Cannot find connection for info!");
    }

    public void setLogWriter(PrintWriter out) throws ResourceException {
        this.out = out;
    }

    public PrintWriter getLogWriter() throws ResourceException {
        return this.out;
    }

}
```

The method `matchManagedConnection` is intended to find a particular connection from a set of available connections using the already described `ConnectionRequestInfo` object. The remaining bookkeeping methods are self-explanatory.

Finally, you will have to write the `ra.xml` deployment descriptor, which contains all the interfaces and implementations.

```xml
<connector xmlns="http://java.sun.com/xml/ns/j2ee"
           xmlns:xsi="http://www.w3.org/2001/XMLSchema-instance"
           xsi:schemaLocation="http://java.sun.com/xml/ns/j2ee
           http://java.sun.com/xml/ns/j2ee/connector_1_5.xsd"
           version="1.5">
    <display-name>Generic JCA</display-name>
    <vendor-name>adam-bien.com</vendor-name>
    <eis-type>Generic JCA</eis-type>
    <resourceadapter-version>1.0</resourceadapter-version>
    <resourceadapter>
```

```xml
        <outbound-resourceadapter>
            <connection-definition>
                <managedconnectionfactory-
class>.genericjca.GenericManagedConnectionFactory</managedconnectionfactory-
class>
<connectionfactory-interface>.genericjca.DataSource</connectionfactory-
interface>
    <connectionfactory-impl-
class>.genericjca.FileDataSource</connectionfactory-impl-class>
                <connection-interface>.genericjca.Connection</connection-
interface>
                <connection-impl-class>.genericjca.FileConnection</connection-
impl-class>
            </connection-definition>
            <transaction-support>LocalTransaction</transaction-support>
            <authentication-mechanism>
    <authentication-mechanism-type>BasicPassword</authentication-mechanism-type>
   <credential-
interface>javax.resource.spi.security.PasswordCredential</credential-interface>
            </authentication-mechanism>
            <reauthentication-support>false</reauthentication-support>
        </outbound-resourceadapter>
    </resourceadapter>
</connector>
```

You start the transactions on the application server and propagate them into the external resource, so it has to be declared as an `outbound-resourceadapter`. The descriptor contains the classes described in this example in the corresponding XML tags. Writing the `ra.xml` deployment descriptor isn't very hard—you can use any XML editor with XSD validation for this purpose. The compiled classes and the `ra.xml` descriptor have to be archived into a .rar file. The connector is deployed just as any other EAR—mainly dropping the archive into an autodeploy directory. The last step is application server specific. You will have to set up the connection pool and deploy the data source under a JNDI name of your choice. The connector should be available in the JNDI tree and ready for use.

The `DataSource` interface can be easily injected into a bean of your choice using the `@Resource` annotation. The value of the attribute `name` or `mappedName` has to correspond to the configured JNDI name. The following example demonstrates how to use of the JCA connector in a session bean:

```java
import com.abien.patterns.integration.genericjca.Connection;
import com.abien.patterns.integration.genericjca.DataSource;
import javax.annotation.Resource;
import javax.ejb.SessionContext;
import javax.ejb.Stateless;

@Stateless
public class JCAClientBean implements JCAClientRemote {

    @Resource(name="jca/FileFactory")
    private DataSource dataSource;
```

```
@Resource
private SessionContext context;

public void accessFile(String content){
        Connection connection = dataSource.getConnection();
        connection.write(content);
        connection.close();
}

public void accessFileAndRollback(String content){
        Connection connection = dataSource.getConnection();
        connection.write(content);
        context.setRollbackOnly();
}

public void accessFileAndThrowException(String content){
        Connection connection = dataSource.getConnection();
        connection.write(content);
        throw new RuntimeException("Force Rollback");
}
}
}
```

To compile the EJB you will only need the `Connection` and `DataSource` interfaces. The generic JCA participates in declarative transactions started by the EJB—it is completely transparent to the developer. The method `accessFile` starts a new transaction, which is propagated to the JCA connector. The `FileConnection` is notified by the container at the commit time and flushes the contents of its buffer to the file.

```
#FileDataSource.getConnection
#GenericManagedConnectionFactory.createManagedConnection
#GenericManagedConnection
#GenericManagedConnection.addConnectionEventListener
#GenericManagedConnectionFactory.matchManagedConnections
#GenericManagedConnection.getConnection
#FileConnection
#GenericManagedConnection.getLocalTransaction
#FileConnection.begin
#FileConnection.write a
#GenericManagedConnection.cleanup
#GenericManagedConnection.getLocalTransaction
#FileConnection.commit
```

The method `accessFileAndRollback` asks for rolling back the current transaction with the invocation of `SessionContext#setRollbackOnly`. The connector is notified as well. the following snippet shows the tracing output:

```
#FileDataSource.getConnection
#GenericManagedConnectionFactory.matchManagedConnections
#GenericManagedConnection.getConnection
#FileConnection
#GenericManagedConnection.getLocalTransaction
#FileConnection.begin
#FileConnection.write a
```

```
#GenericManagedConnection.getLocalTransaction
#FileConnection.rollback
```

Finally the method `accessFileAndThrowException` forces the container to roll back the transaction by throwing a `RuntimeException`.

```
#FileDataSource.getConnection
#GenericManagedConnectionFactory.matchManagedConnections
#GenericManagedConnection.getConnection
#FileConnection
#GenericManagedConnection.getLocalTransaction
#FileConnection.begin
#FileConnection.write a
#GenericManagedConnection.cleanup
#GenericManagedConnection.getLocalTransaction
#FileConnection.rollback
javax.ejb.EJBException
        at
com.sun.ejb.containers.BaseContainer.processSystemException(BaseContainer.java:3
869)
```

The JCA connector works as expected and rolls the transaction back for you.

This custom connector could be easily extended to support XA transactions and more complete file handling. The Apache Commons File Transactions project (http://commons.apache.org/transaction/file/index.html) provides a working implementation for XA-compliant file access. It could be easily wrapped with the generic JCA connector as well.

Rethinking

The JCA connector example I've described here is nothing new. Version 1.0 has been available since 2001 and was one of the first JSRs (JSR 16). Version 1.5 has been available since 2003 and is specified in the JSR 112. The problem is not the actual complexity, rather than the common perception of it.

A custom JCA adapter implementation can be the easiest and the most pragmatic choice. It becomes complex if you are going to implement the entire spec which is neither needed nor required. On the other hand, home-grown workarounds that bypass the container are more complex (and likely to be erroneous) than a straightforward JCA implementation.

Conventions

A JCA adapter implementation is a standard application server extension, not application code. Your applications will use the connector without having the source code and knowing the implementation details. Nonetheless, it is reasonable to follow some conventions:

- The connector implementation belongs to the integration layer, so it should be placed into the `integration` package.

- If you are going to provide a custom connector interface, you should separate the internal implementation from the public API. The public API is needed for the compilation of the client applications, so it will have to be distributed as a standalone library. The connector implementation resides in a separate package, for example, `spi`. It is better to move the JCA implementation into a dedicated package, than to pollute the public API with an additional, meaningless subpackage such as `api` or `contract`.

- Regardless of how complex the internal implementation of the connector really is, the public API should be designed as convenient and simple as possible. The interesting business logic should be accessible in less than three lines of code after the injection.

Participants and Responsibilities

There are three major participants:

- **The application server:** This server is responsible to fulfill the system contracts and propagate the transactions from the application to the connector back (inbound) and forth (outbound). Furthermore it provides a managed runtime for the connector as well as for the application.

- **The connector implementation:** This implementation relies on the provided contracts and interacts with the application server. It is invoked by the container to pass the transaction status and it reports the current connection status back using events. The connector provides a high-level interface to abstract from the incompatible resources to its clients.

- **The application (EJB):** The application uses the public connector API. All the container services (such as transactions, security, pooling, connection management or concurrency) are managed and propagated transparently to the application and even the connector by the application server.

Strategies

There are no noteworthy strategies. Depending on your requirements, you can choose which parts of the JCA specification you are going to implement.

Testing

The JCA's adapter actual integration logic, as well as parts of the JCA glue code, should be unit tested. Integration tests in an environment identical to production are even more important. You should plan some debugging and profiling hours, or even days for more complex JCA adapter implementations. Especially the interaction between the application server, the EJB container, and the JCA connector should be tested. To save time, you should automate the build and deployment process of the connector to your application server.

JCA connectors are shared resources accessed in parallel by several transactions and therefore EJB instances. Load and stress tests are essentially important to validate the stability of the custom JCA implementation. Especially interesting is the behavior in extreme cases, for example, in case the connection pool runs empty and there are still inflight transactions waiting for processing. The exact behavior is hard to predict, it is easier and more efficient to test early and often, than trying to implement a scalable and high-performance solution with a lot of upfront analysis.

Documentation

The SPI does not need extensive and detailed documentation. The description of connection management and transaction concepts should be sufficient to understand the implementation. You can refer to the detailed (five-hundred page) JCA specification document.

You should spend more time on the API documentation instead. Especially useful are tutorial-like descriptions with easy-to-understand working examples. The public API will be exposed to far more developers than the encapsulated and hidden SPI. UML sequence and activity diagrams may be useful for the description of interactions between the application and the connector, as well as the description of system contracts and internal concepts.

Consequences

- **Portability:** The portability of JCA adapters is far better, than EJB 2.x components. It is comparable with the portability of J2EE 1.4 WAR archives. You don't need any vendor-specific extensions.

- **Scalability:** JCA is only a specification. The scalability will only depend on your implementation and the scalability of the legacy resource.

- **Robustness:** The robustness is also highly dependent on the connector implementation, but the availability of system contracts such as lifecycle, transaction, and connection management allows the realization of more robust integrations.

- **Complexity:** The JCA connectors and resource adapter implementation are said to be complex. In fact, a partial implementation of a JCA adapter could be easier and faster than an attempt to build a comparable solution from scratch.

- **Consistency:** JCA resource adapters can participate in local as well as distributed transactions. The application server propagates the transactions to the resource adapter and notifies its implementation about the current status of the transaction. This allows you to integrate a legacy, even non-transactional resource with ACID qualities.

- **Maintainability:** JCA adapter forces reuse. The implementation of the resource adapter is not visible to its clients; they are forced to use the public API. A connector is deployed independently of the applications which encourages reuse and avoids code repetition. The strict separation of public API and internal SPI allows changes of internal connector implementation without breaking its clients.

Related Patterns

The public API is comparable with a DAO or even a service. A JCA resource adapter is used by services or DAOs. Low-level, "inconvenient" JCA implementations are often wrapped by a DAO to make them more accessible. High-level connectors can be accessed by services or even Service Façades.

Asynchronous service integration can be considered as a messaging-specific or narrowed variant of the generic JCA pattern.

Asynchronous Resource Integrator (Service Activator)

Message-driven beans are mapped to a `javax.jms.Destination`. It can be either `Queue` for point to point, or `Topic` for publish-subscribe communication. JMS is only a set of APIs and does not specify the wire protocol. The implementation of the JMS API, the actual message server is responsible for the message transport. Some products such as MQ Series, ActiveMQ (http://activemq.apache.org/) or openMQ (http://openmq.dev.java.net) provide binding for different languages and can be used as integration middleware.

Problem

In most companies the majority of business logic still runs on legacy systems and not on a Java application server. Java applications have to access those resources in a standard way without a lot of proprietary plumbing. Because such logic on back-end systems tends to be essential for the enterprise, nonfunctional qualities such as guaranteed, once and only once delivery, and transactional access to the resources become essential as well.

Older legacy hosts in particular are often based on message-oriented middleware (MOM). The business logic is written in programming languages such as RPG, PL/1, or Cobol which makes the direct integration of such resources even harder.

Fortunately, some message servers allow seamless interaction between Java and the legacy world. The same protocol is used for message delivery, regardless of which language or platform is used to consume and produce messages. A message sent by a PL/1 program is directly consumed by a message-driven bean mapped to a `javax.jms.Queue` or `javax.jms.Destination`. This allows the realization of lean and pragmatic integrations of proprietary resources.

Forces

- You need bidirectional communication between Java EE and the back-end services.
- You need robust access to legacy resources.
- You need a way to access asynchronous services.
- You need a solution to seamlessly integrate your existing Java EE services with back-end services.
- It is important to provide a high level of consistency, scalability, security, and robustness. Transactional access is required.
- You need to exchange messages over protocols such as HTTP, REST, or SOAP.

Solution

If your JMS provider supports the target legacy platform you are basically done. You will only have to agree on a common destination to exchange messages. The message server does the heavy lifting and integrates both worlds for you. The Java EE code remains simple; it is a standard message-driven bean that is mapped to the integrational destination. The message-driven bean is associated with a `Destination` (`Queue` or `Topic`) that is used by the legacy resources as a sink. The application and messaging servers care about the communication, but not the conversion of the message payload. In most cases you can only rely on `javax.jms.TextMessage` and `javax.jms.BytesMessage` for integration purposes. Other types and `javax.jms.ObjectMessage` in particular just cannot work between Java and other programming languages. In rare cases, you can even run into trouble with `javax.jms.TextMessage`, because some legacy hosts work with the EBCDIC [http://en.wikipedia.org/wiki/EBCDIC] character set, which is not compatible with ASCII.

```
@MessageDriven(mappedName = "ajax", activationConfig = {
    @ActivationConfigProperty(propertyName = "acknowledgeMode", propertyValue =
"Auto-acknowledge"),
    @ActivationConfigProperty(propertyName = "destinationType", propertyValue =
"javax.jms.Queue")
    })
public class AJAXListenerBean implements MessageListener {

    @EJB
    private MessageConsumer consumer;

    public void onMessage(Message msg) {
        TextMessage tm = (TextMessage) msg;
        try {
            String message = tm.getText();
            consumer.consume(message);
        } catch (JMSException ex) {
      throw new EJBException("Cannot receive payload : " +ex,ex);
        }
    }

}
```

The responsibility of the message-driven bean is the extraction of the payload, its conversion into meaningful parameters and forwarding to a service. The service is acquired with Dependency Injection and knows nothing about the actual origin of the parameters.

```
@Stateless
@TransactionAttribute(TransactionAttributeType.MANDATORY)
public class MessageConsumerBean implements MessageConsumer {

    public void consume(String message) {
    //business logic...
    }
}
```

The service is deployed, as always, with the `TransactionAttributeType.MANDATORY` configuration, so it can be only invoked in the context of a transaction. The transaction is started by the container before the invocation of the method `onMessage`. It is important to consume the message and invoke the service in the same transaction. The message is deleted from the destination at successful transaction completion.

In case the transaction fails, it will be automatically redelivered. The message-driven bean is therefore only able to delegate the messages to a service and not a Service Façade. A Service Façade would always start a new, independent transaction. The consumption of the message and the execution of the business logic would be decoupled. Even if Service Façade rolls back its transaction, the message-driven bean would still successfully consume the message. The message would just silently disappear from the destination—a hard-to-find error.

Rethinking

The scope of Service Activator in EJB 2.0 changed completely in EJB 3.1. In EJB 2, a message-driven bean was the only way to invoke synchronous EJBs in asynchronous way:

> "Enterprise beans and other business services need a way to be activated asynchronously.

> "...If an application needs synchronous processing for its server-side business components, then enterprise beans are an appropriate choice. Some application clients may require asynchronous processing for the server-side business objects because the clients do not need to wait or do not have the time to wait for the processing to complete. In cases where the application needs a form of asynchronous processing, enterprise beans do not offer this capability in implementations prior to the EJB 2.0 specification.

> "The EJB 2.0 specification provides integration by introducing message-driven bean, which is a special type of stateless session bean that offers asynchronous invocation capabilities. However, the new specification does not offer asynchronous invocation for other types of enterprise beans, such as stateful or entity beans..." [http://java.sun.com/blueprints/corej2eepatterns/Patterns/ServiceActivator.html].

The Service Activator was actually a decorator or adapter [GoF] that misused the message-oriented middleware to invoke synchronous components asynchronously. In EJB 3.1, a simpler and more natural option is available. You only have to annotate a method with the annotation @Asynchronous to be executed in a background thread—no workaround or pattern is required.

The use of message-driven beans as an adapter is still interesting, but only for integrational purposes and decoupling. This is the reason for renaming Service Activator to Asynchronous Resource Integrator.

Rich Internet applications, and AJAX in particular, rely increasingly on asynchronous communication styles with back-end services .JMS is asynchronous by nature, but most messaging servers use binary protocols only, which makes them inappropriate for the web.

Some message providers, such as openMQ (https://mq.dev.java.net/4.3-content/ums/umsMain.html), offer a REST-based front end for internal messaging. openMQ calls it Universal Message Service (UMS). Also, activeMQ provides a similar RESTful bridge(http://activemq.apache.org/rest.html). The solution is in both cases Servlet based. You only have to deploy a WAR, which converts the REST requests into corresponding JMS actions such as login, send, receive, close, commit, or rollback in the case of openMQ.

A RESTful interface can be easily used by all HTTP enabled devices—it is not only restricted to AJAX and browsers. Unfortunately, the RESTful protocol itself is not standardized yet, although you could use, for example, the openMQ bridge to communicate with an activeMQ server. There is a standard Advanced Message Queuing Protocol (AMQP) (http://amqp.org), which tries to standardize the wire protocol as well, but it is not very popular at the moment.

The asynchronous resource integrator pattern can be used for front-end and back-end integration. The only difference is the configuration of the message provider. For the integration of asynchronous resources in the presentation tier, you will need to configure HTTP /RESTful bridges (often available as WARs). The legacy resources, on the other hand, rely already on an existing, binary protocol, which is hard to change.

Conventions

The message-driven bean is only responsible for payload forwarding from a `javax.jms.Message` to the service. It has no domain-specific responsibility and should not contain any business logic. Therefore it should be named as the service with the suffix ASI—the abbreviation of asynchronous service integration, or just Listener, for example, `OrderServiceBean`, `OrderServiceListenerBean` or `OrderServiceASIBean`. It will be hard to find any other meaningful name.

In the case of the integration of asynchronous presentation components, the message-driven bean could reside in the same package as the service (for example, `business.ordermgmt.service.OrderServiceASIBean`). The ASI has similar responsibilities to a Service Façade, so it could be also placed in the subpackage `business.ordermgmt.facade` or `business.ordermgmt.boundary`. The latter approach should be preferred for asynchronous components, where an ASI is used consistently instead of a Service Façade.

For the communication with back-end services, the message-driven bean would actually belong to the integration tier, and therefore the subpackage with the name `integration`. From an implementation perspective, there is no difference between these scenarios. In both cases, the message-driven bean is mapped to a destination—there is no additional integration logic involved. For pragmatic reasons, you could also put the message-driven bean into the same package as the service. In case you need more complex data transformations or conversions, you should move the message-driven bean with the corresponding integration logic into the integration tier.

Participants and Responsibilities

The message-driven bean plays the actual integrator role. It is responsible for:

- Message consumption and service invocation with ACID qualities.
- Payload extraction and conversion into meaningful method parameters.
- Error handling of syntactically incorrect messages AKA poisoned messages. These can be messages with wrong type or unrecognizable payload respectively.

The implementation of the JMS API plays an important role in this pattern as well. The message provider is responsible for providing the glue functionality, and especially client libraries, for both the Java and legacy sides.

The service should not even know about the existence of the message-driven bean. It should be indistinguishable whether it was invoked by the Service Façade or the asynchronous service invoker.

Strategies

From the conceptual point of view, there are two different strategies available. Interestingly the implementation of both strategies is almost identical. The only difference is the source of the incoming events.

Front-end Integration

Front-end integration expects messages from the presentation and even the client tier (the browser). The messages contain user input as payload and have the granularity of Service Façade parameters. Transformations are not required; the payload of the incoming messages often contains JSON or XML objects, which can be directly consumed. The message-driven bean extracts the payload and delegates it as a parameter to a service.

Back-end Integration

A legacy system is the source of the incoming messages in this case. Contrary to front-end integration, you will hardly have influence on the message payload, type, encoding, and content. After the consumption of a legacy message you will probably have to spend some effort to understand the actual payload. The payload itself is often in a proprietary format, which has to be converted into a more handy representation at the beginning. Byte arrays as payload are not uncommon. Complex transformations should not be implemented in the ASI, but be factored out into dedicated, testable conversion service.

Testing

Any conversion and transformation logic should be heavily tested with unit tests. Transformation errors are hard to debug, especially in asynchronous environments. The importance of integration tests in an environment identical to production cannot be emphasized enough. The correct behavior of the ASI cannot be verified with plain unit tests. You will have to deploy it to the application server with properly configured and mapped destinations.

Load tests are important for the verification of the message provider configuration especially thread pooling, thresholds, quotas and dead letter queues in error scenarios. Although message-driven beans are easy to develop and deploy, proper error handling is hard and the debug process a real challenge. Good integration and load tests are essential for robust applications.

Documentation

The invocation of a message-driven bean by an AJAX application isn't obvious and should be therefore documented. Especially the mechanism, any conversions, transaction and error handling are important. A Wiki is perfectly suitable for the description of such concepts. Also, existing naming conventions and patterns for the destination naming should be well documented. As always, the intentions and background information is more important as the actual result.

The destinations should be named after domain concepts (`OrderQueue`) and not technical artifacts (`RequestQueue`). In case of back-end integration the naming conventions are already provided by legacy standards and have to be reused.

In class diagrams, an ASI can be modeled as a service with the additional stereotype <<ASI>>. There is no need for modeling an additional message-driven bean. This information can already be derived from the stereotype.

Consequences

- **Scalability:** Asynchronous communication scales significantly better, than its synchronous counterpart. The transactions are shorter; the client does not have to wait until the transaction completion.

- **Complexity:** Asynchronous communication is only simple for fire-and-forget communication styles. It is hard to build bidirectional communication with asynchronous protocols. It becomes especially complex in case the client needs an immediate feedback. Such pseudo-asynchronous communication is hard to implement without waiting for the response. This would cause blocking in some layer which in turn could lead to duplicate transactions or deadlocks. The first phenomenon can occur by resending a message after a timeout, the second in cases the server forgets to send a response.
In case your legacy resource is able to communicate with the messaging server, ASI becomes the simplest and most robust solution. The alternative would be direct communication with the legacy interfaces with ACID qualities which can become quickly orders of magnitude more complex.

- **Loose coupling:** Messaging decouples the message consumer from the producer with an intermediary destination. The dependency is very weak and only given by the message. The producer can be changed and maintained without affecting the consumer. No recompilation is needed as long as the message remains unchanged.

- **Robustness:** Java is a statically typed language; loose coupling can be only achieved with weakening the type safety by relying on more general contracts. Doing so, you are actually disabling the majority of compiler checks. The application remains longer compilable, but the developer has to provide its runtime robustness. Message-oriented systems are not robust per default; you have to invest a considerable amount of effort to achieve a high level or stability.

- **Testability:** Asynchronous and message-oriented systems in particular are hard to test. Integration tests have to block a certain amount of time to verify the effect of a sent message. Most message servers are not able to be executed in process and started in the @Before method of the unit test. Integration and functional tests are easier to perform and are even more important.

- **Portability:** JMS does not specify the wire protocol. Unless your message server relies on standards like AMQP you are indirectly dependent on the proprietary capabilities of the message server. The application, however, is still only dependent on the JMS API; there are no compile-time dependencies to the JMS implementation.

- **Performance:** Although for the client the response times can become significantly shorter, bidirectional communication requires at least three transactions. The client has to send the message, which becomes consumed, processed, and sent back. The third transaction is the actual consumption of the message. The same business logic could be invoked with a single transaction in synchronous way.

Asynchronous communication needs more transactions and generates significantly more load. This can overwhelm the server and impact performance. You should perform load tests to verify the actual demand on resources (RAM, CPU and so on).

Related Patterns

Asynchronous service invoker is actually a service activator with extended scope and responsibilities. The asynchronous invocation of synchronous services is already provided by the EJB 3.1 specification. The integration of incompatible resources remains the main ASI responsibility.

JMS providers are plugged into the application server using the JCA infrastructure. The ASI can be considered as a specific form of generic JCA. DAOs have similar responsibility as well, but they largely operate synchronously.

ASI forwards the payload to services exclusively. In exceptional cases, it could work directly with DAOs. ASI is triggered by back-end resources or directly by clients. In some cases, services can invoke an ASI by sending JMS messages as well. The message source should be totally transparent for an ASI.

5

Infrastructural Patterns and Utilities

Some patterns are hard to classify because they can be used in every layer. Not all useful patterns are relevant to the bigger picture and can be omitted in the architecture description. This chapter covers such hard-to-classify yet still useful patterns and utilities, including:

- Service Starter
- Singleton
- Bean locator
- Thread tracker
- Dependency injection extender
- Payload extractor
- Resource binder
- Context holder

Service Starter

The Java EE 5 container manages the lifecycle of deployed components. Stateless session beans are created mainly on demand; stateful session beans are created at injection or lookup time. Java EE 5 does support a standardized way to force the container to initialize them at startup time. Stateless session bean pooling is mentioned in the spec and available in most application servers, but the way how the pool is configured is not standardized. You simply cannot rely on the existence of settings such as `pool-initial-size` or min-pool-size on every application server. There is no standardized way to enforce a session bean to start at deployment time.

Problem

Some infrastructural logic and services need to be initialized before the execution of the actual business logic. Such services can be expensive, slow, or unstable (for example, an XML configuration file could be malformed). It is a good strategy to start them at the earliest possible time. Only the introduction of EJB 3.1 provided a standardized solution for the initialization problem. Neither EJB 2.x nor EJB 3.0 supported a direct way to force the container to start session beans at deployment time, with the exception of the introduction of a startup Servlet.

Forces

- You need a portable way to start services eagerly
- The solution should provide extendible hooks with which existing stateless session Beans can be initialized.

Solution

The solution to this problem dependents on the supported EJB version. Prior to EJB 3.1 you could force the initialization of certain components with a Servlet. In EJB 3.1 you can achieve the same with only two additional annotations.

EJB 3.1

The startup problem is solved in the EJB 3.1 specification. You can either initialize the services directly in the Singleton pattern, or even inject and initialize existing session beans for that purpose.

Just annotate a class with the `@Singleton` and `@Startup` annotations and deploy it together with your services. This forces the container to initialize the bean at deployment time, as shown in the following snippet:

```
@Singleton
@Startup
public class ServiceStarter {

    @EJB
    private ExistingServiceBean service;

    @PostConstruct
    public void onInitialize(){
      System.out.println("#" + this.getClass().getSimpleName() + " @PostConstruct");
      service.pleaseInitialize();
```

```
        }
}
```

The container initializes the bean, but won't invoke your business logic or services. You can easily force the container to invoke your hook by designating the initialization method with the @PostConstruct annotation. This method (onInitialize in the example below) is invoked just after the construction of the ServiceStarter and the invocation of a default constructor, as demonstrated in the following example:

```
@Stateless
public class ExistingServiceBean {

    @PostConstruct
    public void onInitialize(){
      System.out.println("#" + this.getClass().getSimpleName() + "
@PostConstruct");
    }

    public void pleaseInitialize(){
  System.out.println("#" + this.getClass()… + " pleaseInitialize()");
    }

    public String someBusinessLogic(){
        return "Hello from bean";
    }
}
```

You can put the initialization logic right into the Singleton's @PostConstruct method. At this point Dependency Injection is already performed, so you can rely on the existence of the injected resources. You could even use the ServiceStarter as a wrapper to initialize common session beans. You only have to inject the reference and invoke any method you like. This eventually will force the container to inject and initialize the session bean. During the initialization the container creates the bean (if it not already exists); it then executes the @PostConstruct method and invokes your business method. This can be easily reproduced with the previous sample; it generates the following output:

```
#ServiceStarter @PostConstruct
#ExistingServiceBean @PostConstruct
#ExistingServiceBean pleaseInitialize()
```

You can even influence the order in which dependent Singletons will perform their initialization. To demonstrate this, you can introduce another Singleton, the Initializer:

```
@Singleton
public class Initializer {

    @PostConstruct
    public void onInitialize(){
      System.out.println("#" + this.getClass().getSimpleName() + "
@PostConstruct");
    }
}
```

The declaration of the dependency to another Singleton can be specified with the `@DependsOn` annotation. This annotation has only one attribute of type `String[]`. It represents the names of the beans that have to be initialized before the annotated class:

```
@Singleton
@Startup
@DependsOn("Initializer")
public class ServiceStarter {
In this example, the Initializer is  initialized before the ServiceStarter:
#Initializer @PostConstruct
#ServiceStarter @PostConstruct
#ExistingServiceBean @PostConstruct
#ExistingServiceBean pleaseInitialize()
```

Workaround for older EJB versions

There is no standard way to enforce the initialization of session beans prior EJB 3.1. The Web container, however, was able to provide this functionality for Servlets during the J2EE days. To initialize a service, you have to provide a Servlet with an overwritten `init` method as shown in the following snippet:

```
public class ServiceStarter extends HttpServlet {
    @EJB
    private InfrastructureService service;

    @Override
    public void init() throws ServletException {
      System.out.println("#" + this.getClass().getSimpleName() + " init()");
        this.service.dummyMethod();
    }
}
```

Just inject a session bean of your choice into the Servlet. A plain injection isn't enough to enforce the creation of the bean; it's the same problem as in the case of the `@Singleton`. The invocation of any arbitrary method, however, will cause the container to initialize the session bean.

The remaining task is configuring the Servlet in the `web.xml` (or with annotations), to be started at deployment time. For that purpose you will have to provide a value, higher than zero, in the `load-on-startup` tag.

```
<web-app>
    <servlet>
        <servlet-name>ServiceStarter</servlet-name>
        <servlet-class>...servicestarter.ServiceStarter</servlet-class>
        <load-on-startup>1</load-on-startup>
    </servlet>
 </web-app>
```

The value influences the initialization order—the higher the value, the earlier (relatively to others) a Servlet is initialized. The result is comparable to the `@DependsOn` annotation. The deployment of the Servlet results in the following output:

```
#ServiceStarter init()
#InfrastructureService @PostConstruct
```

Rethinking

Rethinking is not required, but refactoring is. With the availability of EJB 3.1 support by your production server, you can transform your existing startup Servlets into Singleton beans and get rid of superfluous WARs.

Participants and Responsibilities

The process is started either by the Servlet or a Singleton bean, the service starter. In both cases, the container initiates the process and invokes the `init` or `@PostConstruct` method, respectively. The initialization is either performed in the startup hooks directly, or delegated to session beans by invoking dummy methods.

Testing

Proper startup behavior can only be tested during deployment time. Unit tests, however, are recommended to test the initialization logic itself. Service starter is an exception from the rule; load and stress tests are irrelevant here.

Documentation

Startup service is irrelevant for the bigger picture, so it should not appear in the overview diagrams. In EJB 3.1, you could even omit JavaDoc, because the initialization responsibility is already well documented with the `@Startup` annotation.

Consequences

The service starter improves runtime robustness of the system starting critical services eagerly. There are no other impacts on non-functional requirements.

Related Patterns

The service starter invokes existing services , Service Facades, or Gateways to enforce their initialization. It is not related to other patterns regarding its responsibility. The Singleton, however, is technically identical to the service starter.

Singleton

The single-threaded programming model is one of the main features of EJBs. The realization of the idea leads to the elimination of shared instances and state among threads. Every user request (that is, every thread) operates on a single session bean instance. An instance can be accessed only by one thread at a time. Stateful session beans are even more restrictive. They not only have to be accessible by one thread a time, but every request has to be associated with the same user.

Problem

The simplified programming is superb for scalability and multi-core programming, but it makes management of limited resources hard. The amount of active session bean instances is only dependent on the number of parallel user requests and the proprietary application server configuration. Pool settings, the configuration of max, min pool size, and its resize ability in particular are not backed by the spec. It is therefore not possible to implement a Singleton in a portable way; you can neither rely on the availability of the max pool size parameter, nor on its expected behavior.

Furthermore, without a central instance, it is impossible to implement an efficient read-only cache. Caching is especially interesting for master data and configuration.

Forces

- The solution has to be portable across servers.

- A Singleton is shared across user requests per definition. Either it is accessed in read-only mode or a synchronization mechanism has to be provided by the container.

- A Singleton must not influence the garbage collection; it must not be realized with static and synchronized modifiers.

Solution

A Singleton was standardized with the EJB 3.1 spec. It is a bean that only exists once in a JVM. In a clustered environment, however, you will still get multiple Singleton instances. The Singleton can be started at the container's boot time. The Service Starter pattern leverages this capability. From a technical point of view, a Singleton is identical to the Service Starter. Its main responsibility is not the delegation of its boot capabilities to interesting services, but to provide shared state and concurrency management. The following example shows a simple caching Singleton.

```
@Singleton
public class MasterDataCache {

    private Map<String,Object> cache;

    @PostConstruct
    public void initCache(){
        this.cache = new HashMap<String, Object>();
    }

    public Object get(String key){
        return this.cache.get(key);
    }
```

```
    public void store(String key,Object value){
        this.cache.put(key, value);
    }
}
```

According to spec, a Singleton comes already with suitable, but restrictive defaults: `@ConcurrencyManagement(ConcurrencyManagementType.CONTAINER)` and `@Lock(LockType.WRITE)`. The concurrency is managed by the container, but without any parallelism. The `LockType.WRITE` is exclusive, so only one thread at a time can access the Singleton instance. This default setting provides a high level of consistency, comparable with the serializable isolation level, but at a high cost—it is a bottleneck.

The `LockType.WRITE` is not appropriate for read-only master data caches or caching of, for example, parsed XML configuration. If you are only reading cached data stored in the Singleton, the `LockType.READ` is the right solution for you. It allows simultaneous access to methods designated with this `LockType`.

You could even take over the concurrency management and implement it with standard Java means such as synchronized modifiers or blocks. You will gain more control. In most cases, however, the container's concurrency management is absolutely sufficient.

For a more serious cache implementation, you should rely on frameworks such as JBoss-Cache (http://www.jboss.org/jbosscache/) or EHCache (http://ehcache.sourceforge.net/), which are more powerful, well tested, and provide additional services such as refreshing, eviction of stale elements, distribution, replication ,invalidation, and even disc persistence. Some of the cache implementations, however, might not be compliant with the EJB 3.1 specification.

Rethinking

The use of static, non-final fields is restricted. It was extremely difficult to implement a Singleton without violating the spec. As a workaround, MBeans or JCA connectors could be used for this purpose. The access to JMX from session beans is not specified and error-prone, whereas implementing a JCA connector just to have a Singleton is a slightly overengineered solution.

Instead of designing esoteric solutions with EJB 3.1, you should leverage the container capabilities and use Singleton beans. They are simple, concise, powerful, and fully independent of a concrete application server implementation. They are almost independent from the EJB API itself, only one annotation tights them to the spec.

Participants and Responsibilities

The Singleton bean provides already added value and implements, for example, caching or configuration services. It can access existing Service Façades , services, and resources to fetch needed information and cache it later.

Strategies

Gatekeeper

A Singleton can be effectively used to throttle concurrency to back-end resources. Especially legacy systems have only limited scalability, or the concurrency has to be restricted because of licensing issues. In general, throttling is the responsibility of a Java Connector Architecture (JCA) adapter, if available for the specific back-end system. A JCA connector could also be implemented from scratch for this purpose. It is, however, a lot more work than implementing a simple Singleton.

Even easier to implement is the sequentialization of access to legacy resources. Especially native legacy services are not thread-safe. A Singleton designated with `LockType.WRITE` provides sequential access to its methods and is the perfect solution for accessing single-threaded resources.

Throttling, as well as sequentialization of access to a back-end resource is only given in a single-node environment. Cluster is a logical group of identical nodes, so that you will get one instance of a Singleton per node, and several Singleton instances per application. Cluster-wide Singletons are not specified in EJB 3.1.

Caching Singleton

A more common use case for Singletons is wrapping or even the implementation of caching solutions. Complex XML configuration, internationalization messages, or master data caches can be loaded at startup time and do not change at runtime. Caching Singletons can be deployed with the `LockType.READ` configuration—only then can the cache be accessed in parallel. In the following example, a Singleton wraps `EHCache` and exposes it to other services or even the presentation layer.

```
@Singleton
@Startup
@Lock(LockType.READ)
public class CachingSingleton {

    public static final String DEFAULT_CACHE_NAME = "memory";
    private CacheManager cacheManager;
    private Cache cache;

    @PostConstruct
    void initializeCache(){
        this.cacheManager = CacheManager.create();
        this.cache = this.cacheManager.getCache(DEFAULT_CACHE_NAME);
        if(this.cache == null)
            throw new IllegalStateException("..: " + DEFAULT_CACHE_NAME);
    }

    public Serializable get(long id){
        Element element = this.cache.get(id);
        if(element == null)
            return null;
        return element.getValue();
    }

    public void put(long id, Serializable cache){
```

```
            this.cache.put(new Element(id, cache));
    }

    @PreDestroy
    void shutdownCache(){
        this.cacheManager.shutdown();
    }
}
```

The `CachingSingleton` is rather purist—its only responsibility is caching and not the actual data retrieval. An injected Service, however, could fetch the data in case of a cache miss and provide a caching façade. Alternatively, a `CacheService` could use the `CachingSingleton` just for caching, and populate the cache on demand.

With frameworks such as EHCache it would even be possible to read the cache and let the framework transparently populate it.

A `CachingSingleton` should be eagerly initialized. In case the cache was not properly configured (for example, `ehcache.xml` not found or inconsistent), the application server would throw an exception and the application wouldn't be available at all.

Furthermore, the method `@PreDestroy` is implemented to shut down the cache gracefully. This is important for caches with disc or persistent storage in particular. They use this hook to flush the contents of the memory cache into the persistent store.

Testing

Singletons do not require any testing per se. What you should test, however, is their behavior under a heavy load in a production environment. Especially important is the throttling functionality of the `Gatekeeper`. What you are actually testing is not your code, rather than the container implementation and the impact of `LockTypes` on your performance and scalability.

Documentation

The nature of Singletons is rather technical and not conceptual, so they are less interesting for architectural documentation. In case Gatekeepers or caching Singletons are a recurring pattern in your architecture, it is worth to describe them once in a conceptual meta model, and then reuse this pattern over and over again.

At code level, Singletons are already very well documented with the `@Singleton` and (if applicable) `@Startup` annotations. You should concentrate in your JavaDoc comments on more essential responsibilities such as a description of how the cache works and how to use it. The Singleton itself is already well documented in the EJB 3.1 specification.

Consequences

- **Scalability:** A Singleton exists only once per JVM. Therefore it is a natural bottleneck, especially with the default configuration: `LockType.WRITE`. Already the need for the introduction of a Singleton may indicate design problems in your application. Even the

`LockType.READ` may cause problems because the Singleton's implementation may block and impact the scalability. On the other hand, caching Singletons can save database roundtrips and improve the scalability significantly.

- **Testability:** In general, classic Singletons are not very well unit testable. It is very hard to un-initialize them after the test. This is not true for EJB 3.1 Singletons. Outside the container, these Singletons are just regular Java classes, so you can test them as any other POJO. For integration tests you will have to deploy the ejb-jar to the container; the undeployment will clean up the Singletons, so you could easily repeat the test.

- **Performance:** Caching Singletons can improve the performance significantly. Instead of accessing the JPA layer, or even database, the required object can be served directly from memory. This is a lot faster than accessing a database.

- **Robustness:** The Singleton instance will remain in memory until the undeployment or shutdown of the application. So every referenced object will also remain in memory until the Singleton gets garbage collected itself. This can become a potential problem for caches. Cached objects will never be garbage collected, so the application can run out of memory. You should configure or implement your cache properly and set the maximum amount of objects to a reasonable (load-tested) value.

- **Portability:** An EJB 3.1 Singleton instance is guaranteed to exist only once in a single JVM. In a clustered environment, you will get multiple Singleton instances. Some vendors already provide cluster-wide Singletons. These extensions are proprietary and not portable across application servers.

Related Patterns

A Caching Singleton can access services and can itself be accessed by Service Façades or Services. The Gatekeeper strategy accesses back-end resources and integration services.

From a technical perspective, a Singleton is closely related to a Service Starter (Java EE). There was no support for Singleton beans in EJB prior 3.1.

Bean Locator

Dependency injection works in managed classes only. From POJOs, you will still have to use JNDI / `InitialContext` to access the deployed EJBs. A stateful session bean instance's life starts when a client obtains a reference to the bean instance through Dependency Injection or JNDI lookup. A stateful class cannot be injected to Servlets, request scoped backing beans and so on; you will have to use JNDI lookup to control the creation time and associate, for example, the stateful session bean with the HTTP session. Sometimes a lookup of a resource instead of Dependency Injection is necessary as a workaround for potential application server bugs.

Problem

The JNDI specification (`javax.naming` package) is older than J2EE itself. It is part of the JDK and not of the Java EE specification. Its use is simple, but comes with some plumbing. The `Context#lookup` throws `javax.naming.NamingException`, which is checked. The JNDI API was designed long before the availability of generics, so you will have to cast the result as well.

EJB 3.1 introduced the global JNDI naming of EJB components. The JNDI names come with the following syntax: `java:global[/<app-name>]/<module-name>/<bean-name>#<fully-qualified-interface-name>`. The `app-name` and `fully-qualified-interface-name` are optional.

Neither the use of the JNDI API itself nor the construction of the JNDI names are convenient. The encapsulation of both in a utility class (`BeanLocator`) makes the `lookup` not only more convenient, but also decouples the application from the JNDI details.

Forces

- The JNDI API details should be hidden. The user should be independent of the JNDI API.
- The global JNDI name should be built as conveniently as possible; the error-prone construction of the JNDI name should be simplified.
- The `BeanLocator` should be capable to be used inside as well as outside the EJB container.

Solution

The solution for this problem is straightforward: the JNDI access as well as the construction of the JNDI names is going to be encapsulated inside a utility class, the `BeanLocator`.

This class is responsible for locating the EJBs and construction of the global JNDI names. The simplest possible solution would be the encapsulation of the lookup invocation:

```
try {
    return new InitialContext().lookup(jndiName);
}catch(NamingException ex){
    //...error escalation
}
```

The `BeanLocator` is actually almost as simple as the sample above. In addition, it closes the `InitialContext` after every use. Some application servers require this approach to release the internal `InitialContext` resources. The `lookup` method relies on generics to avoid casting:

```
public class BeanLocator {

    public static <T> T lookup(Class<T> clazz, String jndiName) {
        Object bean = lookup(jndiName);
        return clazz.cast(PortableRemoteObject.narrow(bean, clazz));
    }

    public static Object lookup(String jndiName) {
        Context context = null;
        try {
            context = new InitialContext();
            return context.lookup(jndiName);
        } catch (NamingException ex) {
            throw new IllegalStateException("...");
        } finally {
            try {
                context.close();
            } catch (NamingException ex) {
                throw new IllegalStateException("...");
            }
        }
    }
}
```

Only the checked exceptions are transformed and the `InitialContext` closed after every use. In addition, the return value is casted for convenience reasons.

More interesting is the creation of the JNDI name itself. It is error-prone and repetitive; you have to pass the application and module name (the name of the EJB JAR or WAR archives) over and over again. The `GlobalJNDIName` class is a builder, which creates the JNDI name internally and passes it to the `BeanLocator`. The classes `GlobalJNDIName` and `BeanLocator` are responsible for different tasks. A standalone use of the `GlobalJNDIName`, just for the creation of the JNDI names, is not very useful. For convenience reasons, the `GlobalJNDIName` was moved into the `BeanLocator`, it is a static inner class.

```
public static class GlobalJNDIName {

        //declarations omitted
        public GlobalJNDIName() {
            this.builder = new StringBuilder();
            this.builder.append(PREFIX).append(SEPARATOR);
            this.config = new Properties();
            try {
                this.config.load(this.getClass().getResourceAsStream(PROPERTY_FI
LE));
            } catch (Exception ex) {/*escalation*/}
        this.appName = this.config.getProperty(APP_NAME_KEY);
                        this.moduleName =
this.config.getProperty(MODULE_NAME_KEY);
        }

        public GlobalJNDIName withAppName(String appName) {
```

```java
            this.appName = appName;
            return this;
        }

        public GlobalJNDIName withModuleName(String moduleName) {
            this.moduleName = moduleName;
            return this;
        }

        public GlobalJNDIName withBeanName(String beanName) {
            this.beanName = beanName;
            return this;
        }

        public GlobalJNDIName withBeanName(Class beanClass) {
            return withBeanName(computeBeanName(beanClass));
        }

    public GlobalJNDIName withBusinessInterface(Class interfaze) {
            this.businessInterfaceName = interfaze.getName();
            return this;
        }

        String computeBeanName(Class beanClass) {
Stateless stateless = (Stateless) beanClass.getAnnotation(Stateless.class);
            if (stateless != null && isNotEmpty(stateless.name())) {
                return stateless.name();
            }
            Stateful stateful = (Stateful)
beanClass.getAnnotation(Stateful.class);
            if (stateful != null && isNotEmpty(stateful.name())) {
                return stateful.name();
            }
        Singleton singleton = (Singleton)
beanClass.getAnnotation(Singleton.class);
            if (singleton != null && isNotEmpty(singleton.name())) {
                return singleton.name();
            }
            return beanClass.getSimpleName();
        }

        private boolean isNotEmpty(String name){
            return (name != null && !name.isEmpty());
        }

        public String asString() {
            if (appName != null) {
                this.builder.append(appName).append(SEPARATOR);
            }
            this.builder.append(moduleName).append(SEPARATOR);
            this.builder.append(beanName);
            if (businessInterfaceName != null) {
                this.builder.append("#").append(businessInterfaceName);
```

```
        }
        return this.builder.toString();
    }

    public <T> T locate(Class<T> clazz) {
        return BeanLocator.lookup(clazz, asString());
    }

    public Object locate() {
        return BeanLocator.lookup(asString());
    }
}
```

Now you only have to create the `GlobalJNDIName` in the context of `BeanLocator` and invoke the builder methods:

```
@Override
public void init() throws ServletException {
    this.testSingleton = (TestSingleton) new BeanLocator.GlobalJNDIName().
        withBeanName(TestSingleton.class).
        locate();
}
```

You do not even have to pass the application and module names. Unfortunately they cannot be derived from the Bean class or the business interface itself. The `BeanLocator` searches for the `global.jndi` property file in the classpath. It contains only two entries:

`module.name=BeanLocatorModule`

`application.name=BeanLocatorApp`

The `application.name` is optional; it should correspond with the EAR name. The `module.name` represents the name of the EJB JAR or WAR archives and is mandatory.

The `Properties` are read on every creation of the `GlobalJNDIName`, and could therefore become a performance hotspot. The creation and parsing of `java.util.Properties` is surprisingly fast. The `global.jndi` was loaded and parsed and the values fetched in less than five milliseconds.

It turns out, that there is another, real hotspot. The first invocation of the method `Class#getAnnotation` takes about 55 milliseconds to complete and is about 10 times slower, than the parsing of `global.jndi`.

```
String computeBeanName(Class beanClass) {
    Stateless stateless = (Stateless) beanClass.getAnnotation(Stateless.class);
    if (stateless != null && isNotEmpty(stateless.name())) {
        return stateless.name();
    }
    Stateful stateful = (Stateful) beanClass.getAnnotation(Stateful.class);
    if (stateful != null && isNotEmpty(stateful.name())) {
        return stateful.name();
    }
    Singleton singleton = (Singleton) beanClass.getAnnotation(Singleton.class);
```

```
    if (singleton != null && isNotEmpty(singleton.name())) {
            return singleton.name();
    }
            return beanClass.getSimpleName();
}
```

The method `computeBeanName` looks for Stateless, Stateful, or Singleton annotations and accesses the `name()` property for this purpose. The existence of this property overrides the default naming and should be considered in the construction of the `GlobalJNDIName`.

The annotations, as well as the already located stateless and Singleton beans could be easily cached inside the `BeanLocator` to improve performance.

Before you start to optimize the performance and introduce internal bean caching with the Singleton pattern, keep in mind that the `BeanLocator` is used at the creation time of the components. The creation happens eagerly at the deployment or application start time.

Bad `BeanLocator` performance would only hit the deployment or application server startup time. At runtime, all references should be resolved already. In all other cases you could still cache the references outside the `BeanLocator` as well.

With caching of the `java.util.Properties` some further minor optimization is possible. The module and application archive names are stable and do not change, even between deployments. Instead of using `Properties` you could hard-code both values inside the `BeanLocator` and keep them in sync with the actual archive names.

Rethinking

`BeanLocator` can be considered as a specific form of the J2EE service locator. The service locator was designed to be able to fetch all sorts of JNDI resources such as JMS destinations, data sources, and session beans in particular.

Dependency injection was not available in J2EE, so the service locator provided a general approach to locate components and resources. In Java EE, the `BeanLocator` is an exception from the rule, rather than a common pattern or best practice. The `BeanLocator` should be used only in classes where Dependency Injection does not work or is not available.

In the process of migration from J2EE projects to Java EE the service locator can be replaced with Dependency Injection where available. In the remaining few cases, the service locator can be replaced with the `BeanLocator`.

There is another difference between both patterns; the service locator fetched the home interfaces, whereas the `BeanLocator` returns the business interfaces or bean instances (in case of no-interface view).

Participants and Responsibilities

The `BeanLocator` is used by classes when Dependency Injection is not available. `BeanLocator` returns remote or local stateless, stateful, and Singleton beans. The `BeanLocator` delegates the lookup calls to the JNDI `InitialContext` which is configured within the `jndi.properties`.

Strategies

`BeanLocator` is a useful utility that can be extended in many ways. The flavor presented here is just an idea ; you can customize utility to suit your needs.

Testing

The more sophisticated version of `BeanLocator` reads the application and module name from the configuration file and uses reflection to access the metadata stored in annotations. This requires some processing time and impacts performance. You should load and stress test your application with the `BeanLocator` and search for potential bottlenecks as well as memory leaks. The introduction of `BeanLocator` should be neutral to the runtime performance and only influence the startup time of the application. Sometimes, however, even too long startup time is critical for high-availability applications. A long startup time has impact on the computation of Mean Time Between Failures (MTBF). Bad startup performance makes downtime longer than necessary, which is crucial for patching and update strategies of HA applications. Short offline-periods can be acceptable, whereas longer downtimes could make the introduction of a parallel cluster necessary.

Documentation

`BeanLocator` is reusable, so it is worth to provide good JavaDoc documentation with some how-to-use examples. More interesting, however, is the reason why you actually need a `BeanLocator` at all. In Java EE, Dependency Injection is sufficient in most cases, so the existence of lookup-utilities is suspicious. The reason for its use should be well documented. The mechanism behind `BeanLocator` is rather obvious and does not require extensive documentation.

Consequences

- **Portability:** `BeanLocator` relies on global JNDI names. It is portable across servers.

- **Performance and scalability:** There should be no impact on the runtime performance. The use of `BeanLocator` can affect the startup time though.

- **Testability:** You could achieve the same level of testability with `BeanLocator` as with pure Dependency Injection. In both cases, the user relies on an interface. The Dependency Injection mechanism is configurable, but you could make the `BeanLocator` configurable as well. For unit testing, you could skip the `BeanLocator` entirely and rely on mocking frameworks instead.

- **Robustness:** If the `BeanLocator` is used eagerly, it has no negative impact on robustness. With this "fail fast" strategy the application will either start consistently or not at all. This is comparable with the usual Dependency Injection mechanism.

Related Patterns

Dependency injection can be considered as `BeanLocator` 2.0. Dependency Injection uses a generic version of `BeanLocator`, factored out from the application code into the framework.

Such a generic `BeanLocator` is configured with metadata derived from conventions, class files, annotations, and, optionally, XML. The located bean is automatically injected by the framework.

The J2EE service locator is also closely related to `BeanLocator`. Its implementation was somehow limited because of the lack of global JNDI names, generics, and annotations.

Thread Tracker

Session bean instances are always executed by exactly one thread. For the entire execution time of a method, a single thread is associated with the bean instance and probably the whole call tree.

The application server pools the threads and reuses them between calls to the session beans. The threads have arbitrary, application server-specific names, and are often numbered, for example, httpSSLWorkerThread-8080-0, httpSSLWorkerThread-8080-1 (Glassfish v2) and so on.

Problem

Because the threads are pooled and have generic names, it is hard to associate a method in deadlock scenario with a stuck thread. If you connect to the application server with JConsole or VisualVM, you will only see a bunch of threads with random names.

For troubleshooting purposes it would be helpful to name the threads after the method for the duration of its execution, and roll back this change just after the method call.

Forces

- The solution should be portable across servers.
- The extension of the monitoring capabilities should be clearly separated from the business code.
- The thread tracking should be easily activated and deactivated.
- It should be easy to remove all additional monitoring functionality (and class files as well) before production deployment.
- The thread tracking should be generic enough to be applied to already existing beans.

Solution

The business methods of the bean are executed in a pooled thread. The challenge is to change the thread name to something human readable, such as the name of the bean with concatenated method name, and change it to the origin after the call. You will have to intercept the call before the actual method execution. This is actually a perfect task for an EJB 3 interceptor. It is even executed in the same transaction, thread, and security context as the EJB, and has even access to the Bean instance.

An interceptor wraps the bean instance and can also easily change the name of the thread.

```
public class ThreadTracker {
    @AroundInvoke
    public Object annotateThread(InvocationContext invCtx) throws Exception{
        String originName = Thread.currentThread().getName();
        String beanName = invCtx.getTarget().getClass().getName();
  String tracingName = beanName + "#" + invCtx.getMethod().getName() + " " +
originName;
        try{
            Thread.currentThread().setName(tracingName);
            return invCtx.proceed();
        }finally{
            Thread.currentThread().setName(originName);
        }
```

```
        }
}
```

The `ThreadTracker` can be attached to a particular class using annotations or XML. The choice is highly dependent on your deployment intentions. In case you are planning to use the `ThreadTracker` in production, annotations is the way to go. If you are using `ThreadTracker` just for troubleshooting, it is better to use XML deployment descriptors. In the latter case, you don't even have to touch the existing code.

```
@Stateless
@Interceptors(ThreadTracker.class)
public class DummyBean implements DummyRemote {

    public String sayHello(String message){
        try {
                                //actually not allowed in EJB container
                                //only needed to simulate a dead lock
            Thread.sleep(50000);
        } catch (InterruptedException ex) {  }
        return "Echo: " + message;
    }
}
```

After the activation of the `ThreadTracker` you should be able to identify slow or deadlocked methods already by the name of the thread (see Figure 1).

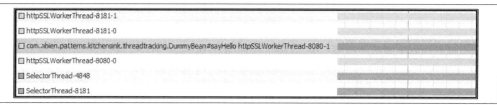

Figure 1. *Renamed thread in the VisualVM*

Changing the thread name is also useful for the monitoring of business transactions. A Service Façade starts a new transaction for every incoming call. The transaction is propagated to all services , DAOs, and other participants. The name of the method is actually the name of the transaction, which is in turn executed in a single thread.

The `ThreadTracker` applied on a Service Façade changes the name of the thread to the name of the currently executed Service Façade method. This method represents the business transaction, so we can easily monitor its throughput, performance, and write transaction-specific logs.

Even more useful is the `ThreadTracker` for message-driven beans monitoring. They are executed asynchronously in a separate transaction and thread. The threads could even originate from a distinct pool. The `ThreadTracker` could help you find potential bottlenecks and slow `onMessage` methods. You only have to attach the `ThreadTracker` to a suspicious message-driven bean—they can be intercepted since EJB 3.0.

Rethinking

In J2EE 1.x crosscutting interceptors (`javax.servlet.Filter`) were only available for the Servlet APIs. There was no standardized way to decorate beans. With the advent of EJB 3 and the introduction of interceptors, crosscutting concerns can be easily factored out from the business logic. This can be achieved without third-party frameworks or libraries.

Participants and Responsibilities

The `ThreadTracker` can be applied to session beans and message-driven beans. POJOs are not managed and therefore cannot be intercepted by the container. For POJOs with interfaces the regular dynamic proxy can be applied instead and the `ThreadTracker` implementation largely reused.

Testing

Interceptors can be tested outside of the container with mocking. You will need to provide an implementation of the `InvocationContext`, which checks whether the name of the current thread has changed.

```java
public class ThreadTrackerTest {

    private ThreadTracker threadTracker;
    private String threadName;

    @Before
    public void setUp() {
        this.threadTracker = new ThreadTracker();
    }

    @Test
    public void testAnnotateThread() throws Exception {
            InvocationContext ic = new InvocationContext() {

            public Object getTarget() {
                return ThreadTrackerTest.this;
            }

            public Method getMethod() {
                try {
                    return
ThreadTrackerTest.class.getMethod("testAnnotateThread", (Class[])null);
                } catch (NoSuchMethodException ex) {
                    throw new IllegalStateException("Cannot find method "
+ex,ex);
                }
            }

            public Object proceed() throws Exception {
                ThreadTrackerTest.this.setThreadName(Thread.currentThread().getN
ame());
                return null;
            }
```

```
      //... irrelevant methods omitted
        };
        this.threadTracker.annotateThread(ic);

        assertNotNull(this.threadName);
        assertTrue(this.threadName.startsWith(this.getClass().getName()));
        //...some asserts omitted
    }

    public void setThreadName(String threadName) {
        this.threadName = threadName;
    }
}
```

Yet more important are integration and load tests. Even when the interceptor works and the names of the threads are changed as expected in the unit test, you could encounter some problems in the target environment. Actually changing the name of the thread is restricted by the EJB spec: "The enterprise bean must not attempt to manage threads. The enterprise bean must not attempt to start, stop, suspend, or resume a thread, or to change a thread's priority or name. The enterprise bean must not attempt to manage thread groups."

The application server could change the name back or even throw an `AccessControlException` (or `java.security.SecurityException`), which would roll back the current transaction and destroy the affected component.

The `ThreadTracker`, as every indirection, influences the performance as well. Interception works on most application servers with reflection. Reflective access to methods is significantly slower, than a direct call, but still irrelevant in a distributed environment. A database access or call to a legacy host is a lot slower than a local call with reflection.

In cases where methods are called several times per second, the `ThreadTracker` could become a bottleneck. It is better, faster, and easier to perform the load test and analyze the results, instead of trying to predict the behavior and optimize in advance.

Documentation

Annotations document already very well the interception points. In case you are using XML deployment descriptors to activate the `ThreadTracker`, you should document the reason for doing so and it should be clear which components are running with `ThreadTracker`, and which are not.

Consequences

- **Portability:** There is nothing application server–specific in the `ThreadTracker`. However, it violates the programming restrictions by changing the current thread's name. The violation of the spec is always problematic; you could even run into trouble upgrading or patching an application server. Strictly speaking the `ThreadTracker` cannot be considered as a portable solution. It is good enough for a single project, but has to be carefully evaluated for a multi-server environment.

- **Performance:** Every indirection slows down the performance. This is also true for the `ThreadTracker`. Although the overhead of the actual algorithm (changing the thread's name) is negligible, the interception itself is several times slower when compared to a direct local call.

Related Patterns

All intercepting patterns such as Dependency Injection Extender are similar. `ThreadTracker` is applied on Service Façades and message-driven beans. For finer monitoring and search for hotspots you could deploy Services with `ThreadTracker` as well.

Dependency Injection Extender

Inversion of control (IoC) frameworks such as Guice or Spring have their own semantics for Dependency Injection (DI). Both frameworks provide richer DI capabilities than EJBs. IoC frameworks need bootstrapping mechanism to load the first class before the Dependency Injection becomes transparent.

Problem

The DI mechanism of frameworks such as Guice is not compatible with EJBs. Guice uses the `@Inject` annotation to indicate injection points and supports constructor injection, which is not available in EJBs. Because of different semantics and mechanisms, it is not possible to directly deploy existing Guice or Spring components as EJBs. They have to be integrated instead.

Forces

- You want to deploy an existing Guice (other frameworks works similarly) component without modification in an EJB application.
- The legacy DI component has to participate in EJB transactions and the security context.
- The integration should be transparent for the legacy DI component.
- EJBs should co-exist with managed classes from the integrated framework.
- The managed classes from the "legacy" DI frameworks should be directly injected into EJBs.

Solution

Bootstrapping and injection is a common, reusable task. It is also independent from the business logic—it's a cross-cutting concern. The injection logic is a perfect candidate to be implemented as an interceptor. It could then be applied to any session bean you want. Guice is similar to EJB; a managed component is comprised of an interface and a class, whereas the injection always relies on the interface and the framework is responsible for the creation and management of the implementation. The association between the interface and its implementation is performed in a fluent way with the implementation of the `com.google.inject.Module` interface.

```
public class MessagingModule implements Module{
    public void configure(Binder binder) {
        binder.bind(MessageProvider.class).to(MessageProviderImpl.class);
    }
}
```

The `Module` implementation is used for the creation of the injector instance, which is used for the bootstrapping process.

```
public class MessageProviderTester {

    public static void main(String[] args) {
        Injector injector = Guice.createInjector(new MessagingModule());
        MessageProvider provider = injector.getInstance(MessageProvider.class);
        String message = provider.getMessage();
        System.out.println("The message is: " + message);
    }
}
```

Guice will inject all dependencies into the `MessageProvider` implementation transparently, no additional steps are necessary. It is enough just to inject the root class of each `Module` into a service or Service Façade. We use Guice-specific annotations for this purpose, to differentiate this type of injection from usual EJB injection.

```
@Stateless
public class ServiceFacadeBean {

    @Inject
    private MessageProvider message;

    public String getHello(String msg){
        return msg + " " + message.getMessage();
    }
}
```

If you compile and start the `ServiceFacadeBean`, you will run into a `NullPointerException`. An EJB is created by the container and not Guice—the `Injector` wasn't able to process and inject the dependencies yet. You need a way to inject the instance managed by Guice before the invocation of any business method.

You could achieve that by coding the injection in every method, which is error-prone and violates the separation of concerns idea. Interceptor is a more natural place for automated injection. It is always invoked before the actual business method call and it is strictly separated from the business logic.

Furthermore, an interceptor can react to lifecycle events such as `@PostConstruct` or `@PreDestroy`. The `@PostConstruct` callback is perfectly suitable for the bootstrapping of the `Injector`. When using this callback, every Service Façade or Service instance will get its dedicated `Injector` instance.

```
public class PerMethodGuiceInjector{

    private Injector injector;

    @PostConstruct
    public void startupGuice(InvocationContext invocationContext) throws
Exception{
        invocationContext.proceed();
     this.injector = Guice.createInjector(new MessagingModule());
    }

    @AroundInvoke
public Object injectDependencies(InvocationContext ic) throws Exception{
        this.injector.injectMembers(ic.getTarget());
        return ic.proceed();
    }
}
```

The `@AroundInvoke` method `injectDependencies` performs the actual injection. For that purpose it fetches the instance of the intercepted bean from the `InvocationContext` and passes it to the method `Injector#injectMembers`.

The Guice components are injected before every invocation of a business method. Stateless session bean instances are interchangeable between the client's method calls. You must not rely on their states. Alternatively, you could inject proxies into the session bean once at creation time and replace the real subjects in the Dependency Injection framework.

If the legacy components are stateless and idempotent, you could even inject them once at the creation time of each stateless or stateful session bean instance. The interceptor becomes even simpler—you don't need the `@AroundInvoke` method any more.

```
public class PerInstanceGuiceInjector{

    @PostConstruct
  public void startAndInject(InvocationContext invocationContext) throws
Exception{
 invocationContext.proceed();
 Injector injector = Guice.createInjector(new MessagingModule());
 injector.injectMembers(invocationContext.getTarget());
  }
}
```

Regardless of the strategy you are choosing, you will have to declare and associate the interceptor with a bean. You can use annotations or XML for that purpose. Annotations at class level do already document this pattern in code and are better supported by standard IDEs. This makes the injection process more explicit and easier to understand.

```
@Stateless
@Local(ServiceFacade.class)
@Interceptors(PerMethodGuiceInjector.class)
public class ServiceFacadeBean implements ServiceFacade{
    @Inject
    private MessageProvider message;

    public String getHello(String msg){
        return msg + " " + message.getMessage();
    }

}
```

Rethinking

EJB 3 are flexible enough to integrate proprietary DI frameworks. The Dependency Injection Extender opens new ways for the co-existence of different frameworks behind a Service Façade.

The integration of legacy components with EJBs is simple and almost seamless; it doesn't require any XML configuration. This makes the Dependency Injection Extender approach even interesting for reuse of smaller chunks of existing functionality.

Participants and Responsibilities

The interceptor plays the most important role. It is the actual bridge between EJBs and legacy components. The Interceptor is reusable across services and Service Facades. It is responsible for:

- The configuration of the DI framework.

- The bootstrapping of the legacy DI framework.
- Per-instance or per-method injection of components into the service or Service Façade.

The session bean has only to declare dependencies to managed classes using the legacy framework's semantics and declare the interceptor. The injection and bootstrapping are transparent for the application developer.

Strategies

Stateful Session Bean Injector

A stateful session bean remains associated for its lifetime with its client. There is a one-to-one relationship between the client and the stateful session bean. The state of a stateful session bean is never shared between clients. In that case you can use per-instance injectors without any problems. The injected components can be cached for the duration of the session; you don't have to inject fresh members before every method call.

The legacy framework, however, becomes responsible for creating stateful components at injection time as well. Otherwise different stateful session bean could access the same shared state, which can lead to inconsistencies.

Stateless Session Bean Injector

In stateless session beans you cannot rely on any relation between the bean instances and its clients. All the members have to be injected either every time before a method call or you have to use smart proxies, which react, for example, to transactions. Idempotent components, however, can be injected once and reused between session bean instances. In general per-method injectors are a good choice.

Transactional Integration

The injected components already participate in a transaction started in the session bean. The transactional resources are enlisted in the transaction by the EJB container automatically; the managed classes only haveto look up or inject transactional resources (for example, `DataSource`, `EntityManager`, or a `Destination`) from the JNDI context and use it.

You could even inject the same resource into a regular session bean without losing consistency. In the same transaction, both the session bean and the managed class access the resource in the same transactional context and thus see the current transaction state.

Testing

There is no logic other than integration in the DIE pattern. Integration tests become essentially important. The injection process slows down the application, so you should perform load and stress tests as well.

Documentation

Although the DIE implementation is easy, there is still some "magic" involved. You should well explain the concepts and mechanics behind the DIE and especially the reasons for such integration. DIE is highly reusable, so it is enough to document it once.

Not only the pattern, but especially its use should be documented. This can be achieved in an elegant way using the @Interceptor annotation instead of the XML configuration. The annotation not only documents the occurrence of the DIE in your code, but enables the developer to navigate from the service or Service Façade into the interceptor using standard IDE features (such as a CTRL-click in Eclipse and NetBeans).

Consequences

- **Performance:** Both interceptors and DI rely on reflection which is relatively slow. This only matters for the runtime performance, if you are injecting the members before every business method invocations. Even in this case, the injection process will be much faster than an average database access.

- **Portability:** The Dependency Injection Extender relies on interceptors only and does not use any proprietary application server features. It is portable across Java EE 5 application servers.

- **Testability:** Dependency Injection Extender interceptor implementation is hard to test, because it relies on the existing EJB and DI framework infrastructure. Applications that use the Dependency Injection Extender are easy to test, even outside of the container. All you have to do is instantiate the bean as a POJO and use the interceptor logic to inject the members. This is only required for EJB 3.0 containers, in EJB 3.1 the embeddable container can be used for unit testing.

Related Patterns

All interceptor-based patterns are somehow related to the Dependency Injection Extender, especially the SOA strategy of the Service Façade and Payload Extractor. DIE is often applied on Service Façades or, in larger components on services, to expose the legacy framework in an EJB way to the presentation tier. DAO could also rely on proprietary resources and integrate Guice or Spring components this way.

Payload Extractor

The message-driven bean's method onMessage expects the interface javax.jms.Message as a parameter that has to be cast into a more concrete representation to extract the payload. The method onMessage is transactional. Messages are only considered as delivered if the transaction is going to be committed without any unhandled unchecked exceptions.

Problem

The extraction of the payload requires you to check the message type, cast it, extract the payload, potentially cast it again (for example, casting the ObjectMessage payload from Serializable to something more meaningful), and catch and properly handle checked exceptions. These tasks are repetitive, verbose, and error-prone.

Especially hard to implement is proper handling of wrong message types. All destination instances are identical—they are only distinguished by their names and not the message type. Nothing prevents other producers to put a message with unexpected types into the destination.

Such unexpected messages could cause ClassCastExceptions, which leads to the rollback of the current transaction. The message would be put back to the destination and redelivered again. The number of attempts depends on the message providers configuration.

If you just ignore such messages, it will disappear from the destination and with it the chance to find the actual configuration error. Syntactically incorrect or messages with wrong types are often called *poisoned messages*.

Forces

- Poisoned messages have to be handled properly. At least they have to be redirected into a dedicated dead letter queue.
- The type checking and error handling is reusable and has to be factored out from the message-driven beans into a dedicated component.
- Error handling has to be configured and implemented outside of the business logic.
- The solution should be transactional.

Solution

An interceptor is an obvious candidate for error handling and payload extraction. Message-driven beans can be decorated with interceptors, the onMessage method can be entirely wrapped. Hence interceptor has access to the method's parameter, here an instance of javax.jms.Message, it can perform the casts and extract the payload for you.

The extracted payload is passed to the method consume with corresponding parameter type. It's only a convention. Alternatively, you could pick a method annotated with, for example, @MessageSink or @MessageConsumer annotation and pass the payload to it as parameter as well. A message-driven bean should not implement any business methods, so that such flexibility is actually superfluous.

The message-driven bean only has to declare the interceptor on the class level or the `onMessage` method. In this case, it will have exactly the same effect. Annotation of the `onMessage` method is, however, more clear and explicit so it should be preferred.

```
@MessageDriven(mappedName = "ajax", activationConfig =  {
       @ActivationConfigProperty(propertyName = "acknowledgeMode",
propertyValue = "Auto-acknowledge"),
       @ActivationConfigProperty(propertyName = "destinationType",
propertyValue = "javax.jms.Queue")
    })
public class MessageConsumerBean implements MessageListener {

    @Override
    @Interceptors(PayloadExtractor.class)
    public void onMessage(Message message) {
        /* the work is done in interceptor */
    }

    public void consume(String message){
        System.out.println("Payload received: " + message);
    }
}
```

The interceptor `PayloadExtractor` is invoked before the method `onMessage`, it receives the actual message and detects its type. Depending on the type, it casts the message, extracts its contents, and invokes the method `consume` using reflection.

```
public class PayloadExtractor {
    public static final String CONSUME_METHOD = "consume";
    @EJB
    private DeadLetterHandler dlh;

    @AroundInvoke
public Object audit(InvocationContext invocationContext) throws Exception{
       Object mdb = invocationContext.getTarget();
       Method method = invocationContext.getMethod();

       if("onMessage".equals(method.getName())){
                          Message jmsMessage = (Message)
messageParameter(invocationContext);
          invokeMethodWithSingleParameter(jmsMessage,mdb);
       }
         return invocationContext.proceed();
    }

    private void escalateError(Message originMessage) {
        this.dlh.wrongMessageType(originMessage);
    }

    private void invokeMethodWithSingleParameter(Message jmsMessage,Object mdb)
{
         if(jmsMessage instanceof ObjectMessage){
           try {
```

```
                ObjectMessage om = (ObjectMessage) jmsMessage;
                Serializable payload = om.getObject();
                invokeConsumeMethod(mdb, jmsMessage, payload);
            } catch (JMSException ex) {
                throw new IllegalStateException("Cannot get payload from
ObjectMessage " +ex,ex);
            }
        }else if(jmsMessage instanceof TextMessage){
            try {
                TextMessage tm = (TextMessage) jmsMessage;
                String payload = tm.getText();
                invokeConsumeMethod(mdb, jmsMessage, payload);
            } catch (JMSException ex) {
                throw new IllegalStateException("Cannot get payload from
TextMessage " +ex,ex);
            }
        }else{
            escalateError(jmsMessage);
        }
    }

    private void invokeConsumeMethod(Object mdb,Message message,Object
methodParameter){
        try {
         mdb.getClass().getMethod(CONSUME_METHOD,methodParameter.getClass()).inv
oke(mdb, methodParameter);
        } catch (NoSuchMethodException ex) {
          escalateError(message);
        } catch (Exception ex) {
            throw new IllegalStateException("Cannot access the consume method "
+ ex, ex);
        }
    }
    private Object messageParameter(InvocationContext context){
        return context.getParameters()[0];
    }
}
```

DeadLetterHandlerBean is responsible for handling already consumed messages that
cannot be processed by the application. It sends the message into a dedicated dead letter queue.
These poisoned messages are handled either manually by a system administrator or more likely,
they are passed to an emergency management system, which generates a ticket and escalates it.

```
@Stateless
public class DeadLetterHandlerBean implements DeadLetterHandler {
    @Resource(name = "jms/DeadLetterQueue")
    private Queue deadLetterQueue;
    @Resource(name = "jms/DeadLetterQueueFactory")
    private ConnectionFactory deadLetterQueueFactory;

    @Override
    public void wrongMessageType(Message message) {
        try {
```

```java
            this.sendJMSMessageToDeadLetterQueue(message);
        } catch (JMSException ex) {
            //exception handling...
        }
    }

    private void sendJMSMessageToDeadLetterQueue(Message message) throws
JMSException {
        Connection connection = null;
        Session session = null;
        try {
            connection = deadLetterQueueFactory.createConnection();
            session = connection.createSession(false, Session.AUTO_ACKNOWLEDGE);
            MessageProducer messageProducer =
session.createProducer(deadLetterQueue);
            messageProducer.send(message);
        } finally {
            if (session != null) {
                try {
                    session.close();
                } catch (JMSException e) {
  //exception handling
                }
            }
            if (connection != null) {
                connection.close();
            }
        }
    }
}
```

The `DeadLetterHandlerBean` should not exclusively rely on messaging to escalate the errors. `DeadLetterHandlerBean` might be called by problems with the JMS server, so you should log the messages or even send them via email as a fallback solution and not exlusively rely on the JMS infrastructure. The dead letter queue should be configured as persistent; otherwise all unconsumed messages are lost on every server restart.

Rethinking

In J2EE 1.4 it was impossible to decorate message-driven beans relying on built-in functionality without byte code extension. Instead of factoring out the crosscutting concerns, you had to move them in an abstract superclass, which was comparable to the `PayloadExtractor`. This approach was more intrusive and complex.

Interceptors introduced a more pragmatic and lightweight alternative. You can just apply an interceptor, which will cast the message, extract the payload, and invoke the `consume` method. The method `onMessage` remains empty, but will still be invoked.

The only overhead is the introduction of the method `consume`. In case you need a specific treatment of messages, you can remove the `@Interceptors` tag and provide your own extraction and error-handling logic. With `PayloadExtractor` you can start immediately with the default behavior and implement custom code on demand.

Participants and Responsibilities

The interceptor `PayloadExtractor` is the key part of this pattern. It is responsible for:

- The interception of the method `onMessage` and hijacking its parameter.
- Casting the `Message` into a concrete interface (`ObjectMessage`, `TextMessage`, `BytesMessage`, `StreamMessage` or `MapMessage`).
- Payload extraction.
- The invocation of a business method with the payload as parameter.
- Proper escalation of unrecoverable errors by invoking the `DeadLetterHandlerBean`.

The `DeadLetterHandlerBean` only has to forward the poisoned message with context information to an emergency management system or other resource.

The remaining responsibility of the message-driven bean is only the delegation of the extracted payload to a service.

Strategies

There is only one strategy (@Interceptors) for intercepting the message-driven bean, but countless error handling strategies, which are highly dependent on your IT management infrastructure.

Testing

`PayloadExtractor` is a highly reusable pattern, which implements the repetitive plumbing for you. Especially the error handling and forwarding of the poisoned messages are already implemented in a central place. Integration tests are still important, because you will have to test the escalation of errors as well.

It is entirely based on reflection, so that it will definitely slow down your system. In the entire context, the overhead is probably negligible in general, but should be verified with load and performance tests.

The method `consume` should always beunit tested to verify the proper transformation and delegation of messages.

Documentation

Empty `onMessage` methods and standalone `consume` methods are not obvious and can cause confusion. You should describe the idea of `PayloadExtractor` in a tutorial-like format with some working hello world examples.

The use of this pattern does not require a lot of documentation, the @Interceptors annotation with the `PayloadExtractor` as a value is explicit enough. No additional JavaDoc is required—it would only repeat the facts that the tutorial already describes.

Consequences

- **Performance:** Both the interception and the invocation of the method `consume` heavily rely on reflection. When compared to the straight method invocation (less than one millisecond), reflection is very slow (a few milliseconds). If you are using a distributed protocol, or even XML as payload, it will take a few hundred milliseconds to consume and process the message. In high-performance systems, interception could become an issue, but instead of trying to prematurely optimize your system, you should perform some load tests and measure the actual overhead.

- **Maintenance:** `PayloadExtractor` greatly simplifies the code and centralizes error handling and plumbing as a cross-cutting concern. It is non-intrusive; you can easily deactivate the interception and provide your own extraction logic.

- **Testability:** The extraction is cleanly separated from the actual business logic. The method `consume` is easily unit-testable. Testing of the actual `PayloadExtractor` implementation is still hard, but it has to be performed only once.

- **Complexity:** The recurring extraction and error-handling logic are implemented once and factored out into the interceptor as a common cross-cutting concern. The message-driven beans are almost empty. This greatly reduces the code complexity.

Related Patterns

From an implementation point of view, the `PayloadExtractor` is similar to the Dependency Injection Extender. `PayloadExtractor` forwards the content of the message to services, which are injected to the message-driven bean.

Resource Binder

Java Naming and Directory Interface (JNDI) is a JDK API for which many SPIs (such as CORBA, RMI, LDAP or even File System) already exist. It is used in a Java EE context to register (`Context#bind`, `Context#rebind`) and find (`Context#lookup`) deployed components and resources. The application servers tend to use the CORBA implementation of the JNDI API. The EJB 3 Dependency Injection also relies on JNDI behind the scenes.

Problem

The application server registers the components at the startup (deployment) time of the application. Resources and services such as `DataSources`, `Destination` services, or JCA connectors are registered using the administration console. In both cases the application servers perform the binding of a resource to a JNDI name and thus the entire registration process. There are no standard hooks for the registration of custom resources.

Forces

- You need a convenient and robust way to register custom resources.

- The registration should be application server independent.

- The resources should be injectable into EJBs.

- No sophisticated lifecycle management is required: the resources are stateless and can be maintained as a Singleton, or more precisely, Flyweight (GoF) pattern.

Solution

EJB 3.1 Singletons can be initialized at application startup time. You only have to designate the Singleton with the `@Startup` annotation and provide a `@PostConstruct` method. The `@PostConstruct` method will be invoked at server's startup, or at the deployment time, so it is the perfect place for the registration of custom resources.

```
@Startup
@Singleton
public class ResourceBinder {
    @PostConstruct
    public void bindResources(){
        try {
            Context context = new InitialContext();
  context.rebind(CustomResource.JNDI_NAME, new CustomResource());
        } catch (NamingException ex) {
            throw new IllegalStateException("Cannot bind resource " +ex,ex);
        }
    }
}
```

The actual logic is trivial: you only have to instantiate your resource, then `InitialContext`, and register the newly created resource using the `Context#bind` or `Context#rebind` methods. The method `bind` throws `javax.naming.NameAlreadyBoundException` in case an object with the passed name is already registered; the method `rebind` just overwrites any already existing object.

The custom resource can be an ordinary POJO without any special requirements. Some application servers may have special requirements for the resources (such as implementing `java.io.Serializable` or `javax.naming.Referenceable`), but it should work out of the box (this example works with the Java EE reference implementation, Glassfish v2 and v3).

```java
public class CustomResource{

    public final static String JNDI_NAME = "theName";

    public void doSomething(){
        System.out.println("#Done !");
    }
}
```

The registered resource can be directly injected to all Java EE managed classes and EJBs in particular. You have only to declare the dependency and annotate it with the `@Resource` annotation. The JNDI name is passed as `name`, and should correspond with the name used for the registration of the custom resource. The following example shows an injection of custom resources into a session bean with `@Resource` annotation:

```java
@Singleton
@Startup
@DependsOn("ResourceBinder")
public class CustomResourceClient {

    @Resource(name=CustomResource.JNDI_NAME)
    private CustomResource resource;

    @PostConstruct
    public void invokeResource(){
        this.resource.doSomething();
        System.out.println("Resource invoked");
    }
}
```

The Dependency Injection works even in Singleton beans, if they are created after the `ResourceBinder`. This can be achieved with the `@DependsOn` annotation. It will force the container to instantiate the `ResourceBinder` before the designated class. For all other resources (session beans, Servlets, backing beans and so on) the Dependency Injection of custom resources should work without any limitations.

Rethinking

With eagerly startable Singletons Java EE lets you register custom resources before the initialization of the actual business logic. This makes them interesting for a variety of initialization tasks. Prior to EJB 3.1, the initialization was only possible in a Servlet or using proprietary startup classes.

Dependency injection makes the `ResourceBinder` an interesting option. Before the availability of DI the resource had to be looked up first, then cast, and associated with the field in the `setSessionContext` method. The method `Context#lookup` throws a checked `NamingException`.

The use of JNDI without DI is too verbose, error-prone, and complex. Java EE fixed the problem with injection and makes JNDI interesting for the registration of custom resources.

Participants and Responsibilities

Startup Singleton `ResourceBinder` plays the main role; it is responsible for:

- The initialization of needed resources before any business logic invocation.
- Lifecycle management of the custom resource.
- Resource registration in the application server JNDI tree.
- Resource cleanup and deregistration at server shutdown time.

The custom resource can be any arbitrary Java class, without knowledge of the JNDI registration process. The class should be designed in reentrant way—it should be idempotent. With transactional and stateful resources the state of the business logic can become inconsistent, because all transactions will share the same state.

Session beans and other managed classes just inject the class as any other standard Java EE resource using the `@Resource` annotation.

Strategies

The `ResourceBinder` is just too simple to be viable for different strategies. The proprietary JNDI implementations of the different application servers may require specific steps to bind a POJO to the JNDI tree. In extreme cases, you will have to implement additional interfaces such as `java.io.Serializable` and `javax.naming.Referenceable`. You could register an adapter that implements the required interfaces and holds the particular resource. In this case, the adapter, and not the resource, will be injected. The resource client will have to ask the adapter to get the actual reference to the custom resource.

If your resources are reusable across different applications, you could package the `ResourceBinder` with all the resources in a dedicated archive. The `ResourceBinder` implementation could be maintained separately, but you will still need to have the custom resources in the classpath.

Testing

The registration of a custom resource requires a single line of code; nothing can go wrong here. You could, of course, mock out the `Context` interface and check whether this method was invoked properly, but it is better to invest more time into integration tests.

The application servers may have additional requirements for the registration of POJOs in the JNDI tree. The `ResourceBinder` pattern shouldn't have any effect on the runtime performance, it could at most slow down the startup time of the application. There is only one instance of the injected resource, so it could become a bottleneck in case the code is synchronized. You should perform load tests with performance measurements to verify proper behavior and scalability of the injected resources.

Documentation

Injection of arbitrary POJOs into EJBs is not obvious. You should clearly document and communicate this fact in easily accessible documentation such as a wiki. In addition, you could document the injected field using JavaDoc. UML diagrams are not required for the explanation of this pattern.

Consequences

- **Portability:** JNDI is part of the JDK; nonetheless the SPI of different application servers may behave differently. You should not presume that `ResourceBinder` will work with every application server out of the box.

- **Maintenance:** The injection of custom resources significantly reduces the amount of infrastructural code. You don't have to maintain the exception handling of lookup methods or service locators.

- **Performance:** `ResourceBinder` has no effect on the runtime performance, however, it can affect startup time. The registration of the resource, as well as the injection, is performed before any business call.

- **Scalability:** `ResourceBinder` has no effect on the scalability as well. However, it is a Singleton and the POJOs are registered globally at application start up (that is, the Flyweight pattern). The scalability of the solution is dependent on the scalability of the injected resource.

- **Testability:** The injected resource can be easily mocked out during the unit tests. `ResourceBinder` increases the testability of session beans.

Related Patterns

Service locator is inversely related to the `ResourceBinder`. Service locator is responsible for actively fetching resources from the JNDI tree, whereas the `ResourceBinder` enables the Dependency Injection of custom resources.

The resources exposed by the `ResourceBinder` are consumed in session beans and therefore in services, Service Façades, and DAOs.

Context Holder

The application server is managing concurrency and threads for you. The invocation context such as transaction and security information are associated with the current execution thread by the EJB container.

Problem

It is hard to pass additional information between transaction participants. EJB 3.1 does provide a simple API (`javax.interceptors.InvocationContext#getContextData`) for managing the invocation context, but only to pass information between interceptors. There is no standardized way to pass information between EJB instances participating in the same transaction.

Forces

- You need to attach additional objects (security tokens, messages) to the current thread without violating the programming restrictions.

- Your application server may use several dedicated thread pools, so information stored in `ThreadLocal` may get lost.

- You don't want to enhance the method signatures with an additional parameter to be able to pass the context.

- You need a portable solution.

Solution

The problem is not solved by the EJB 3.1 specification, rather than by the Java EE 5/6 spec itself. The `TransactionSynchronizationRegistry` can be injected in any managed class using the plain `@Resource` annotation—it comes already with a map-like API: `Object getResource(Object key)` and `putResource(Object key, Object value)` methods.

The `TransactionSynchronizationRegistry` is already associated with the current transaction, so you can safely use it as a context-transport mechanism. An interceptor already participates in a transaction started in a session bean (for example, in a Service Façade), so you could even inject the `TransactionSynchronizationRegistry` into it. The interceptor could store additional information, which would be accessible not only to the Service Façade, but also to all artifacts behind such Services, DAOs, and indirectly even PDOs.

```
import static ...kitchensink.contextholder.RegistryKey.*;
public class CurrentTimeMillisProvider {

    @Resource
    private TransactionSynchronizationRegistry registry;

    @AroundInvoke
    public Object injectMap(InvocationContext ic) throws Exception{
        registry.putResource(KEY, System.currentTimeMillis());
        return ic.proceed();
    }
}
```

The `TransactionSynchronizationRegistry` is key-value based, so you will need a key to store and access the context information. An `enum` is perfectly suitable for this purpose. The key can be even statically imported.

```
public enum RegistryKey {
    KEY
}
```

You don't have to access or even inject the `TransactionSynchronizationRegistry` in every layer. The information remains accessible as long as your session bean participates in the same transaction. If there is nothing to do in a Service Façade, you could just skip it and access the contextual information from a service.

```
@Stateless
@Interceptors(CurrentTimeMillisProvider.class)
public class ServiceFacadeBean implements ServiceFacade {

    @EJB
    private Service service;

    public void performSomeWork(){
        service.serviceInvocation();
    }

}
```

To access the context information, you will have to inject the `TransactionSynchronizationRegistry` again and fetch the data using the `getResource` method.

```
@Stateless
public class ServiceBean implements Service {

    @Resource
    private TransactionSynchronizationRegistry tsr;

    public void serviceInvocation() {
        long timeMillis = (Long)tsr.getResource(KEY);
        //...
        System.out.println("Content is " + timeMillis);
    }
}
```

You will have to cast the object stored in the `TransactionSynchronizationRegistry` to proper type after fetching. The API is available since JTA 1.1, before the availability of generics.

Rethinking

The `TransactionSynchronizationRegistry` was even available within the J2EE 1.4 timeframe. It wasn't a very attractive solution, because of the lack of Dependency Injection. It had to be fetched using the JNDI lookup mechanism with a standardized name: `java:comp/TransactionSynchronizationRegistry`. This required several lines of code with proper exception handling or the use of a service locator, which encapsulated the plumbing. `TransactionSynchronizationRegistry` was not widely used as storage of contextual information.

Java EE 5 introduced Dependency Injection, which dramatically simplified access to JNDI resources. In fact, you will need only two lines of code to either store or access the information (the actual injection and the invocation of `putResource` or `getResource`, respectively).

Participants and Responsibilities

The actual context holder is provided either by the container (`TransactionSynchronizationRegistry`) or Java SE (`ThreadLocal`). In both cases, it is initiated before the first business method invocation of a Service Façade or Gateway. This can be achieved with an interceptor, dynamic proxy, or Servlet filter (the injector). The injector extracts or creates the contextual information (such as security, time, or cache) and stores it in the context holder. All other participants only have to fetch the context holder to access the information. An explicit injector is optional; the context holder can be injected in the business logic as well and be used as a convenient transport of technical, crosscutting data.

Strategies

TransactionSynchronizationRegistry Strategy

This should be the preferred strategy for the `ContextHolder`—it is portable across application servers and independent of the individual and proprietary thread pool settings. The current transaction is used as the transport mechanism for storing additional data.

ThreadLocal Strategy

Although less portable, this strategy is far more popular. It works very well if the entire invocation is executed in a single thread. If you defined distinct thread pools for a Service Façade and Service, your context self-healing settings, a hard-to-find bug.

This strategy relies on the `ThreadLocal` functionality. The `ThreadLocal` is wrapped by the `ThreadLocalContextHolder` just for convenience reasons.

```
import java.util.HashMap;
import java.util.Map;

public class ThreadLocalContextHolder {

    private static final ThreadLocal<Map<String,Object>> THREAD_WITH_CONTEXT =
new ThreadLocal<Map<String,Object>>();

    private ThreadLocalContextHolder() {}

    public static void put(String key, Object payload) {
        if(THREAD_WITH_CONTEXT.get() == null){
            THREAD_WITH_CONTEXT.set(new HashMap<String, Object>());
        }
        THREAD_WITH_CONTEXT.get().put(key, payload);
    }
```

```java
    public static Object get(String key) {
        return THREAD_WITH_CONTEXT.get().get(key);
    }

    public static void cleanupThread(){
        THREAD_WITH_CONTEXT.remove();
    }
}
```

`ThreadLocalContextHolder` creates at first access an instance of the
`Map<String,Object>`, which is used in subsequent calls as the actual registry. The public
API is very similar to the `TransactionSynchronizationRegistry`, the names were
shortened to `get` and `put` instead of `getResource` and `putResource`.

The utility `ThreadLocalContextHolder` exposes its API as static methods that can be
statically imported. This further simplifies the management of the contextual information. The
following example shows an interceptor working with the `ThreadLocal` strategy:

```java
import javax.interceptor.AroundInvoke;
import javax.interceptor.InvocationContext;
import static ...kitchensink.contextholder.RegistryKey.*;
import static
...kitchensink.contextholder.threadlocal.ThreadLocalContextHolder.*;

public class CurrentTimeMillisProvider {


    @AroundInvoke
    public Object injectMap(InvocationContext ic) throws Exception{
        put(KEY.name(), System.currentTimeMillis());
        return ic.proceed();
    }
}
```

The `ThreadLocalContextHolder` does not require Dependency Injection so it is not limited
to Java EE managed classes. It can even be used in a web container for data transport. Similarly to
the `TransactionSynchronizationRegistry` based solution you can skip any number of
layers and access the contextual data wherever you want, for as long as you stay in the same
thread. This strategy does not even depend on transactions.

```java
@Stateless
@Interceptors(CurrentTimeMillisProvider.class)
public class ServiceFacadeThreadLocalBean implements ServiceFacadeThreadLocal {

    @EJB
    private ServiceThreadLocal service;

    public void performSomeWork(){
        service.serviceInvocation();
    }
}
```

The information can be easily accessed using the statically imported method ThreadLocalContextHolder#get.

```
import static ...threadlocal.ThreadLocalContextHolder.*;
import static ...kitchensink.contextholder.RegistryKey.*;
@Stateless
public class ServiceThreadLocalBean implements ServiceThreadLocal{

    public void serviceInvocation() {
        Long millis = (Long) get(KEY.name());
        System.out.println("Content is: " + millis);
    }
}
```

The payload can be any object you want, so casting is still required. This sample is a generic solution, in a concrete project the key values could be provided as concrete classes in a type-safe manner.

Testing

This utility is very simple; the complexity is similar to using the java.util.Map interface. The ContextHolder relies on the EJB container, so it is essentially important to test it in a production-like environment. Integration and load tests should be performed in very early stages.

Documentation

ContextHolder does not have any impact on architecture; it is rather a design or even implementation artifact. Nonetheless the principle of attaching the data to threads or transactions is not obvious and should be clearly documented.

Consequences

- **Portability:** The TransactionSynchronizationRegistry based solution is backed by the Java EE 5/6 spec and has to be portable across application servers. The ThreadLocal based strategy works as long as the entire invocation is executed in a single thread of execution. Proprietary application server extensions such as thread pools could break the solution, because one request could be executed by more than one thread.

- **Performance:** The performance of the ThreadLocal strategy is highly dependent on the Java SE version. The newer (Java 6 SE+) ThreadLocal implementations are very fast. TransactionSynchronizationRegistry, on the other hand, is an interface that is implemented by the application server. The performance of the TransactionSynchronizationRegistry based solution is dependent on the particular application server implementation. The performance of both strategies should be verified with basic load tests and attached profiler.

- **Testability:** TransactionSynchronizationRegistry is an interface; its implementation is going to be injected by the container. During unit tests a mock implementation of this interface has to be provided and the Dependency Injection mechanism has to be implemented. The Dependency Injection can be either solved with reflection or direct-field setting. The implementation of a dedicated setter is only plumbing and makes the code less readable.

The `ThreadLocal` based solution is easily testable, because the `ThreadLocal` implementation is not dependent on any application server classes or services. It can be directly executed in the unit test and will work as expected.

- **Maintainability:** `ContextHolder` greatly reduces the amount of code and plumbing required for the transport of crosscutting contextual data. The request can be easily enriched with additional information without changing the existing infrastructure and method signatures.

- **Flexibility:** The `ThreadLocal` strategy does not need transactions or JTA APIs to pass data between objects. It can even be used in a plain web container. It is, however, limited to the 1:1 association between the request and the thread for the entire invocation. `TransactionSynchronizationRegistry` doesn't have this limitation but it is dependent on the existence of transactions.

Related Patterns

`ContextHolder` is used by Service Façades and their interceptors to pass data to services and DAOs down the chain. The `ThreadLocal` based strategy can even be applied in a web container to pass contextual information from the UI layer back to the service components. Because the Context Holder uses interceptors as well, it is similar to the Thread Tracker, Payload Extractor, and Dependency Injection Extender.

Pragmatic Java EE Architectures

In the field, a unrelated collection of patterns doesn't solve anything. A constrained combination of patterns – or a patterns language are more useful. The right pattern combination depends on the context of the project, individual use cases, and, most importantly, nonfunctional requirements. In this chapter I discuss two contrary approaches: service- and domain-driven design styles.

Premature Encapsulation Is the Root of All Evil

The vast majority of J2EE applications was poisoned by too many leaky abstractions, layers, and indirections. This questionable best practice didn't really pay off. The abstractions themselves became problematic and resulted in a lot of plumbing. The motivation for using extensive abstractions and layering was driven by the intrusive J2EE programming model. The business logic was dependent on the J2EE API. Java EE eliminates most of these infrastructural dependencies. The business logic does not extend the Java EE framework, instead it is decorated with annotations. The business logic is already separated from the infrastructure by its very nature. These fact have a radical impact on the Java EE architecture and allow not only leaner implementation, but also modeling.

Entity Control Boundary (ECB) – The Lean Way

Service-oriented and domain-driven architectures can be expressed using so-called robustness diagrams, championed by Doug Rosenberg and Kendall Scott. A robustness diagram is in essence a simplified UML diagram that depicts Entity, Control, and Boundary elements (as defined on the Agile Modeling web site [www.agilemodeling.com]). The Boundary element is the user interface, the Control element represents the actual process or activity, and the Entity element is a concept from an enterprise context.

These three elements are generic enough to be mapped either to service-oriented or object-oriented architectures. The ECB approach can even be refined for Java EE—you can put more semantical information into these elements:

- **Boundary** is the façade (Service Façade or Gateway) that exposes the functionality of a component and directly interacts with the user interface.
- **Control** is a reusable, fine-grained Service behind a Boundary. It can be optional or generic in simple use cases such as CRUD or master data management.

- **Entity** refers to object-oriented or procedural domain objects. In most cases, this conceptual Entity is persistent and mapped to a single JPA entity and its supportive infrastructure such as a (Data) Service or DAO. In rare cases (for example, optimization), the Entity can be indirectly mapped to a stored procedure `ResultSet` or `RowSet` as well.

The ECB elements are suitable for modeling any business logic or use case. In both worlds, the *cohesion* or elements play the most important role. Wikipedia defines cohesion as follows:

> "In computer programming, cohesion is a measure of how strongly-related and focused the various responsibilities of a software module are. Cohesion is an ordinal type of measurement and is usually expressed as "high cohesion" or "low cohesion" when being discussed. Modules with high cohesion tend to be preferable because high cohesion is associated with several desirable traits of software including robustness, reliability, reusability, and understandability whereas low cohesion is associated with undesirable traits such as being difficult to maintain, difficult to test, difficult to reuse, and even difficult to understand."

In short, you should aim for highly cohesive systems, but in order to do so, you need a vehicle to express a group of cohesive elements. In Java (EE) the main responsibility of a business component is the exposure of its specification or contracts with additional business value and hiding its realization, which is comprised of a group of cohesive elements (see Figure 1).

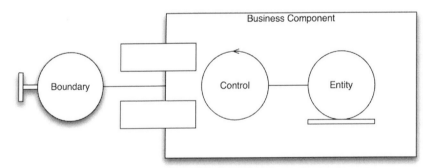

Figure 1: ECB and a business component

A business component is directly mapped to a Java package and therefore a file system folder. The external component interface is realized by a Boundary, whereas the Control and the Entity comprises its realization.

From a technical point of view, this model is not perfect. In practice, the Boundary is not just an interface—it somehow has to be realized as well. Only the Boundary interface represents the component's external interface and its implementation belongs to the business component's realization. The interface as well as its implementation have to be stored inside the component (see Figure 2).

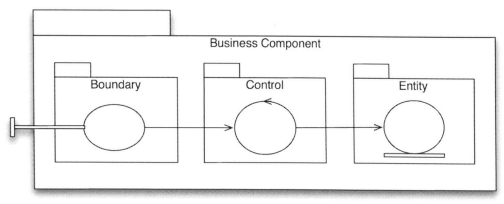

Figure 2: Internal layering of a business component

Instead of storing them directly in the package representing the business component, put each of the ECB elements in a subpackage with the same name. You will find the components inside the component subpackages with the names: `boundary`, `control`, and `entity`. You could even further emphasize the isolation of a component's realization and store the Boundary interface directly in the component package and its implementation in the `boundary` package. This subpackaging strategy facilitates greatly the implementation of metrics and quality assurance with tools such as jdepend, sonarj, dependometer, or xradar.

The ECB-driven naming would be consistent across the service-oriented and domain-driven approaches. Alternatively, you could use the already introduced naming conventions derived from the pattern names. In this case, you would recognize the components type just by looking at the subpackage names. Each approach has its pros and cons. With the ECB naming, you can reuse metrics across different component types. It is harder, however, to implement type-specific refinements. The pattern-driven naming is exactly the opposite—already implemented rules are harder to reuse, but you can be more specific for each architectural style.

Lean Service-Oriented Architectures

Thanks to e simplified Java EE 6 development model, a few interfaces and annotated classes are all you need to implement the Service Façade, Service, and Persistent Domain Object that constitute a lean service-oriented architecture.

Although Java EE 6 is far less complex than previous platform versions, it can still be misused for the creation of exaggerated and bloated architectures.

The Essential Ingredients of SOAs

The crucial artifact in any SOA is an exposed service. A service can be considered as a contract with significant business value. A clear relation should exist between the service contract and a business requirement, a use case, or even a user story. A service can be realized as a single action or a set of cohesive actions. For example, an `OrderService` might comprise a single action that performs the actual order, or a group of related operations that also include canceling the order and receiving the order status. An SOA does not reveal any details about how a service must be implemented; it aims for services to be technology- and even location-agnostic.

SOA principles can be mapped to Java EE artifacts. The most important ingredients in a Java-based SOA implementation are interfaces and packages. Everything else is only a refinement, or design. Only one artifact in the language—a plain Java interface—meets the requirements of a service contract. It is often used to decouple the client from the service implementation. It can also be used to expose the functionality of a component.

Component-based design (CBD) is the evolutionary predecessor of SOAs. Component contracts are comparable to SOA services, except for their heavier dependence on particular technology and a general lack of operations-related metadata (such as service-level agreements [SLAs]) or strong governance principles. A component is built on the *maximal cohesion, minimal coupling* principle. A component should be highly independent of other components, and the implementation should consist of related (cohesive) elements. In a Java EE SOA implementation, a component is a Java package with these strong semantics. The package's functionality is exposed with a single interface or, in rare cases, multiple interfaces.

The Essential Complexity of SOAs

SOA implies distribution of services, which is not always necessary or desirable in a Java EE application. It would be foolish to access a local service remotely just to satisfy some high-level SOA concepts. Direct local access should always be preferred over remote services. A local call is not only much faster than a remote one; the parameters and return values can also be accessed per reference and need not be serialized.

Whether the service is local or remote, the business logic should be always be executed consistently. A component needs a dedicated remoting and transaction boundary interface, which acts as a gatekeeper. The main responsibility of such a façade is to keep the granularity of the methods coarse and the persistent state of the component consistent (see Figure 3).

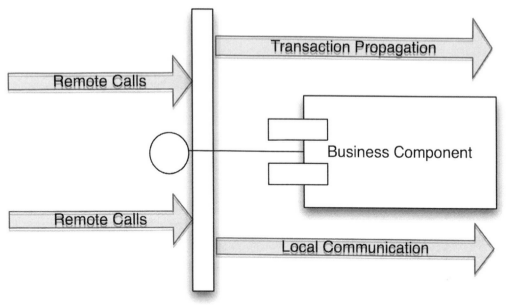

Transaction / Remoting Boundary

Figure 3: Remoting/transactions boundary

The right granularity can only be achieved by carefully crafting the interface so that consistency can be easily ensured with built-in transactions. That is the essential responsibility of the Service Facade pattern. Its the Boundary of a service-oriented business component as shown in the following example:

```
package ...bookstore.business.ordermgmt.facade;
@Stateless
@Remote(OrderService.class)
@TransactionAttribute(TransactionAttributeType.REQUIRES_NEW)
public class OrderServiceBean implements OrderService {
    @EJB
    private CrudService crudService;
    @EJB
    private VatCalculator vatCalculator;
    @EJB
    private PriceCalculator pc;
    @EJB
    private OrderProcessor op;
    @EJB
    private ShipmentService shipmentService;


public Shipment orderBook(int customerId, int isbn){
```

```
    BigDecimal priceNoVat = this.pc.computePrice(customerId, isbn);
    BigDecimal price = this.vatCalculator.computeVat(priceNoVat);
    Order o = this.op.processOrder(customerId, customerId, price);
    return this.shipmentService.deliver(o);
}

public Shipment findShipment(long shipmentId){
        return this.shipmentService.find(shipmentId);
}
//some methods omitted
}
```

Applying the `TransactionAttributeType.REQUIRES_NEW` annotation to a Service Façade causes all methods to inherit this setting automatically. You could also rely on the default (which is `TransactionAttributeType.REQUIRED`) and not specify a transaction setting . However, the `OrderService` is the transaction and remoting boundary. It is accessed exclusively by the user interface, which must not start any transactions. Using the `REQUIRES_NEW` attribute is more explicit. It always starts a new transaction, which is what you would expect from a boundary. The `REQUIRED` configuration, if it were invoked within a transaction context, would reuse an existing transaction or start a new one. A boundary, however, will never be invoked in an existing transaction, which makes the default setting more confusing.

A Service Façade is the standardized implementation of the here described semantics—it is the Boundary of a service-oriented component.

Separation of Concerns, or Divide and Conquer

`OrderServiceBean` emphasizes the business logic and hides the component's implementation. These are the responsibilities of the classic Façade and also the already introduced Service Façade patterns. Furthermore, the `OrderServiceBean` ensures the component's consistency by starting a transaction before every method is exposed over the business interface. Transactions are a cross-cutting concern—an *aspect*—already implemented by the EJB container. The façade already has enough responsibilities, so it has no more room for the implementation of the actual business logic.

The intention of a Controller (AKA Service) is the actual realization of the business logic. In an SOA world, it is of a procedural nature. A Service resides behind the Service Façade, so it can never be accessed directly by the user interface or other presentation components. A service is stateless and can only be called by the Service Façade. Every Service Façade method starts a new transaction, so a Service can safely rely on the existence of the transaction. The following code shows an example of the transaction and remoting configuration of a Service pattern:

```
@Stateless
@Local(OrderProcessor.class)
@TransactionAttribute(TransactionAttributeType.MANDATORY)
public class OrderProcessorBean implements OrderProcessor {
```

```
    @PersistenceContext
    private EntityManager em;

 public Order processOrder(int customerId, int productId, BigDecimal
price) {
        Order order = new Order(customerId, productId, price);
        this.em.persist(order);
        return order;
    }
}
```

In this example, the concerns are clearly separated. The façade provides the cross-cutting functionality and plays the coordinator role, and the service focuses on the actual domain logic implementation. The clearly separated roles and responsibilities make it possible to predefine a service's structure and configuration easily. A service is a stateless session bean with a local business interface. It is always invoked by the façade in a transaction, so it can be deployed with the MANDATORY setting. This restrictive TransactionAttribute further emphasizes the encapsulation; it is not possible to call it directly without a transaction. The bean implementation exposes the business interface with the @Local annotation, so the interface is independent of the EJB API.

Domain Objects or Structures?

Since Services implement the actual business logic, and the Service Façade cares about the cross-cutting concerns, there is no more functionality left to be implemented in the Persistent Domain Objects (PDOs). The Java Persistence API (JPA) entities consist only of annotated attributes and getters/setters; they contain no business logic. The following example shows such an anemic domain object:

```
@Entity
@Table(name="T_ORDER")
@NamedQueries({
@NamedQuery(name=Order.findByCustomerId,query="SELECT o FROM Order o where
o.customerId = :customerId")
})
public class Order {

 public final static String PREFIX ="..ordermgmt.domain.Order";
 public final static String findByCustomerId = PREFIX +
"findByCustomerId";

    @Id
    @GeneratedValue(strategy = GenerationType.AUTO)
    private Long id;

    private int customerId;
```

```java
    private int productId;
    private double price;

    public Order() { }


    public Order(int customerId, int productId, BigDecimal price){
        this.customerId = customerId;
        this.productId = productId;
        this.price = price.doubleValue();
    }

    public Long getId() {
        return id;
    }

    public double getPrice() {
        return price;
    }

    public void setPrice(double price) {
        this.price = price;
    }

    public int getProductId() {
        return productId;
    }

    public void setProductId(int productId) {
        this.productId = productId;
    }
}
```

Although the anemic object model is considered to be an antipattern, it fits very well into an SOA. Most of the application is data-driven, with only a small amount of object-specific or type-dependent logic. For simpler applications, anemic JPA entities have advantages too:

- Dumb entities are easier to develop—no domain knowledge is required.
- Anemic JPA entities can be generated more easily. The necessary metadata can be derived entirely from the database. You can just maintain the database, and the existing entities can be safely overwritten by newly generated entities.
- The persistent entities can be detached and transferred to the client. Aside from the classic "lazy loading" challenges, there are no further surprises. The client will only see the accessors and will not be able to invoke any business methods.

Thinking About Internal Structure

I've already identified some key ingredients of a service-oriented component:

- **Boundary (Service Façade):** Provides simplified, centralized access to the component and decouples the client from the concrete services. It is the network and transaction boundary.

- **Control (Service):** The actual implementation of the business logic.

- **Entity (domain structure, PDO):** It's a structure rather than an object. It implements the component's persistence and exposes all of its state to the services, without any encapsulation.

You will find these three layers in most components. The component structure manifests itself as internal packages named by the key ingredients (see Figure 4).

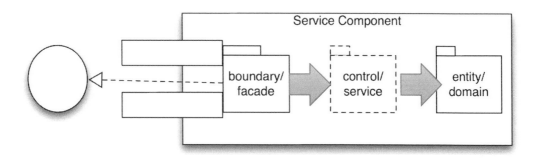

Figure 4. Internal structure of a service component

The `ordermgmt` component consists of the `boundary/facade`, `control/service`, and `entity/domain` packages.

DAOs: Dead or Alive?

Behind the motivation for this pattern was the desire to achieve the greatest possible decoupling from the concrete realization of the data store mechanics.

The question to ask is how often you've had a concrete requirement to switch among relational databases, object-oriented databases, flat files, and so on in a project. In the absence of such a requirement, you should ask yourself how likely such a replacement of the data store really is. Even if it is likely to happen, data store abstractions are rather leaky. The JPA `EntityManager` class is comparable to a domain store and works with managed entities. Other data stores are more likely to use the per-value approach and therefore return a new copy of a persistent entity on every request in a single transaction. This is a huge semantic difference; with the `EntityManger`, there's no need to merge attached entities, whereas it is absolutely necessary in the case of a DAO with Data Transfer Objects.

Even a perfect database abstraction is leaky. Different databases behave differently and have specific locking and performance characteristics. An application might run and scale perfectly on one database but encounter frequent deadlocks with another product. Such a variation just cannot be abstracted with any abstractions or design patterns. The only possible way to survive such a migration is to tweak the isolation levels, transactions, and database configuration. These issues can't be hidden behind a DAO interface, and it's likely that the DAO implementation would not even change. The DAO abstraction would be only useful if the actual JPA QL or SQL statements change, which is a minor problem.

So neither the original definition nor a database migration use case justifies the implementation of a dedicated DAO. Does this mean that DAOs are dead? For standard use cases, yes. But you still need a DAO in most applications to adhere to the principles of DRY (don't repeat yourself) and separation of concerns. It is more than likely that an average application uses a set of common database operations over and over again. Without a dedicated DAO, the queries will be sprinkled through your business tier. Such duplication significantly decreases the application's maintainability. But the redundant code can be easily eliminated with a DAO that encapsulates the common data access logic. In other words, even though DAOs still exist, they can no longer be considered as a general best practice. They should be created in a bottom-up instead of a top-down fashion. If you discover data access code duplication in your service layer, factor it out to a dedicated DAO and reuse it. Otherwise it is just fine to delegate to an EntityManager from a service. The enforcement of an empty DAO layer is even more harmful, because it requires you to write dumb code for even simple use cases. The more code is produced, the more time you must spend to write tests and to maintain it.

With JDK 1.5 and the advent of generics, it is possible to build and deploy a generic, convenient, and type-safe DAO once and reuse it from variety of services. Such a DAO should come with a business interface to encourage unit testing and mocking.

A small pattern language for SOA

The essential ingredient of a service component is not the Service, but a Service Façade. Its main responsibility is the (as tight as possible) encapsulation of the component's realization and the (as convenient as possible) exposure of a component's functionality to the outside world.

The Service Façade acts as a firewall (a really strict Boundary), it separates the component's specification from its realization. The best way to achieve that in Java is to separate the implementation from the contract using distinct packages. The artifacts of the component's API can be located in the component's root package, whereas the realization artifacts are placed into the the boundary, control, and domain subpackages respectively.

The strict separation between the components outside view from the internal realization makes the Transfer Object pattern mandatory. The direct exposure of PDOs to the client would break the business component encapsulation. Every change to the PDOs could potentially break the users. The Transfer Object belongs to the service component's API, so it is located at the top-level package (for example, ordermgmt). Not only PDOs, but all other classes that are required for the interaction with the component, have to be placed in that package. Exceptions and everything that is needed for the compilation of the contract and client, has to be located in the API package as well.

Services are optional artifacts and have to be introduced only in case the Service Facade will not degrade to a dumb delegate. As a rule of thumb, you should have at least two Service implementations, otherwise the Service Façade will not be eligible to be called a coordinator or even façade. Especially simplistic use cases such as CRUD can be efficiently realized with a Service Façade and a Data Access Object (DAO).

PDOs are not mandatory elements, but you will find them in most components with a persistent state. Contrary to the domain components, PDOs in a service component mainly consist of state without any business logic. The logic is located in Services. A Service with the particular PDO can be considered as an atomic unit.

Fetching of the PDOs can be implemented either in a Service or a dedicated DAO. Ever since the release of JDK 1.5, generic DAO implementations have been easy to implement. A DAO can be used as a convenient decorator of the `EntityManager` (which is optional), or an integration adapter that talks directly to the data store. The latter example should be considered mandatory for all integration scenarios of Java EE incompatible resources (stored procedures inclusively).

Integrational DAOs are not able to return attached PDOs—they expect and return Transfer Objects. With the introduction of an integrational DAO, you will get Transfer Objects in the component's realization as well.

A Paginator is fully optional. In case it is needed, it should be introduced in a stateless configuration. Service components are inherently stateless, so there is no need to make them stateful just because of simple iteration logic.

The Fluid Logic pattern is more interesting. In the domain-driven component, the Fluid Logic is mostly used for the introduction of more fluent access to the domain objects, or for building DSLs. In a service-oriented world, dynamic languages can be used efficiently for integration purposes. The Fluid Logic pattern is perfect for the realization of a flexible adapter or glue between incompatible services or for data transformations.

Service-oriented components are contract driven—every single invocation is routed through the Service Façade. In addition, SOA promotes the reuse of existing components and services—a once deployed service might be reused by several clients with different nonfunctional requirements.

An SOA service needs a certain level of quality to be interesting for reuse. Otherwise the failure of a single service may cause the outage of several clients. Some service-level agreement configuration such as performance or simple statistics can be attached to the service as annotations and proactively monitored by an interceptor. The Service Façade may be decorated by additional aspects for the purpose.

Also, existing legacy Spring or Guice services can be easily injected into the Service Façade using the Dependency Injection Extender, another interceptor-based pattern. The Context Holder makes the transport of additional resources, also into POJOs or legacy components (such as principal, transactional resources or additional metadata) possible. Figure 5 shows such a service component built on patterns.

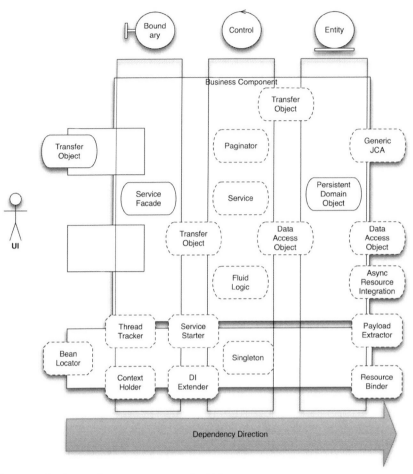

Figure 5: A service component build on patterns

SOA aims for reuse, which causes more overhead and requires additional patterns. Service components are, on average, more complex than comparable domain components.

A touch of pragmatism

Most service components are not complicated and consist mainly of basic data operations. In these cases the façade would just delegate to a service, which in turn delegates to the `javax.persistence.EntityManager` class or a generic `CrudService` session bean to perform its persistence tasks. Otherwise you will end up getting two dumb delegates: the façade would only delegate to the Service, and the Service to the `CrudService` (AKA DAO). Delegates without additional responsibilities are just dead code. They only increase the code complexity and make maintenance more tedious. You could fight this bloat by making the service layer optional. The Service Façade would manage the persistence and delegate the calls to the

`EntityManager` instance. This approach violates the separation-of-concerns principle, but it's a very pragmatic one. It is still possible to factor reusable logic from the façade into the services with minimal effort.

If you really want to encapsulate the data access in a dedicated layer, you can easily implement it once and reuse the generic access in different projects. Such a generic DAO does not belong to a particular business component. It would violate the cohesion. It could be deployed as a standalone technical component with the name `dataservice`.

As Lean as Possible, but Not Leaner

It would be hard to streamline this architecture further without sacrificing its maintainability. I know of no other framework that lets you express a service-based architecture in such a lean and straightforward manner. No XML configuration, external libraries, or specific frameworks are needed. The deployment consists of only a single JAR file with a short `persistence.xml` configuration file.

The entire architecture is based on a few annotated Java classes with pure interfaces (that is, interfaces that are not dependent on the EJB API). With EJB 3.1 you could even remove the interfaces and inject the bean implementation directly. Services and DAOs could be deployed without any interfaces, which would cut the total number of files in half and make the component significantly leaner. However, you would lose the ability to mock out the service and DAO implementation easily for plain unit tests.

Objects- or Domain-Driven Design

Domain-driven design and service-oriented design are opposite approaches. Domain-driven design relies mainly on encapsulated objects with state and behavior, whereas SOA emphasizes the procedure (a service). Object-oriented applications tend to be stateful, SOA tend to be stateless. The best practices in one case become antipatterns in the other.

The Essential Ingredients of Domain-Driven Designs

Both architectures can be modeled with the same ECB approach. The responsibility of the ECB artifacts changes dramatically, however—ECBs become mapped to other patterns:

- **Entity (PDO)**: The Entity is the main and most important ingredient of the domain-driven architectural style. It unifies the behavior and state management in a single class. An Entity is persistent in most cases. A real domain-driven architecture should actually only be comprised of Entities with aspects. All other artifacts should (in theory) be superfluous. The Entity is mapped to the PDO and by extension a JPA entity.

- **Control (Service)**: The Control degrades to a supportive class which only cares about cross-cutting aspects. The DAO may be considered as a special kind of a Control. A Control is fully optional and is only introduced in case there is some Entity-independent, reusable logic available. In practice, a Control is often used for the implementation of reusable queries, data warehouse jobs, reports and so on.

- **Boundary (Gateway)**: As in the service-oriented flavor, the Boundary represents the border between the user interface and the business logic. The responsibilities of both Boundaries, however, are exactly inverted. The service-oriented Boundary tries to encapsulate as tight as possible the component's realization, whereas the domain-driven Boundary exposes the Entities (PDOs) as directly and as conveniently as possible. Furthermore, the object-oriented Boundary is in most cases stateful, whereas the service-oriented Boundary is mostly stateless. Nevertheless, the Boundary in the domain-driven setup is only necessary because of the Java EE 5/6 shortcomings. At least a single active component (a session bean) is needed. It provides the context for the execution of JPA entities. In an ideal environment, a Gateway could also be implemented as an aspect, or even a static method on a PDO. In practice, the Boundary (Gateway) is used as an entry point to the business logic and contacted first by the user interface.

As in the service-oriented example, the business component is comprised of three internal subpackages named after the ECB approach or the patterns (`facade/gateway`, `control/service`, `entity/domain`). The business component also hosts cohesive elements only. There is, however, no separation between the specification and the realization. Because the PDOs are already well encapsulated, they are directly available to the user interface. There is no need for further encapsulation.

The Essential Complexity of Domain-Driven Designs

The domain-driven approach is nothing else than object-oriented principles applied to the Java EE world. The essential complexity is tackled with well-defined and encapsulated PDOs. The Gateway is relatively easy and can also be introduced at a later point with the bottom-up approach. The Service is optional and is often created in bottom-up fashion, after the first refactoring cycles to cut redundancies.

The big difference between the service-oriented and domain-driven approaches is the state management. The SOA-like approaches are often request-response or even fire-and-forget based. The client sends a request and receives an answer, mostly in an asynchronous way. The parameters as well as the return values becomes detached after every call. This behavior (passing the parameters and return objects per value) is desired by an SOA, so that the business component can remain stateless.

The domain-driven approach relies on a PDO's state—the client would like to access the objects directly, without synchronizing the state with the back-end database. The PDOs have to remain attached for the duration of the conversation. The PDOs remain attached in the `EntityManager` and the transactions initiate the synchronization with the persistent store.

This can be achieved only with a stateful Gateway, which holds a reference to an attached root PDO. The statefulness itself isn't a scalability problem, rather than the amount of attached entities during the transaction. Every entity that was found or referenced will remain in the `EntityManager` cache for the length of the session.

The essential complexity of service-oriented applications is the synchronization of the PDO graph with the persistent store. Both write and read operations are complicated. The write operations are performed on the server when the client sends back the changed object graph. The read operations are mostly performed on the client side, when the view tries to follow the relations and load detached objects.

A stateful, domain-driven component solves both issues for you, but you will have to think about freeing the resources and detaching superfluous PDOs. This could become as complex as the synchronization of detached entities or loading of lazy relations in a service-oriented component. With the default configuration of most JPA providers, all read PDOs will remain in memory for the length of the session. You will either change the cache settings or work with proxies (for example, OIDs) and load objects as needed to address the issue. Before starting any optimization, you should perform load and stress tests first. Whether the aggressive caching behavior of your provider becomes a problem or not depends on many factors, including the number of concurrent sessions, the session length, and the number of accessed PDOs per session.

Monolithic or Loosely Coupled?

A business component is build according to the maximal cohesion/minimal coupling principle. It contains elements that realize a single aspect of the target domain. Regardless of how decoupled a component is from its neighbors, its elements will have to communicate with each other.

In theory, this direct dependency between business components should be eliminated, or at least factored out into the client. In practice, this means that container-managed relations between PDOs could not be spanned across components. Although it seems reasonable it is not practicable.

A `Customer` PDO from `customermgmt` component would not be able to directly access the `Address` PDO from the `addressmgmt` components. The alternative is to cut the direct dependencies between PDOs and use queries to build the relations lazily. This cannot only have a huge impact on performance, but it also makes the implementation far more complicated.

The main advantage of the stateful domain-driven approach is the transparent synchronization and lazy loading of dependent entities. To leverage this advantage you will have to realize direct dependencies between PDOs.

The entity/domain layer of one component should be able to access the PDOs directly from the other one. It is, however, not necessary for the remaining layers to communicate with each other.

If you allow direct dependencies between the entity/domain layers you will probably run into the next problem: circular dependencies between components and even single PDOs (see Figure 6). In JPA, bidirectional dependencies are common and are used heavily in JPA 1.0 (to get rid off the intermediary mapping table in `@OneToMany` relations).

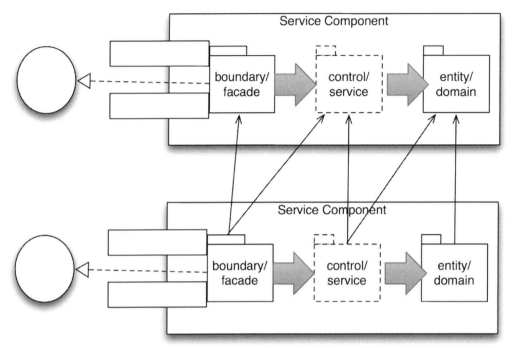

Figure 6: Possible dependencies between layers.

This fact causes long discussions and frequent meetings and leads eventually to the following compromises:

- **Documented exceptions:** Few bidirectional dependencies between components are harmless. It's pragmatic to allow them instead of introducing complex and hard-to-maintain workarounds such as additional lookups, queries, or resolving services.

- **Proxying:** This is the SOA way of re-solving the dependencies. Instead of pointing directly to the target entity, you could use a proxy that can be resolved by a query service on demand. The dependent PDO will have to be processed by a specific service to resolve the proxy on demand. This approach is less transparent; it actually only obfuscates the dependency between two entities.

- **Component refactoring/restructuring:** This is the most popular and convenient solution for the resolution of unwished dependencies. The dependent elements are grouped in a single business component. The bidirectional dependency between the PDOs still exists, but is isolated in a single business component. This approach is convenient, but breaks the maximal cohesion/minimal coupling rule. The PDOs (for example, `Customer` with its `Address`) do not have to be cohesive. The first indicator of a non-cohesive component are difficulties to find the right name (for example, `customeraddressmgmt`).

A Small Pattern Language for Domain-driven Components

There are only two mandatory patterns in a domain-driven component, the PDO and the Gateway. All other patterns and layers are optional and have to be introduced only in case there is a reasonable need. Even the `control` subpackage (and by extension a Service) are optional.

A typical domain-driven component consists of a single Gateway and few (five to ten) PDOs. The remaining patterns (boxes with a dashed outline in Figure 7) can be understood as workarounds:

- **Transfer object (TO):** A TO is needed for optimization purposes. The client is often only interested in a tiny subset of the entire PDO. This is common for pre-filling combo boxes for the iuser interface at the beginning of use cases, for example. Instead of returning full-fledged PDOs, you can let the `EntityManager` populate a TO and return it to the client. Sometimes a client needs a different view of the data, as it is provided by the PDOs. A TO can meet that requirement by holding the results of a queries spanning multiple PDOs.

- **Service:** A Service is only needed to realize procedural logic, which cannot be associated with a particular PDO without negatively influencing its cohesion. Therefore a Service is an exception in the domain-driven world—you should realize most of the business logic in PDOs and crosscutting aspects in Gateways. There is almost no room for procedural Sevice in domain-driven world.

- **Paginator:** A Paginator is a specific kind of service that is able to iterate efficiently over a collection of PDOs. A Paginator is also an optimization, which should only be introduced in case the iteration over a collection of attached PDOs causes performance or resource problems.

- **Fluid Logic:** This pattern is more likely to be used in conjunction with domain objects. A Fluid Logic pattern is able to integrate dynamic languages for the manipulation of static PDOs. Languages such as Groovy, JRuby, or Scala are well suitable for the definition of domain-specific languages, which can be applied to manipulate attached PDOs.

- **Data Access Object (DAO):** Whether a DAO is required is almost a religious question. In fact the `EntityManager` is already a generic DAO. In most projects, however, you will still find a DAO that builds and executes reusable queries. It is mostly created as a product of refactoring, instead of being introduced upfront. You can consider a DAO as a *domain repository*.

- **Integrational/Infrastructural patterns:** The use of integrational and infrastructural (kitchen sink) patterns is a lot harder to predict. The need for those patterns is highly dependent on your environment and its Java EE compliance. The more incompatible resources you have to integrate, the more hacking is required. Patterns such as DAO, Asynchronous Resource Integrator, or Generic JCA may help you to cleanly integrate a incompatible resource and encapsulate the (often ugly) glue code. The infrastructural patterns are even more dependent on you particular situation.

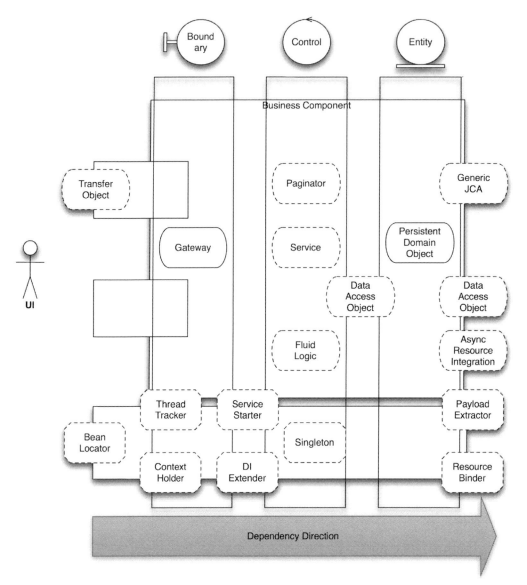

Figure 7: A domain-driven component built on patterns

Alphabetical Index